LIVING RELIGIONS
EASTERN TRADITIONS

LIVING RELIGIONS

EASTERN TRADITIONS

MARY PAT FISHER

SPECIALIST CONSULTANTS

Dr. Owen Cole, Chichester Institute of Higher Education

Dr. Eugene Gallagher, Connecticut College

Dr. Livia Kohn, Boston University

Dr. Jane Marie Law, Cornell University

Sandhya S., Mata Amritanandamayi Mutt

PRENTICE-HALL
Upper Saddle River, N.J. 07458

Published 2003 by Prentice-Hall Inc.
A Division of Pearson Education
Upper Saddle River, N.J. 07458

10 9 8 7 6 5 4 3 2 1

ISBN 0-13-182986-6

This book was designed and produced by
Laurence King Publishing Ltd, London
www.laurenceking.co.uk

The material in this volume is taken from *Living Religions* (5th edition),
copyright © Mary Pat Fisher, 2002
Acquisitions editors: Ross Miller (Prentice Hall) and
Melanie White (Laurence King Publishing)
Marketing manager: Clare Bitting
Project manager (5th edition): Jessica Spencer
Designer (5th edition): Richard Foenander
Picture researcher (5th edition): Bridget Tily
Maps: Andrea Fairbrass, Advanced Illustration Ltd, Cheshire
Typeset by Fakenham Photosetting, Norfolk

Printed in Hong Kong

Cover: *The Sun Rises While the Moon Sleeps* (detail), 1990,
Peter Davidson (contemporary artist),
Private Collection/Bridgeman Art Library, London
Half title: Boy about to become a monk, Myanmar.
Frontispiece: Novice monks receiving alms, Laos

CONTENTS

Unique FREE online resource for world religion!
www.prenhall.com/fisher

Prentice Hall's exclusive Companion Website™ that accompanies *Living Religions* offers tools and support for teachers and students alike to learn more about world religion. Tied directly to the text, the Companion Website™ is a comprehensive online resource that features a variety of learning and teaching activities, including:

For Students:

- **Chapter learning objectives** that help students organize key concepts
- **Online quizzes** which include instant scoring and coaching
- **Writing activities** that foster critical thinking
- **Essay questions** that test students' critical thinking skills
- **Video essays** for many chapters, based on Quicktime™
- **Video clips** of important elements of that faith
- **Dynamic web links** that provide a valuable source of supplemental information
- **Communication tools** such as chat rooms and message boards to facilitate online collaboration and communication
- **Key word searches** that are easy to use and feature built-in search engines
- **Built-in routing** that offers students the ability to forward essay responses and graded quizzes to their instructors

For Instructors:

- **Syllabus Manager**™ tool provides an easy-to-follow process for creating, posting, and revising a syllabus online that is accessible from any point within the companion website.
  Faculty resources: Located by chapter, instructors have access to the Instructor's manual which contains lecture outlines and material. Plus, most chapters have Powerpoint™ slides with maps and images for use in classroom presentations.
- **Faculty Resources** for each chapter offers lectures, detailed overviews, activities, and other resources for instructors. Also included are maps and images in Powerpoint™ format for use in classroom presentations.

Also new and available free on the Companion Website is eThemes of the New York Times! This up-to-date archive from the world's leading newspaper on current topics in religion will help students witness first-hand the relevance of religion in the 21st Century.

The Companion Website makes integrating online resources into your course exciting and easy! Join us online and enter a new world of teaching and learning.

PREFACE

Religion is not a museum piece. As the twenty-first century unfolds, religion is a vibrant force in the lives of many people around the world, and many religions are presently experiencing a renaissance.

Living Religions: Eastern Traditions is a sympathetic approach to what is living and significant in the world's major religious traditions and new religious movements that have originated in the East. This book provides a clear and straightforward account of the development, doctrines, and practices of these faiths. It ends with conclusions about trends that are now being seen in all religions. The emphasis throughout is on the personal consciousness of believers and on their own accounts of their religion and its relevance in contemporary life.

Special features

One of the unique features of this text is personal interviews with followers of each faith. This material provides interesting and informative first-person accounts of each religion as perceived from within the tradition. This volume includes special boxes featuring interviews with a Hindu grandmother, a Jain "semi-nun," a Thai Buddhist trying to incorporate meditation into worldly life, a Chinese scholar living abroad and witnessing social changes as they affect the religious values of her parents, and a Shinto practitioner trying to restore faith in his ancient religion. In addition, first-person accounts have been interwoven throughout the text.

Living Religions: Eastern Traditions also includes feature boxes on "Religion in Public Life." These portray the spiritual roots of Dr. Karan Singh and His Holiness the Dalai Lama, followers of Eastern religions who are making significant contributions to modern society. In their stories, one recognizes that deep religiosity can go hand-in-hand with deep social commitment.

There are also feature boxes on "Religion in Practice," such as the Swadhyaya Movement and Life in a Western Zen Monastery, and "Teaching Stories", such as "The Monkeys Take Care of the Trees", which can serve as take-off points for discussions about core values imbedded in each faith.

Violence perpetrated in the name of religion is often in the news these days. *Living Religions: Eastern Traditions* includes probing discussions of this disturbing factor. Distinctions are made between the basic teachings of religions, none of which condones wanton violence, and the ways in which religions have been politicized. There is extensive coverage of the socio-political context of the contemporary practice of religions, particularly with reference to emergent Hindu nationalism. The final chapter examines the current tensions between the hardening of inter-religious boundaries and efforts to bring harmony among religions.

Throughout the book, women's contributions and women's issues are carefully considered. Women's voices, including those of female religious leaders and scholars, are woven into the discussions.

The opening chapter, "The Religious Response," brings critical scholarship to bear on underlying issues in the study of religion. Throughout the book the latest scholarship has been applied. The text incorporates extensive quotations from primary sources to give a direct perception of the thinking and flavor of each tradition. Particularly memorable brief quotations are set off in boxes.

One of the most engaging features of Living Religions: Eastern Traditions is its illustrations. I have been glad to have the chance to use 114 illustrations, 61 of them in color, to help bring religions to life. Narrative captions accompanying the illustrations offer additional insights into the characteristics and orientation of each tradition and the people who practice it.

Learning aids

I have tried to present each tradition clearly and without the clutter of less important names and dates. Key terms, defined and highlighted in boldface when they first appear, are included in an extensive glossary. Because students are often unfamiliar with terms from other cultures, useful guides to pronunciation of words that may be unfamiliar are included in the glossary.

Maps are used throughout the text to give a sense of geographical reality to the historical discussions, as well as to illustrate the present distribution of the religions. Timelines are used to recapitulate the historical development of each of the major religions, up to the present.

I assume that readers will want to delve further into the literature. At the end of each chapter, therefore, I offer an annotated list of books that might be particularly interesting and useful in deeper study of that religion.

Acknowledgments

The material in this volume is based on my well-received textbook on the religions of the world, *Living Religions*, which has now gone through five editions. In order to try to understand each religion from the inside, I have traveled for many years to study and worship with devotees and teachers of all faiths, and to interview them about their experience of their tradition. People of all religions also come to the Gobind Sadan Institute for Advanced Studies in Comparative Religions, where it is my good fortune to meet and speak with them about their spiritual experiences and beliefs.

In preparing the fifth edition, I worked directly with consultants who are authorities in specific traditions and who offered detailed suggestions and resources. I was ably helped by Dr. Livia Kohn, of Boston University; Dr. Owen Cole of Chichester Institute of Higher Education; Dr. Jane Marie Law of Cornell University; Sandhya S. of Mata Amritanandamayi Mutt and Dr. Eugene Gallagher of Connecticut College. I am extremely grateful for their generous and enthusiastic help, and for the assistance of the many scholars who have served as consultants to the previous editions and are specially acknowledged therein.

Living Religions has been extensively reviewed by professors teaching courses in world religions. Reviewers of the first edition included George Braswell, Southeastern Baptist Theological Seminary; Howard R. Burkle, Grinnell College; James Carse, New York University; Frances Cook, University of California; Ronald Flowers, Texas Christian University; Rita Gross, University of Wisconsin; Willard Johnson, San Diego State University; Anjum Khilji, Institute of Parapsychology at Durham Technical Community College; Dennis Klass, Webster University; Robert Minor, University of Kansas; Kusumita P. Pederson, New York University; Lynda Sexson, Montana State University; Paul Schwartz, San Francisco State University; Herb Smith, McPherson College. In addition, Reverend Stan Possell, Rabbi Steven Razin, Mohammad T. Mehdi, and Prajapati O'Neill read and commented on specific chapters.

Reviewers of the second edition included: Gary Alexander, University of Wisconsin; Howard R. Burkle, Grinnell College; Francis H. Cook, University of California (retired); Ronald B. Flowers, Texas Christian University; Eugene V. Gallagher, Connecticut College; John A. Grim, Bucknell University; Marcia K. Hermansen, San Diego State University; Wayne R. Husted, Penn State University; John P. Keenan, University of Pennsylvania; Lynn Ross-Bryant, University of Colorado; Larry D. Shinn, Bucknell University; H. Michael Simmons, Center for Zoroastrian Research; Maurine Stein, Prairie State College; James D. Tabor, University of North Carolina. In addition, Robert Carter of Trent University and Balkar Singh of Punjabi University at Patiala offered suggestions on the chapters on Shinto and Sikhism, respectively, and S. A. Ali of Hamdard University and R. P. Jain of Delhi were very helpful in guiding me to literature on Islam and Jainism.

Reviewers of the third edition included: William R. Goodman, Jr., Lynchburg College; Robert Imperato, Saint Leo College; Barbara Ring Kotowski, University of Texas at El Paso and El Paso Community College; Scott Lowe, University of North Dakota; Elizabeth Neumeyer, Kellogg Community College; Maurine Stein, Prairie State College. Lee Bailey of Ithaca College was also generous in his help. Many Russian scholars reviewed the text, and their comments were very helpful in preparing additions particularly with concern to the contemporary and historical situations in the former Soviet Union.

Reviewers of the fourth edition included: Professor Philip C. Schmitz, Eastern Michigan University; Dr. Christopher S. Queen, Harvard University; Dr. Ted J. Solomon, Drake University; Dr. Nancy A. Hardesty, Clemson University; Dr. Krishna Mallik, Bentley College; Dr. Guy L. Beck, College of Charleston; Dr. David Chappell, University of Hawaii at Manoa.

Reviewers for the fifth edition offered extremely detailed constructive suggestions. They include: Robert Imperato, Saint Leo University; Sallie King, James Madison University; Jonathan Brumberg-Kraus, Wheaton College; George Mummert, Moberly Area Community College; Bob Badra, Kalamazoo Valley Community College; Hugh Urban, Ohio State University; John Gilman, San Diego State University; David Suter, St. Martin's College; Jeffrey

Brodd, California State University, Sacramento; Mark MacWilliams, St. Lawrence University; Mark Webb, Texas Technical University. Other people who have generously helped with source material for this edition include Rev. Marcus Braybrooke, Shivaprakash, Dr. M. A. Pradhani, Marianne Vandiver, Michelle Brand, Galina Ermolina, Edward Fisher, Vladimir Sova, William Beeman, Yale Partlow, Alexandra Engel, Jean Armour Polly, Wolfgang Hecker, G. Gispert-Sauch, S.J., Mohammed Rafiq Shariq Warsi, and Swami Dharmanand.

As always, Laurence King Publishing has provided me with excellent editorial help. Melanie White and Jessica Spencer have guided this edition through its development and production with loving and patient skill, and Bridget Tily has worked very hard to track down the many new illustrations I requested.

Finally, I cannot adequately express my gratitude to my own revered teacher, Baba Virsa Singh of Gobind Sadan. People of all faiths from all over the world come to him for his spiritual blessings and guidance. In the midst of sectarian conflicts, his place is an oasis of peace and harmony. Now more than ever, we are learning from Babaji to regard each other as members of one human family. May God bless us all to move in this direction.

Mary Pat Fisher
Gobind Sadan Institute for Advanced Studies
in Comparative Religion, New Delhi

THE RELIGIOUS RESPONSE

Before sunrise, members of a Muslim family rise in Malaysia, perform their purifying ablutions, spread their prayer rugs facing Mecca, and begin their prostrations and prayers to Allah. In a French cathedral, worshippers line up for their turn to have a priest place a wafer on their tongue, murmuring, "This is the body of Christ." In a South Indian village, a group of women reverently anoint a cylindrical stone with milk and fragrant sandalwood paste and place around it offerings of flowers. The monks of a Japanese Zen Buddhist monastery sit cross-legged and upright in utter silence, broken occasionally by the noise of the *kyosaku* bat falling on their shoulders. On a mountain in Mexico, men, women, and children who have been dancing without food or water for days greet an eagle flying overhead with a burst of whistling from the small wooden flutes they wear around their necks. After the terrorist attacks on the World Trade Center in New York, there is a common response everywhere: People gather for prayer.

These and countless other moments in the lives of people around the world are threads of the tapestry we call "religion." The word is probably derived from the Latin, meaning "to tie back," "to tie again." All of religion shares the goal of tying people back to something behind the surface of life—a greater reality, which lies beyond, or invisibly infuses, the world that we can perceive with our five senses.

Attempts to connect with this greater reality have taken many forms. Many of them are organized institutions, such as Buddhism or Christianity, with leaders, sacred scriptures, beliefs, rituals, ethics, spiritual practices, cultural components, and historical traditions. Others are private personal experiences of individuals who belong to no institutionalized religion but nonetheless have an inner life of prayer, meditation, or direct experience of an inexplicable presence.

In this introductory chapter, we will try to develop some understanding of religion in a generic sense—why it exists, its encounters with modern science, and what general forms it takes—before studying the characteristics of the particular group religions that are practiced today.

Why are there religions?

In many cultures and times, religion has been the basic foundation of life, permeating all aspects of human existence. But from the time of the European Enlightenment, there has been a Western tendency to regard religion as a separate compartment of human life. Travelers brought the news that religious

behaviors of various sorts could be found everywhere that there are people, triggering attempts to explain their origin. Religion has become an object to be studied, rather than an unquestioned basic fact of life. Cultural anthropologists, sociologists, philosophers, psychologists, and even biologists have peered at religion through their own particular lenses, trying to explain what religion is and why it exists, to those who no longer take it for granted. In the following pages we will briefly examine some of the major theories that have evolved.

From candles and oil lamps to sacred fires, light is universally used to remind worshippers of an invisible reality. At Gobind Sadan, outside New Delhi, worship at a sacred fire continues twenty-four hours a day.

Materialistic perspective: humans invented religion

During the past two centuries, scientific **materialism** gained considerable prominence as a theory to explain the fact that religion can be found in some form in every culture around the world. The materialistic point of view is that the supernatural is imaginary; only the material world exists. From this point of view, religions have been invented by humans.

An influential example of this perspective can be found in the work of the nineteenth-century philosopher Ludwig Feuerbach (1804–1872). He reasoned that there are no supernatural entities; deities are simply projections, objectifications of people's fears and desires. What we can neither understand nor control, we fear; thus, according to Feuerbach, people living close to the land made gods of the most fearsome aspects of nature, such as lightning and death.

Following this line of reasoning, twentieth-century psychoanalyst Sigmund Freud described religion as a collective fantasy, a "universal obsessional neurosis"—a cosmic projection and replaying of the loving and fearful relationships that we had (and have) with our parents. Religious belief gives us an external God who is so powerful that He or She can protect us from the terrors of life, and will reward or punish us for obedience or nonobedience to social norms. From

Some religions try to transcend the mundane, glimpsing what lies beyond. Others, such as the Zen Buddhism that influenced this 18th-century drawing of The Meditating Frog, *find ultimate reality in the here and now, intensely experienced.*

Freud's extremely sceptical point of view, religious belief is an illusion springing from people's infantile insecurity and neurotic guilt; as such it closely resembles mental illness.

Others believe that religions have been created or at least used to manipulate people. Historically, religions have often supported and served centers of secular power. The nineteenth-century socialist philosopher Karl Marx argued that a culture's religion—as well as all other aspects of its social structure—springs from its economic framework. In Marx's view, religion's origins lie in the longings of those who suffer from oppression. It may have developed from the desire to revolutionize society and combat exploitation, but in failing to do so, it became otherworldly, an expression of unfilled desires for a better, more satisfying life:

> *Man makes religion: religion does not make man. . . . The religious world is but the reflex of the real world. . . . Religion is the sigh of the oppressed creature, the sentiment of a heartless world, and the soul of soulless conditions. It is the opium of the people. . . .*[1]

According to Marx, not only do religions pacify people falsely; they may themselves become tools of oppression. He observed that religious authorities claim to possess absolute truth and then permit that claim to be wielded as a weapon by social and political forces. For instance, he charged Christian authorities of his times with supporting "vile acts of the oppressors" by explaining them as due punishment of sinners by God. Other critics have made similar complaints against Eastern religions that blame the sufferings of the poor on their own misdeeds in their previous lives. Such interpretations and uses of religious teachings lessen the perceived need for society to help those who are oppressed and suffering. Marx's ideas thus led toward atheistic communism, for he had asserted, "The abolition of religion as the *illusory* happiness of the people is required for their real happiness."[2]

Functional perspective: religion is useful

Another line of reasoning has emerged in the search for a theory explaining the universal existence of religions: They are found everywhere because they are useful.

Pioneering work in this area was done by French sociologist Emile Durkheim (1858–1917). He proposed that humans cannot live without organized social structures, and that religion is a glue that holds a society together. He attempted to analyze Australian tribal religions, assuming them to be as simple as the material culture of their practitioners, to show the relationship between beliefs and group life. From this effort, he deduced a definition of religion, as "a unified system of beliefs and practices relative to sacred things, that is to say, things set apart and forbidden—beliefs and practices which unite into one single moral community called a church, all those who adhere to them."[3] To Durkheim, religious phenomena were symbols and reinforcers of the social order.

This kind of thinking about religion as functional system persists to today. John Bowker, author of the 1995 book *Is God a Virus?*, asserts that religions are organized systems that serve the essential biological purpose of bringing people together for their common survival, as well as giving their lives a sense of meaning. To Bowker, religion is universal because it protects gene replication and the nurturing of children. He proposes that because of its survival value, the potential for religiosity may even be genetically inherent in human brains.

The twentieth-century psychoanalyst Erich Fromm (1900–1980) looked at the usefulness of religion for individuals and concluded that humans have a need for a stable frame of reference, and that religion fulfills this need. As Mata Amritanandamayi, a contemporary Indian spiritual teacher, explains:

> Faith in God gives one the mental strength needed to confront the problems of life. Faith in the existence of God is a protective force. It makes one feel safe and protected from all the evil influences of the world. To have faith in the existence of a Supreme Power and to live accordingly is a religion. When we become religious, morality arises, which, in turn, will help to keep us away from malevolent influences. We won't drink, we won't smoke, and we will stop wasting our energy through unnecessary gossip and talk. ... We will also develop qualities like love, compassion, patience, mental equipoise, and other positive traits. These will help us to love and serve everyone equally. ... Where there is faith, there is harmony, unity and love. A nonbeliever always doubts. ... He cannot be at peace; he's restless. ... The foundation of his entire life is unstable and scattered due to his lack of faith in a higher principle.[4]

Research conducted by the Center for the Study of Religion/Spirituality and Health at Duke University indicates that religious faith is also beneficial for our physical health. They have found that those who attend religious services or read scriptures frequently are significantly longer lived, less likely to be depressed, less likely to have high blood pressure, and nearly ninety percent less likely to smoke.

Many of our psychological needs are not met by the material aspects of our life on earth. For example, we have difficulty accepting the commonsense notion that this life is all there is. We are born, we struggle to support ourselves, we age, and we die. If we believe that there is nothing more, fear of death may inhibit enjoyment of life and make all human actions seem pointless. Confronting mortality is so basic to the spiritual life that, as the Christian monk Brother David Steindl-Rast observes, whenever monks from any spiritual tradition meet, within five minutes they are talking about death.

> *It appears that throughout the world man has always been seeking something beyond his own death, beyond his own problems, something that will be enduring, true and timeless. He has called it God, he has given it many names; and most of us believe in something of that kind, without ever actually experiencing it.*
>
> *Jiddu Krishnamurti*[5]

Many of us seek an assurance that life continues in some form beyond the grave. But we may also want this present life to have some meaning. For many, the desire for material achievement offers a temporary sense of

The Golden Temple in Amritsar, India. Religious edifices attempt to reflect the sacred realm.

purposefulness. But once achieved, these material goals may seem hollow. The Buddha said:

Look!
The world is a royal chariot, glittering with paint.
No better.
    Fools are deceived, but the wise know better.[6]

All religions help to uncover meaning in the midst of the mundane. The influential twentieth-century scholar of comparative religion, Mircea Eliade (1907–1986), wrote of the distinction between the **profane**—the everyday world of seemingly random, ordinary, and unimportant occurrences—and the **sacred**—the realm of the extraordinary and supernatural, the source of the universe and its values, which is charged with significance. Religions open pathways to the sacred by exploring the **transpersonal** dimension of life—the eternal and infinite, beyond limited personal or communal concerns.

Religions propose ideals that can radically transform people. Mahatma Gandhi was an extremely shy, fearful, self-conscious child. His transformation into one of the great political figures of our time occurred as he meditated single-mindedly on the great Hindu scripture, the ***Bhagavad-Gita***. Gandhi was particularly impressed by the second chapter, which he says was "inscribed on the tablet of my heart."[7] It reads, in part:

He is forever free who has broken
Out of the ego-cage of I and mine
To be united with the Lord of Love.
This is the supreme state. Attain thou this
And pass from death to immortality.[8]

People long to gain strength for dealing with personal problems. Those who are suffering severe physical illness, privation, terror, or grief often turn to the divine for help. Agnes Collard, a Christian woman near death from four painful years of cancer, reported that her impending death was bringing her closer to God:

I don't know what or who He is, but I am almost sure He is there. I feel His
presence, feel that He is close to me during the awful moments. And I feel love.
I sometimes feel wrapped, cocooned in love.[9]

Religious literature is full of stories of miraculous aid that has come to those who have cried out in their need. Rather than what is construed as divine intervention, sometimes help comes as the strength and philosophy to accept burdens. The eighteenth-century Hasidic Jewish master known as the Baal Shem Tov (c. 1700–1760) taught that the vicissitudes of life are ways of climbing toward the divine. Islam teaches patience, faithful waiting for the unfailing grace of Allah. Despite his own trials, the Christian apostle Paul wrote of "the peace of God, which passeth all understanding."[10] Gandhi was blissful in prison, for no human could bar his relationship with the Lord of Love.

Rather than seeking help from without, an alternative approach is to gain freedom from problems by changing our ways of thinking. According to some Eastern religions, the concept that we are distinct, autonomous individuals is an illusion;

what we think of as "our" consciousnesses and "our" bodies are in perpetual flux. From this point of view, freedom from problems lies in recognizing and accepting the reality of temporal change and devaluing the "small self" in favor of the eternal self. The ancient sages of India referred to it as "This eternal being that can never be proved, ... spotless, beyond the ether, the unborn Self, great and eternal, ... the creator, the maker of everything."[11]

Many contemplative spiritual traditions teach methods of turning within to discover and eradicate all attachments, desires, and resentments associated with the small earthly self, revealing the purity of the eternal self. Once we have found it within, we begin to see it wherever we look. This realization brings a sense of acceptance in which, as philosopher William James observed:

> *Dull submission is left far behind, and a mood of welcome, which may fill any place on the scale between cheerful serenity and enthusiastic gladness, has taken its place.*[12]

Kabir, a fifteenth-century Indian weaver who was inspired alike by Islam and Hinduism and whose words are included in Sikh scripture, described this state of spiritual bliss:

> *The blue sky opens out farther and farther,*
> *the daily sense of failure goes away,*
> *the damage I have done to myself fades,*
> *a million suns come forward with light,*
> *when I sit firmly in that world.*[13]

Some people feel that their true selves are part of that world of light, dimly remembered, and long to return to it. The nineteenth-century Romantic poet William Wordsworth wrote:

> *Our birth is but a sleep and a forgetting;*
> *The Soul that rises with us, our life's Star*
> *Hath had elsewhere its setting*
> *And cometh from afar;*
> *Not in entire forgetfulness,*
> *And not in utter nakedness,*
> *But trailing clouds of glory do we come*
> *From God, who is our home.*[14]

We look to religions for understanding, for answers to our many questions about life. Who are we? Why are we here? What happens after we die? Why is there suffering? Why is there evil? Is anybody up there listening? For those who find security in specific answers, some religions offer **dogma**—systems of doctrines proclaimed as absolutely true and accepted as such, even if they lie beyond the domain of one's personal experiences. Absolute faith provides some people with a sense of relief from anxieties, a secure feeling of rootedness, meaning, and orderliness in the midst of rapid social change. Religions may also provide rules for living, governing everything from diet to personal relationships. Such prescriptions are seen as earthly reflections of the order that prevails in the cosmos. Some religions, however, encourage people to explore the perennial questions by themselves, and to live in the uncertainties of not knowing intellectually, breaking through old concepts until nothing remains but truth itself.

A final need that draws some people to religion is the discomforting sense of being alone in the universe. This isolation can be painful, even terrifying. The divine may be sought as a loving father or mother, or as a friend. Alternatively, some paths offer the way of self-transcendence. Through them, the sense of isolation is lost in mystical merger with the One Being, with Reality itself.

Faith perspective: Ultimate Reality exists

From the point of view of religious faith, there truly is an underlying reality that cannot readily be perceived but that some people in all cultures have experienced. Human responses to this Supreme Reality have been expressed and institutionalized as the structures of religions.

Religious belief often springs from mystical experience—the overwhelming awareness that one has been touched by a reality that far transcends ordinary life. Those who have had such experiences find it hard to describe them, for what has touched them lies beyond the world of time and space to which our languages refer. These people usually know instantly and beyond a shadow of doubt that they have had a brush with spiritual reality. Pierre Teilhard de Chardin (1881–1955), a highly respected French paleontologist and Jesuit priest, became convinced that God is "the heart of All" because of his fiery personal encounters with "the unique Life of all things."[15] George William Russell (1867–1935), an Irish writer who described his mystical experiences under the pen name "AE," was lying on a hillside:

not then thinking of anything but the sunlight, and how sweet it was to drowse there, when, suddenly, I felt a fiery heart throb, and knew it was personal and intimate, and started with every sense dilated and intent, and turned inwards, and I heard first a music as of bells going away ... and then the heart of the hills was opened to me, and I knew there was no hill for those who were there, and they were unconscious of the ponderous mountain piled above the palaces of light, and the winds were sparkling and diamond clear, yet full of colour as an opal, as they glittered through the valley, and I knew the Golden Age was all about me, and it was we who had been blind to it but that it had never passed away from the world.[16]

The existential loneliness some feel is hauntingly depicted by the sculptures of Alberto Giacometti, such as his Walking Man, *c. 1947–48.*

Encounters with a **transcendent** reality are given various names in spiritual traditions: enlightenment, God-realization, illumination, *kensho*, awakening, self-knowledge, **gnosis**, ecstatic communion, coming home. They may arise spontaneously, as in near-death experiences in which people seem to find themselves in a world of unearthly radiance, or may be induced by meditation, fasting, prayer, chanting, drugs, or dancing. To the frustration of many who now try these techniques in search of enlightenment without seeing immediate results, it seems that we cannot grasp the Ultimate Reality solely by our own efforts. Rather, it grasps us.

This spontaneous experience of being grasped by Reality is the essential basis of religion, according to the influential German professor of theology, Rudolf Otto (1869–1937). The experience is ineffable, "*sui generis* and irreducible to any other;

and therefore, like every absolutely primary and elementary dictum, while it admits of being discussed, it cannot be strictly defined."[17] This experience of the Holy, asserts Otto, brings forth two general responses in a person: a feeling of great awe or even dread, and a feeling of great attraction. These responses, in turn, have given rise to the whole gamut of religious beliefs and behaviors.

Though ineffable, the nature of genuine religious experience is not unpredictable, according to the research of Joachim Wach (1898–1955), a German scholar of comparative religion. In every religion, it seems to follow a certain pattern: (1) It is an experience of what is considered Ultimate Reality; (2) It involves the person's whole being; (3) It is the most shattering and intense of all human experiences; and (4) It motivates the person to action, through worship, ethical behavior, service, and sharing with others in a religious grouping.

These predictable, if dramatic and transformative, results cannot be rigidly schematized, however, according to the Canadian scholar, Wilfred Cantwell Smith (1917–2000). He asserted that what are commonly called "religions" are themselves elusive, complex systems that do not fit neatly into labeled, reified categories such as "Hinduism" and "Christianity." And the experiential basis of religion means that it cannot be fully described and analyzed as an object. Smith proposed: "Fundamentally it is the outsider who names a religious system. . . . The participant is concerned with God; the observer has been concerned with 'religion.' "[18]

A sense of the presence of the Great Unnamable may burst through the seeming ordinariness of life. (Samuel Palmer, The Waterfalls, Pistyll Mawddach, North Wales, 1835–36.)

> *[The "flash of illumination" brings] a state of glorious inspiration, exaltation, intense joy, a piercingly sweet realization that the whole of life is fundamentally right and that it knows what it's doing.*
>
> *Nona Coxhead*[19]

Modes of encountering Ultimate Reality

We have two basic ways of apprehending reality: rational thought and non-rational modes of knowing. To reason is to establish abstract general categories from the data we have gathered with our senses, and then to organize these abstractions to formulate seemingly logical ideas about reality. Reason may lead different people to different conclusions, however. The seventeenth-century English rationalist philosopher Thomas Hobbes (1588–1679) reasoned that God is simply an idea constructed by the human imagination from ideas of the visible world. His contemporary, the rationalist French philosopher René Descartes (1596–1650), asserted that his awareness of his own existence and his internal reasoning were indications of the existence of God.

Some people come to religious convictions indirectly, through belief in what has been uttered by great religious figures or what has been established as doctrine by religious tradition. Other people develop faith only after their own questions have been answered. Martin Luther, father of the Protestant branches of Christianity, recounted how he searched for faith in God through storms of doubt, "raged with a fierce and agitated conscience."[20]

The human mind does not function in the rational mode alone; there are differing modes of consciousness. In his classic study, *The Varieties of Religious Experience*, William James concluded:

> *Our normal waking consciousness, rational consciousness as we call it, is but one special type of consciousness, whilst all about it, parted from it by the flimsiest of screens, there lie potential forms of consciousness entirely different . . .*
>   *No account of the universe in its totality can be final which leaves these other forms of consciousness quite disregarded.*[21]

In some religions, people are encouraged to develop their own intuitive abilities to perceive spiritual truths directly, beyond the senses, beyond the limits of human reason, beyond blind belief. This way is often called **mysticism**. In the ancient *Upanishads* (teachings given by great Indian masters of meditation to their students), the pupils are urged to sit in deep meditation and, with their minds fully absorbed in love, direct their consciousness toward the eternal One. In indigenous traditions, people may be taught to undergo austerities and then cry out for a sacred vision from the unseen to help guide their actions.

Many religions have developed meditation techniques that encourage intuitive wisdom to rise from the depths—or the voice of the divine to descend into individual consciousness. Whether this wisdom is perceived as a natural faculty within or an external voice, the process is similar. The consciousness is initially turned away from the world and even from one's own feelings and thoughts, letting them all go. Often a concentration practice, such as watching the breath or

staring at a candle flame, is used to collect the awareness into a single, unfragmented focus. Once the mind is quiet, distinctions between inside and outside drop away. The seer becomes one with the seen, in a fusion of subject and object through which the inner nature of things often seems to reveal itself.

Our ordinary experience of the world is that our self is separate from the world of objects that we perceive. But this dualistic understanding may be transcended in a moment of enlightenment in which the Real and our awareness of it become one. The *Mundaka Upanishad* says, "Lose thyself in the Eternal, even as the arrow is lost in the target." For the Hindu, this is the prized attainment of **moksha**, or liberation, in which one enters into awareness of the eternal reality known as **Brahman**. This reality is then known with the same direct apprehension with which one knows oneself. The Sufi Muslim mystic Abu Yazid said, "I sloughed off my self as a snake sloughs off its skin, and I looked into my essence and saw that 'I am He.' "[22]

This enlightened awareness cannot be communicated to those who have not had a similar experience, although our sacred literature is full of attempts to do so. Neither human language nor human logic, both of which deal with the experience of a world of separate forms, is adequate to describe the unitary experience of Ultimate Reality.

Understandings of Ultimate Reality

Approached by different ways of knowing, by different people, from different times and different cultures, the sacred has many faces. The Ultimate Reality may be conceived as **immanent** (present in the world) or transcendent (existing above and outside of the material universe). Many people perceive the sacred as a personal being, as Father, Mother, Teacher, Friend, Beloved, or as a specific deity. Religions based on one's relationship to the Divine Being are called **theistic**. If the being is worshipped as a singular form, the religion is **monotheistic**. If many attributes and forms of the divine are emphasized, the religion may be labeled **polytheistic**. Religions that hold that beneath the multiplicity of apparent forms there is one underlying substance are called **monistic**.

Ultimate Reality may also be conceived in **nontheistic** terms. It may be experienced as a "changeless Unity," as "Suchness," or simply as "the Way." There may be no sense of a personal Creator God in such understandings.

Some people believe that the sacred reality is usually invisible but occasionally appears visibly in human **incarnations**, such as Christ or Krishna, or in special manifestations, such as the flame Moses reportedly saw coming from the center of a bush but not consuming it. Or the deity that cannot be seen is described in human terms. Theologian Sallie McFague thus writes of God as "lover" by imputing human feelings to God:

God as lover is the one who loves the world not with the fingertips but totally and passionately, taking pleasure in its variety and richness, finding it attractive and valuable, delighting in its fulfilment. God as lover is the moving power of love in the universe, the desire for unity with all the beloved.[23]

Opposite *Many religions use ritual cleansing with water to help remove inner filth that obscures awareness of Ultimate Reality.*

Throughout history, there have been religious authorities who have claimed that the deity they worship is the true one and that all others are worshipping false gods. They have labeled others as "pagans" or "nonbelievers." For their part, the others apply similar negative epithets to them. When these rigid positions are taken, often to the point of violent conflicts or forced conversions, there is no room to consider the possibility that all may be talking about the same indescribable thing in different languages or referring to different aspects of the same unknowable Whole.

Atheism is the belief that there is no deity. Following Karl Marx, many communist countries in the twentieth century discouraged or suppressed religious beliefs, attempting to replace them with secular faith in supposedly altruistic government. The distinguished Protestant theologian Reinhold Niebuhr (1892–1971) described atheistic communism as "an irreligion transmuted into a new political religion, canonized precisely in the writings of Marx (and the later Lenin) as sacred scripture" with Marx cast as "the revered prophet of a new world religion."[24] It was not uncommon for people of all faiths in all continents of the world to embrace as a new religion of sorts Marx's message of collectivism in contrast to the dehumanizing effects of modern industry and capitalism, and with it, his stinging criticism of oppression of the people in the name of religion.

Atheism may also arise from within, in those whose experiences give them no reason to believe that there is anything more to life than the mundane. One American college student articulates a common modern form of unwilling atheism:

To be a citizen of the modern, industrialized world with its scientific worldview is to be, to a certain extent, an atheist. I myself do not want to be an atheist; the cold mechanical worldview is repugnant to my need for the warmth and meaning that comes from God. But as I have been educated in the secular, scientistic educational system—where God is absent but atoms and molecules and genes and cells and presidents and kings are the factors to be reckoned with, the powers of this world, not a divine plan or a divine force as my ancestors must have believed—I cannot wholly believe in God.[25]

Agnosticism is not the denial of the divine but the feeling, "I don't know whether it exists or not," or the belief that if it exists it is impossible for humans to know it. Religious scepticism has been a current in Western thought since classical times; it was given the name "agnosticism" in the nineteenth century by T. H. Huxley, who stated its basic principles as a denial of metaphysical beliefs and of most (in his case) Christian beliefs since they are unproven or unprovable, and their replacement with scientific method for examining facts and experiences.

These categories are not mutually exclusive, so attempts to apply the labels can sometimes confuse us rather than help us understand religions. In some polytheistic traditions there is a hierarchy of gods and goddesses with one highest being at the top. In Hinduism, each individual deity is understood as an embodiment of all aspects of the divine. In the paradoxes that occur when we try to apply human logic and language to that which transcends rational thought, a person may believe that God is both a highly personal being and also present in all things. An agnostic may be deeply committed to moral principles. Or mystics may have personal encounters with the divine and yet find it so unspeakable that they say it is beyond human knowing. The Jewish scholar Maimonides (1135–1204) asserted that:

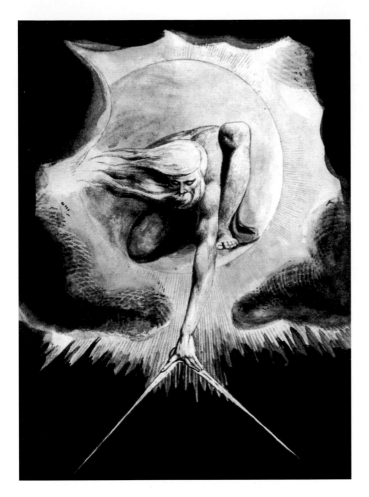

The concept of God as an old man with a beard who rules the world from the sky has been supported by the art of patriarchal monotheistic traditions, such as William Blake's frontispiece to "Europe," The Act of Creation, *1794.*

the human mind cannot comprehend God. Only God can know Himself. The only form of comprehension of God we can have is to realize how futile it is to try to comprehend Him.[26]

Jaap Sahib, the great hymn of praises of God by the Tenth Sikh Guru, Guru Gobind Singh, consists largely of the negative attributes of God, such as these:

Salutations to the One without colour or hue,
Salutations to the One who hath no beginning.
Salutations to the Impenetrable,
Salutations to the Unfathomable . . .
O Lord, Thou art Formless and Peerless
Beyond birth and physical elements. . . .
Salutations to the One beyond confines of religion. . . .
Beyond description and Garbless
Thou art Nameless and Desireless.
Thou art beyond thought and ever Mysterious.[27]

Some people believe that the aspect of the divine that has revealed itself to them is the only one. Others feel that there is one being with many faces, that all religions come from one source. Father Bede Griffiths, a Catholic monk who lived in a community in India, attempting to unite Eastern and Western traditions, was among those who feel that if we engage in a deep study of all religions we will find their common ground:

> In each tradition the one divine Reality, the one eternal Truth, is present, but it is hidden under symbols. ... Always the divine Mystery is hidden under a veil, but each revelation (or "unveiling") unveils some aspect of the one Truth, or, if you like, the veil becomes thinner at a certain point. The Semitic religions, Judaism and Islam, reveal the transcendent aspect of the divine Mystery with incomparable power. The oriental religions reveal the divine Immanence with immeasurable depth. Yet in each the opposite aspect is contained, though in a more hidden way.[28]

Worship, symbol, and myth

No matter how believers conceive of the Ultimate Reality, it inspires their reverence. The outer forms of religions consist in large part of human attempts to express this reverence and perhaps enter the sacred state of communion with that which is worshipped. Around the world, rituals, sacraments, prayers, and spiritual practices are used to create a sacred atmosphere or state of consciousness in which people hope to touch or be touched by whispers of the eternal.

> Our religious ceremonies are but the shadows of that great universal worship celebrated in the heavens by the legions of heavenly beings on all planes, and our prayers drill a channel across this mist separating our earthbound plane from the celestial ones through which a communication may be established with the powers that be.
>
> Pir Vilayat Inayat Khan[29]

Group ceremonies often include sharing of food, fire or candles, purification with water, flowers, fragrances, and offerings of some sort. When such worshipful actions are predictable and repeated rather than spontaneous, they are known as **rituals**. Religious rituals usually involve repetition, specific intentions, patterned performance, traditional meanings, and purposefulness. In reference to offerings, Professor Antony Fernando of Sri Lanka explains:

> Even the most illiterate person knows that in actual fact no god really picks up those offerings or is actually in need of them. What people offer is what they own. Whatever is owned becomes so close to the heart of the owner as to become an almost integral part of his or her life. Therefore, when people offer something, it is, as it were, themselves they offer. ... Sacrifices and offerings are a dramatic way of proclaiming that they are not the ultimate possessors of their life and also of articulating their determination to live duty-oriented lives and not desire-oriented lives.[30]

What religions attempt to approach is beyond human utterance. Believers build statues and buildings through which to worship the divine, but these forms are not the divine itself. Because people are addressing the invisible, it can be suggested only through metaphor. Deepest consciousness cannot speak the language of everyday life; what it knows can be suggested only in **symbols**—images borrowed from the material world that are similar to ineffable spiritual experiences. They appeal to the emotions and imagination rather than to the rational mind.

Many peoples have used similar images to represent similar sacred meanings. The sun, for example, is frequently honored as a symbol of the divine because of its radiance; the sky is the abode of many gods, for it is elevated above the earth. A vertical symbol placed at the center of the world—such as a pillar, tree, or mountain—appears in many cultures as a symbol of a basic holy connection between the earthly plane and the unseen heavenly planes.

Myths are stories based on symbols. Religious myths attempt to express ultimate divine reality, basic truths, or the inner meaning of life for believers. A primary function of religious myth is to establish models for human behavior. Stories about the heroic lives of the great founders and saints are held up as examples for molding one's own life. They also establish belief in a superhuman

This symbolic representation of a World Tree comes from 18th-century Iran. It is conceived as a tree in Paradise, about which the Prophet Muhammad reportedly said, "God planted it with His own hand and breathed His spirit into it."

dimension to these lives. Great holy figures are often said to have been born of virgin mothers, for instance, for their seminal source is not human but rather the Invisible One. There are also myths of **cosmogony** (sacred accounts of the creation of the world) and of **eschatology** (beliefs concerning the purported end of the world). These myths form a sacred belief structure that supports the laws, rituals, and institutions of the religion, as well as explaining the cosmic situation and the ways of the community.

While believers may perceive myths and invisible beings as real facts, it is now common for scholars to interpret them metaphorically rather than literally and to see them as serving functions for the society or the individual. For example, the American mythologist Joseph Campbell (1904–1987) speculated that the sacred myths of a group serve basic social purposes: awakening a sense of wonder at creation, incorporating the group's ethical codes, and helping individuals pass harmoniously through life-cycle changes. Following psychoanalyst Carl Jung's lead, Campbell interpreted legends of the hero's journey (stories of separation, initiation, and return bearing truth to the people) as a form of psychological instruction for individuals:

> It is the business of mythology to reveal the specific dangers and techniques of the dark interior way from tragedy to comedy. Hence the incidents are fantastic and "unreal": they represent psychological, not physical, triumphs. The passage of the mythological hero may be overground, [but] fundamentally it is inward—into depths where obscure resistances are overcome, and long lost, forgotten powers are revivified, to be made available for the transfiguration of the world.[31]

Absolutist and liberal interpretations

Within each faith people often have different ways of interpreting their traditions. The **orthodox** stand by an historical form of their religion. They try to be strict followers of its established practices, laws, and creeds. Those who try to resist contemporary influences and affirm what they perceive as the historical core of their religion could be called **absolutists**. In our times, many people feel that their distinctive identity as individuals or as members of an established group is threatened by the sweeping social changes brought by modern industrial culture. The breakup of family relationships, loss of geographic rootedness, decay of clear behavioral codes, and loss of local control may be very unsettling. To find stable footing, some people may try to stand on selected religious doctrines or practices from the past. Religious leaders may encourage this trend toward rigidity by declaring themselves absolute authorities or by telling the people that their scriptures are literally and exclusively true. They may encourage antipathy or even violence against people of other religious traditions.

The term **fundamentalism** is often applied to this selective insistence on parts of a religious tradition and to violence against people of other religions. This use of the term is misleading, for no religion is based on hatred of other people and because those who are labeled "fundamentalists" may not be engaged in a return to the true basics of their religion. A Muslim "fundamentalist" who insists on the veiling of women, for instance, does not draw this doctrine from the foundation of Islam, the Holy Qur'an, but rather from historical cultural practice in some Muslim countries. A Sikh "fundamentalist" who concentrates on externals, such as wearing a turban, sword, and steel bracelet, overlooks the central insistence of the Sikh Gurus on the inner rather than outer practice of religion. A Hindu "fundamentalist" who objects to the presence of Christian missionaries working among the poor ignores one of the basic principles of ancient Indian religion, which is the tolerant assertion that there are many paths to the same universal truth. Rev. Valson Thampu, editor of the Indian journal *Traci*, writes that this selective type of religious extremism "absolutises what is spiritually or ethically superfluous in a religious tradition. True spiritual enthusiasm or zeal, on the other hand, stakes everything on being faithful to the spiritual essence."[32]

A further problem with the use of the term "fundamentalism" is that it has a specifically Protestant Christian connotation. The Christian fundamentalist movement originated in the late nineteenth century as a reaction to liberal trends, such as historical-critical study of the Bible. Other labels may, therefore, be more cross-culturally appropriate, such as "absolutist," "extremist," or "reactionary," depending on the particular situation.

Those who are called religious **liberals** take a more flexible approach to religious tradition. They may see scriptures as products of a specific culture and time rather than the eternal voice of truth, and may interpret passages metaphorically rather than literally. If activists, they may advocate reforms in the ways their religion is officially understood and practiced. Those who are labeled **heretics** publicly assert controversial positions that are unacceptable to the orthodox establishment. **Mystics** are guided by their own spiritual experiences, which may coincide with any of the above positions.

The encounter between science and religion

Divisions among absolutist, liberal, and sceptical interpretations of religion are related to the development of modern science. Like religion, science is also engaged in searching for universal principles that explain the facts of nature. The two approaches have influenced each other since ancient times, when they were not seen as separate endeavors. In both East and West, there were continual attempts to understand reality as a whole.

In ancient Greece, source of many "Western" ideas, a group of thinkers who are sometimes called "nature philosophers" tried to understand the world through their own perceptions of it. By contrast, Plato distrusted the testimony of the human senses. He thus made a series of distinctions: between what is perceived by the senses and what is accessible through reason, between body and soul, appearance and reality, objects and ideas. In Plato's thought, the soul was superior to the body, and the activity of reason preferable to the distraction of the senses. This value judgment dominated Western thought through the Middle Ages, with its underlying belief that all of nature had been created by God for the sake of humanity.

In the seventeenth century, knowledge of nature became more secularized (that is, divorced from the sacred) as scientists developed models of the universe

The Hubble space telescope is revealing an unimaginably vast cosmos, with billions of galaxies in continual flux. The Eagle Nebula shown here is giving birth to new stars in "pillars of creation" which are 6 trillion miles high.

as a giant machine. Its ways, like the running of a clock, could be discovered by human reason, by skillful attempts to study its component parts and mathematically quantify its characteristics and activities. However, even in discovering such features, many scientists regarded them as the work of a divine Creator or Ruler. Isaac Newton, whose gravitational theory shaped modern physics, speculated that space is eternal because it is the emanation of "eternal and immutable being." Drawing on biblical quotations, Newton argued that God exists everywhere, containing, discerning, and ruling all things.

During the eighteenth-century Enlightenment, rational ways of knowing were increasingly respected, with a concurrent growing scepticism toward claims of knowledge derived from such sources as divine revelation or illuminated inner wisdom. The sciences were viewed as progressive; some thinkers attacked institutionalized religions and dogma as superstitions. Scepticism was applied even to science itself, as early modern scientists gave up trying to find absolute certainties. Rather, they developed hypotheses that were seen as only provisionally true, subject to further investigation and revision.

Unitary concepts of science and religion faced their most serious challenge in

1859, when the naturalist Charles Darwin published *The Origin of Species*, a work that propounded the theory of evolution by natural selection. Darwin demonstrated that certain genetic mutations give an organism a competitive advantage over others of its species, and thus its lineage is naturally more likely to survive. According to Darwin's theory, over great lengths of time this process has directed the development of all forms of life. The theory of natural selection directly contradicted a literal understanding of the biblical Book of Genesis, in which God is said to have created all life in only six days. By the end of the nineteenth century, all such beliefs of the Judeo-Christian tradition were being questioned. The German philosopher Nietzsche proclaimed, "God is dead!"

From twentieth-century scientific research, it is clear that the cosmos is mindboggling in its complexity and that what we perceive with our five senses is not Ultimate Reality. For instance, the inertness and solidity of matter are only illusions. Each atom consists mostly of empty space with tiny particles whirling around in it. These subatomic particles—such as neutrons, protons, and electrons—cannot even be described as "things." Twentieth-century theories of quantum mechanics, which tried to account for the tiniest particles of matter, uncovered the Uncertainty Principle—the demonstration that the position and velocity of a subatomic particle cannot be simultaneously determined. Subatomic particles behave like energy as well as like matter, like waves as well as like particles. Their position can be determined only statistically. Their behaviors can best be described in terms of a dynamic, interdependent system which includes the observer. Human consciousness is inextricably involved in what it thinks it is "objectively" studying. As physicist David Bohm puts it, "Everything interpenetrates everything."[33]

Our own bodies appear relatively solid, but they are in a constant state of flux and interchange with the environment. Our eyes, ears, noses, tongues, and skin do not reveal absolute truths. Rather, our sensory organs may operate as filters, selecting from a multi-dimensional universe only those characteristics that we need to perceive in order to survive. Imagine how difficult it would be simply to walk across a street if we could see all the electromagnetic energy in the atmosphere, such as x-rays, radio waves, gamma rays, and infrared and ultraviolet light, rather than only the small band of colors we see as the visible spectrum. Though the sky of a starry night appears vast to the naked eye, the giant Hubble telescope placed in space is revealing an incomprehensibly immense cosmos whose limits have not been found. It contains matter-gobbling black holes, vast starmaking clusters, inter-galactic collisions, and cosmic events that happened billions of years ago, so far away that their light is just now being captured by our most powerful instruments for examining what lies far beyond our small place in this galaxy. We know that more lies beyond what we have yet been able to measure. And even our ability to conceive of what we cannot sense may perhaps be limited by the way our brain is organized.

As science continues to question its own assumptions and theories, various new hypotheses are being suggested about the nature of the universe. "Superstring theory" proposes that the universe may not be made of particles at all, but rather of tiny vibrating strings and loops of strings. According to Superstring theory, whereas we think we are living in four observable dimensions of space and time, there may be ten dimensions, with the unperceived six dimensions "curled up" or "compactified" within the four dimensions that we can perceive. According to "M theory," there may be a total of eleven dimensions, including one called "supergravity."

New branches of science are finding that the universe is not always predictable, nor does it always operate according to human notions of cause and effect. And whereas scientific models of the universe were until recently based on the assumption of stability and equilibrium, physicist Ilya Prigogine observes that "today we see instability, fluctuations, irreversibility at every level."[34]

Science cannot accurately predict even the future orbits of planets within this solar system, for all the relevant factors will never be known to human researchers. Physicist Murray Gell-Mann says that we are "a small speck of creation believing it is capable of comprehending the whole."[35]

Contemporary physics approaches metaphysics in the work of physicists such as David Bohm. He describes the dimensions we see and think of as "real" as the *explicate* order. Behind it lies the *implicate* order, in which separateness resolves into unbroken wholeness. Beyond may lie other subtle dimensions, all merging into an infinite ground that unfolds itself as light. This scientific theory is very similar to descriptions by mystics from all cultures about their intuitive experiences of the cosmos. Indeed, realization of the inadequacy of empirical inquiry came long ago in Eastern religious traditions. They recognized the value of perception and reason for the acquisition of ordinary, utilitarian knowledge, but discounted their use for the acquisition of transcendent knowledge of the mystery of being. This mystery, they hold, can be apprehended only through spiritual experience.

> *The most beautiful and profound emotion that we can experience is the sensation of the mystical. It is the sower of all true science. He to whom this emotion is a stranger, who can no longer wonder and stand rapt in awe, is as good as dead. To know that what is impenetrable to us really exists, manifesting itself as the highest wisdom and the most radiant beauty which our dull faculties can comprehend only in their most primitive forms—this knowledge, this feeling is at the center of true religiousness. . . . A human being is part of the whole. . . . He experiences himself, his thoughts and feelings as something separated from the rest—a kind of optical delusion of his consciousness. . . . Our task must be to free ourselves from this prison by widening our circle of compassion to embrace all living creatures, and the whole [of] nature in its beauty.*
>
> *Albert Einstein*[36]

One of the major controversies between science and religion is the conflict between religious concepts of intentional divine creation and the scientific concept of a universe that has evolved mechanistically by processes such as genetic mutations and random combinations of elements. Scientific research is continually revealing a universe whose perfections are suggestive of purposefulness. They have found, for instance, that stars could never have formed if the force of gravity were ever so slightly stronger or weaker. Biologists find that the natural world is an intricate harmony of beautifully elaborated, interrelated parts. Even to produce the miniature propeller that allows a tiny bacterium to swim, some forty different proteins are required. The huge multinational Human Genome Project has discovered that the basic genetic units that are found in all life forms are repeated 3.1 billion times in complex combinations to create human beings.

The question arises: Can the complex maps that produce life be the consequences of chance arrangements of atoms, or are they the result of deliberate design by some First Cause? Current research has demonstrated that the development of certain complex biochemical systems, such as the Krebs citric acid cycle, which unleashes the chemical energy stored in food and makes it available to support life, can be explained by Darwinian mechanics. Some feel that evolution theory presupposes blind, uncaring mechanics, since so many species that have arisen have become extinct. The feeling is that if there were a Creator God, how could that God be so wasteful or cruel? However, the theory of evolution does not necessarily conflict with religious beliefs, if both are examined carefully. Biology professor Kenneth Miller proposes that:

> Evolution is certainly not so "cruel" that it cannot be compatible with the notion of a loving God. All that evolution points out is that every organism that has ever lived will eventually die. This is not a special feature of Darwinian theory, but an observable, verifiable fact. The driving force behind evolutionary charge is differential reproductive success, the fact that some organisms leave more offspring than others. Yes, the struggle for existence sometimes involves competition and predation, but just as often it involves cooperation, care, and extraordinary beauty.[37]

Geneticist Francis Collins, Director of the United States' National Human Genome Research Institute at the National Institutes of Health, is both a serious scientist and a "serious" Christian. He does not find the two facets to his life incompatible. Rather, he says:

> When something new is revealed about the human genome, I experience a feeling of awe at the realization that humanity now knows something only God knew before. It is a deeply moving sensation that helps me appreciate the spiritual side of life, and also makes the practice of science more rewarding.[38]

According to contemporary "Big Bang" theory, the entire cosmos originated from one point in an explosion whose force is still expanding. Astronomer Fred Hoyle (1915–2001), who originated the term "Big Bang," cautioned that it may not have been a chance happening:

> The universe has to know in advance what it is going to be before it knows how to start itself. For in accordance with the Big Bang Theory, for instance, at a time of 10

Some contemporary scientists feel that the perfect details of the natural world cannot have arisen without some kind of guiding intelligence in the cosmos.

[to the minus 43] seconds the universe has to know how many types of neutrino there are going to be at a time of 1 second. This is so in order that it starts off expanding at the right rate to fit the eventual number of neutrino types. . . . An explosion in a junkyard does not lead to sundry bits of metal being assembled into a working machine.[39]

Religious beliefs that, if interpreted literally, seem to be contradicted by scientific fact can instead be interpreted as belonging to the realm of myth. Myths give us symbolic answers to ultimate questions that cannot be answered by empirical experience or rational thought, such as "What are we here for?"

At the cutting edge of research, scientists themselves find they have no ultimate answers that can be expressed in scientific terms. The renowned theoretical physicist Stephen Hawking asks, "What is it that breathes fire into the equations and makes a universe for them to describe?"[40]

Women and the feminine in religions

Another long-standing dichotomy in the sphere of religion is the exclusion of women and the feminine in favor of male-dominated systems. According to some current though controversial theories, many of the myths surviving in today's religions may be related to the suppression of early female-oriented religions by later male-oriented religious systems. Archaeological evidence from many cultures was re-interpreted during the twentieth century as suggesting that worship of a female high goddess was originally widespread. Although there were, and are now, cultures that did not ascribe gender or hierarchy or personality to the divine, some that did may have seen the highest deity as a female.

Just as today's male high deity goes by different names in different religions (God, Allah), the Great Goddess had many names. Among her many identities, she was Danu or Diti in ancient India, the Great Mother Nu Kwa of China, the Egyptian cobra goddess Ua Zit, the Greek earth goddess Gaia, the sun goddess Arinna of Turkey, Coatlique the Mother of Aztec deities, Queen Mother Freyja of the Scandinavians, Great Spider Woman of the Pueblo peoples of North America, and Mawu, omnipotent creator of the Dahomey. A reverent address to Ishtar, an important Mesopotamian goddess, dating from some time between the eighteenth and seventh centuries BCE suggests some of the powers ascribed to her:

Unto Her who renders decision, Goddess of all things. Unto the Lady of Heaven and Earth who receives supplication; Unto Her who hears petition, who entertains prayer; Unto the compassionate Goddess who loves righteousness; Ishtar the Queen, who suppresses all that is confused. To the Queen of Heaven, the Goddess of the Universe, the One who walked in terrible Chaos and brought life by the Law of Love; And out of Chaos brought us harmony.[41]

Temples and images that seem to have been devoted to worship of the goddess have been found in almost every Neolithic and early historic archaeological site in Europe and West Asia. She was often symbolically linked with water, serpents, birds, eggs, spirals, the moon, the womb, the vulva, the magnetic currents of the earth, psychic powers, and the eternal creation and renewal of life.

An early image of what appears to be the Great Mother, creator and sustainer of the universe. (Tel Halaf, 5th millennium BCE.)

In Hindu tradition, the great goddess Durga (left) is understood as the active principle that can vanquish the demonic forces. She carries symbols of the cosmic energies of other aspects of the divine. (Durga slaying the Buffalo Demon, *India, c. 1760.*)

In the agricultural cultures that may have worshipped the goddess, women frequently held strong social positions. Hereditary lineages were often traced through the mother, and women were honored as priestesses, healers, agricultural inventors, counselors, prophetesses, and sometimes warriors.

What happened to these apparently goddess-oriented religions? Scholars are now trying to piece together not only the reality, extent, and characteristics of Goddess worship, but also the circumstances of its demise. A cross-cultural survey by Eli Sagan (*The Dawn of Tyranny*) indicates that male-dominant social and religious structures accompanied the often violent shift from communal kinship groups and tribal confederations to centralized monarchies. In these kingdoms, social order was based on loyalty to the king and fear of his power. In Europe and West Asia, worship of the goddess was suppressed throughout the third and second millennia BCE by invading Indo-European groups (most probably from the steppes of southern Russia) in which males were dominant and championed worship of a supreme male deity. The Indo-Europeans' major deity was often described as a storm god residing on a mountain and bringing light (seen as the good) into the darkness (portrayed as bad and associated with the female).

In some cases, worship of the goddess co-existed with or later surfaced within male deity worship. In India, the new gods often had powerful female consorts or counterparts or were androgynous (that is, both male and female). The Hindu **Durga**, represented as a beautiful woman riding a lion, is worshipped as the blazing splendor and power of the Godhead. In Christianity, some scholars feel that devotion to Mary, Mother of Jesus, is in some ways a substitute for earlier worship of the goddess.

Nevertheless, as worship of the goddess was suppressed, so was ritual participation of women. In patriarchal societies, women often became property and were expected to be obedient to the rule of men. Although Christ had honored and worked with women, his later male followers limited the position of women within the Christian Church. Not only was women's spiritual contribution cast aside; in replacing the goddess, patriarchal groups may also have devalued the "feminine" aspect of religion—the receptive, intuitive, ecstatic mystical communion that was perhaps allowed freer expression in the goddess traditions. Women have been the major victims of this devaluation of the feminine, but there has also been distrust of mystics of both sexes who dared to reveal their ecstatic and personal relationship with the divine.

Although women are still barred from equal spiritual footing with men in many religions, this situation is now being widely challenged. The contemporary feminist movement includes strong efforts to make women's voices heard in the sphere of religion. Women are trying to discover their own identity, rather than having their identities defined by others. They are challenging patriarchal religious institutions that have excluded women from active participation. They are also challenging gender-exclusive language in holy texts and authoritarian masculine images of the divine. Their protests also go beyond gender issues to question the narrow and confining ways in which religious inspiration has been institutionalized. At prestigious Christian seminaries in the United States, women preparing for the ministry now outnumber men and are radically transforming views of religion and religious practice. Many feminists are deeply concerned about social ills of our times—violence, poverty, ecological disaster—and are insisting that religions be actively engaged in insuring human survival, and that they be life-affirming rather than punitive in approach. Feminist Christian theologian Rosemary Ruether feels that the movement toward greater religious participation by women may help to heal other fragmentations in our spiritual lives:

> *The feminist religious revolution ... reaches forward to an alternative that can heal the splits between "masculine" and "feminine," between mind and body, between males and females as gender groups, between society and nature, and between races and classes.*[42]

The negative side of organized religion

Tragically, religions have often split rather than unified humanity, have oppressed rather than freed, have terrified rather than inspired.

Since the human needs that religions answer are so strong, those who hold religious power are in a position to dominate and control their followers. In fact, in many religions leaders are given this authority to guide people's spiritual lives, for their wisdom and special access to the sacred is valued. Because religions involve the unseen, the mysterious, these leaders' teachings may not be verifiable by everyday physical experience. They must more often be accepted on faith. While faith is one of the cornerstones of spirituality, it is possible to surrender to spiritual leaders who are misguided or unethical. Religious leaders, like secular leaders, may not be honest with themselves and others about their inner motives. They may mistake their own thoughts and desires for the voice and will of God. Some people believe, however, that the most important thing for the disciple is to surrender the ego; even an unworthy leader can help in this goal simply by playing the role of one to whom one must surrender personal control.

Because religions paint pictures of life after death, they may play on people's fear of death or punishment, both here and hereafter. This excerpt from a famous sermon by the New England Calvinist minister Jonathan Edwards illustrates the terrifying images that can be conjured up:

> You are thus [sinners] in the hands of an angry God; 'tis nothing but his mere pleasure that keeps you from being this moment swallowed up in everlasting destruction. The God that holds you over the pit of hell, much as one holds a spider or some loathsome insect over the fire, abhors you, and is dreadfully provoked; his wrath towards you burns like fire; he looks upon you as worthy of nothing else, but to be cast into the fire.[43]

Religions try to help us make ethical choices in our lives, to develop a moral conscience. But in people who already have perfectionist or paranoid tendencies, the fear of sinning and being punished can be exaggerated to the point of neurosis or even psychosis by blaming, punishment-oriented religious teachings. If they try to leave their religion for the sake of their mental health, they may be haunted with guilt that they have done a terribly wrong thing. Religions thus have the potential for wreaking psychological havoc on their followers.

Because some religions, particularly those that developed in the East, offer a state of blissful contemplation as the reward for spiritual practice, the faithful may use religion to escape from their everyday problems. Psychologist John Welwood observes that Westerners sometimes embrace Eastern religions with the unconscious motive of avoiding their unsatisfactory lives. He calls this attempt "spiritual bypassing":

> Spiritual bypassing may be particularly tempting for individuals who are having difficulty making their way through life's basic developmental stages, especially at a time when what were once ordinary developmental landmarks—earning a livelihood through dignified work, raising a family, keeping a marriage together—have become increasingly difficult and elusive for large segments of the population. While struggling with becoming autonomous individuals, many people are introduced to spiritual teachings and practices which come from cultures that assume a person having already passed through the basic developmental stages.[44]

Because religions may have such a strong hold on their followers—by their fears, their desires, their deep beliefs—they are potential centers for political power. When church and state are one, the belief that the dominant national religion is the only true religion may be used to oppress those of other beliefs within the country. As the 1991 World Conference of Religions in Kochi, India, concluded:

> We found that interpretation of religious teachings has often been used to support social injustices, such as the oppression of women, racial oppression, human rights abuses, genocide, and marginalization of the poor. Religion has been misused to manipulate, exploit and divide people, rather than to draw us into compassionate unity.[45]

Religion may also be used as a rallying point for wars against other nations, casting the desire for control as a holy motive. Throughout history, huge numbers of people have been killed in the name of eradicating "false" religions and replacing them with the "true" religion. Our spirituality has the potential for uniting us

Angels Weep

Wherever there is slaughter of innocent men, women, and children for the mere reason that they belong to another race, color, or nationality, or were born into a faith which the majority of them could never quite comprehend and hardly ever practice in its true spirit; wherever the fair name of religion is used as a veneer to hide overweening political ambition and bottomless greed, wherever the glory of Allah is sought to be proclaimed through the barrel of a gun; wherever piety becomes synonymous with rapacity, and morality cowers under the blight of expediency and compromise, wherever it be—in Yugoslavia or Algeria, in Liberia, Chad, or the beautiful land of the Sudan, in Los Angeles or Abuija, in Kashmir or Conakry, in Colombo or Cotabato—there God is banished and Satan is triumphant, there the angels weep and the soul of man cringes; there in the name of God humans are dehumanized; and there the grace and beauty of life lie ravished and undone.

Dr. Syed Z. Abedin, Director of the Institute for Muslim Minority Affairs[46]

all in bonds of love, harmony, and mutual respect. But often it has served instead to divide us by creating barriers of hatred and intolerance.

As institutionalized religions attempt to spread the teachings of their founders, there is also the danger that more energy will go into preserving the outer form of the tradition than into maintaining its inner spirit. Max Weber (1864–1920), an influential early twentieth-century scholar of the sociology of religion, referred to this process as the "routinization of charisma." **Charisma** is the rare quality of personal magnetism often ascribed to founders of religion. Their followers feel that these teachers have extraordinary or supernatural powers. When the founder dies, the center of the movement may shift to people with managerial prowess and those who turn the original inspirations into routine rituals and dogma.

No religion is free from these historical shifts. To keep religion alive, true, and vibrant requires a genuine connection with the unseen, scrupulous honesty, and pure-heartedness. As we survey the various contemporary manifestations of the religious impulse, we will find people and groups—in all traditions—who are keeping the spark of the divine alive today. To find them, we will attempt to drop the lens of seeing from the point of view of our own culture, and try instead to see religions as they see themselves. To use Mircea Eliade's term, we will be delving into the **phenomenology** of religion—its specifically sacred aspects—rather than trying to explain religions only in terms of other disciplines such as history, politics, economics, sociology, or psychology. The phenomenology of religion involves an appreciative—even loving—investigation of religious phenomena in order to comprehend their spiritual intention and meaning. We will also be striving for "thick description," a term used by the cultural anthropologist Clifford Geertz, not only reporting outward behaviors but also attempting to explain their meaning for believers within the faith. To take such a journey through many religions does not presuppose that we must forsake our own religious beliefs or our scepticism. But the journey is likely to broaden our perspective and thus bring us closer to understanding other members of our human family. Perhaps it will bring us closer to Ultimate Reality itself.

Suggested reading

Armstrong, Karen, *The Battle for God*, New York: Alfred A. Knopf, 2000. A readable historical survey of the clash between fundamentalism and modernism in major religions.

Campbell, Joseph, *The Hero with a Thousand Faces*, second edition, Princeton, New Jersey: Princeton University Press, 1968. Brilliant leaps across time and space to trace the hero's journey—seen as a spiritual quest—in all the world's mythologies and religions.

Campbell, Joseph with Bill Moyers, *The Power of Myth*, New York: Doubleday, 1988. More brilliant comparisons of the world's mythologies, with deep insights into their common psychological and spiritual truths.

Capra, Fritjof, *The Tao of Physics*, third edition, Boston: Shambhala, 1991. A fascinating comparison of the insights of Eastern religions and contemporary physics.

Carter, Robert E., ed., *God, The Self, and Nothingness—Reflections: Eastern and Western*, New York: Paragon House, 1990. Essays from major Eastern and Western scholars of religion on variant ways of experiencing and describing Ultimate Reality.

Cenkner, William, ed., *Evil and the Response of World Religion*, St. Paul, Minnesota: Paragon House, 1997. Articles describing ways that religions have attempted to account for suffering and cruelty in human existence.

Eliade, Mircea, *The Sacred and the Profane*, translated by William R. Trask, New York: Harper and Row, 1959. Encompassing all religions, a study of religious myth, symbolism, and ritual as ways of creating a place for the sacred within a secular environment.

Ferguson, Kitty, *The Fire in the Equations: Science, Religion and the Search for God*, New York/London: Bantam Books, 1994. A wide-ranging, perceptive analysis of the implications of scientific research for religious beliefs.

Forward, Martin, *Religion: A Beginner's Guide*, Oxford: Oneworld Publications, 2001. Brief but profound glimpses of underlying issues in religious faith and practice.

Hick, John, *An Interpretation of Religion*, New Haven: Yale University Press, 1992. A leading philosopher of religion offers a rational justification for seeing the major world religions as culturally conditioned forms of response to the great mystery of Being.

King, Ursula, *Women and Spirituality: Voices of Protest and Promise*, second edition, University Park, Pennsylvania: Pennsylvania State University Press, 1993. Excellent cross-cultural survey of feminist theology and spiritual activism.

Marty, Martin E. and R. Scott Appleby, *The Fundamentalism Project*, 5 volumes, Chicago: University of Chicago Press, 1991. Scholarly analyses of fundamentalist phenomena in all religions and around the globe.

Otto, Rudolf, *The Idea of the Holy*, second edition, London: Oxford University Press, 1950. An important exploration of "nonrational" experiences of the divine.

Paden, William E., *Interpreting the Sacred: Ways of Viewing Religion*, Boston: Beacon Press, 1992. A readable introduction to the complexities of theoretical perspectives on religion.

Peacocke, Arthur, *Paths from Science towards God: The End of all our Exploring*, Oxford: Oneworld Publications, 2001. Both a scientist and a theologian, the author explores many issues in the relationship between science and religion.

Sharma, Arvind, ed., *Women in World Religions*, Albany, New York: State University of New York Press, 1987. Analyses of the historic and contemporary place of women in each of the major religions.

Sharma, Arvind and Katherine K. Young, eds., *Feminism and World Religions,* Albany: State University of New York Press, 1999. Leading female scholars analyze their religions from a contemporary feminist point of view.

Shinn, Larry D., ed., *In Search of the Divine: Some Unexpected Consequences of Interfaith Dialogue*, New York: Paragon House Publishers, 1987. Scholars from various religions present a tapestry of understandings of the Sacred Reality.

Stone, Merlin, *When God was a Woman*, San Diego, California: Harcourt Brace Jovanovich, 1976. Pioneering survey of archaeological evidence of the early religion of the Goddess.

Underhill, Evelyn, *Mysticism: The Nature and Development of Spiritual Consciousness*, Oxford: Oneworld Publications, 1999. This classic, originally published in 1911, remains one of the deepest studies of mystical experience in many religions.

Ward, Keith, *God, Chance and Necessity*, Oxford: Oneworld Publications, 1997. A leading Christian theologian critiques scientific theories that deny the existence of God.

Young, Serinity, ed., *An Anthology of Sacred Texts by and about Women*, New York: Crossroad, 1995. Extensive and unusual selections bringing women's religious experiences to light.

CHAPTER 2
HINDUISM

"With mind absorbed and heart melted in love"

In the Indian subcontinent there has developed a complex variety of religious paths. Some of these are relatively unified religious systems, such as Buddhism, Jainism, and Sikhism. Most of the other Indian religious ways have been categorized together as if they were a single tradition named "Hinduism." This term does not appear in any of the old texts. It is derived from a name applied by foreigners to the people living in the region of the Indus River, and introduced in the nineteenth century under colonial British rule as a category for census-taking.

An alternative label preferred today is **Sanatana Dharma** ("eternal religion"). *Sanatana*, "eternal" or "ageless," reflects the belief that these ways have always existed. **Dharma** is often translated as "religion," but its meaning encompasses matters of duty, natural law, social welfare, ethics, health, and transcendental realization. *Dharma* is thus a holistic approach to social coherence and the good of all, corresponding to order in the cosmos.

The spiritual expressions of Sanatana Dharma range from extreme asceticism to extreme sensuality, from the heights of personal devotion to a deity to the heights of abstract philosophy, from metaphysical proclamations of the oneness behind the material world to worship of images representing a multiplicity of deities. According to tradition, there are actually 333 million deities in India. The feeling is that the divine has countless faces.

The extreme variations within Sanatana Dharma are reflections of its great age. Few of the myriad religious paths that have arisen over the millennia have been lost. They continue to co-exist in present-day India. Some scholars of religion argue that these ways are so varied that there is no central tradition that can be called Hinduism proper.

Truth is one; sages call it by various names.   *Rig Veda*

One avenue into understanding this mosaic of beliefs and practices is to trace the supposed chronological development of major patterns that exist today. However, in villages, where the majority of Indians live, worship of deities is quite diverse and does not necessarily follow the more reified and philosophical Brahmanic tradition that is typically referred to as "Hinduism." The Brahmanic tradition tends to be upper class, educated, and male-dominated. Even in this Brahmanic tradition, historians of religion and devotees of its various forms have widely variant ideas about the historical origin of its threads. The archaeological evidence is fragmented, and Indians have not traditionally emphasized chronology. Reports of actual events and people are interwoven with mythological embellishments and symbolism.

Harappan civilization

Many of the threads of Sanatana Dharma may have existed in the religions practiced by the aboriginal Dravidian peoples of India. There were also advanced urban centers in the Indus Valley from about 2500 BCE or even earlier until 1500 BCE. Major fortified cities have been found by archaeologists at Harappa, Mohenjo-Daro, and Dholavira; the culture they represent is labeled "Harappan."

Archaeologists have found little conclusive evidence of temples in the Harappan cities, but the people clearly lavished great care on their plumbing and irrigation systems. The major structure at Mohenjo-Daro, called the Great Bath, is a large, lined tank with steps leading down into it, surrounded by an open courtyard; an adjoining structure has what appear to be private bathing rooms. Historians speculate from this evidence that the early Indus people placed a religious sort of emphasis on hygiene and/or ritual purification.

They also seem to have venerated life-giving power. Although few pieces of ritual art remain, seals have been found depicting an ascetic male figure in cross-legged yogic posture. He has an erect phallus, wears a great horned head-dress, and is surrounded by strong animals such as bulls and tigers. There were also many stone **lingams**, natural elongated oval stones or sculptures up to two feet tall. Both the seals and the lingams suggest that the early Indus people knew about meditation practices and were worshippers of a deity who bore the attributes of the later god **Siva**,[1] who is still one of the major forms of the divine worshipped today.

Even more prominent among the artifacts are terracotta figurines that seem to honor a great goddess. Sacred pots, like those still used in South Indian village ceremonies honoring the goddess, may have been associated then, as now, with the feminine as the receptacle of the primeval stuff of life. There is also considerable evidence of worship of local deities by stone altars placed beneath sacred trees. Each tree is still popularly believed to be the home of a tree spirit, and many are honored with offerings.

Vedic religion

Western historians developed the **Aryan Invasion Theory** that the highly organized cultures of the Indus Valley and the villages in other parts of the subcontinent were gradually overrun by nomadic invaders from outside India. The theory argues that the **Vedas**, the sublime religious texts often referred to as the foundations of Sanatana Dharma, were the product of the invaders, and not of indigenous Indians. These invaders were identified as **Aryans**, who were among

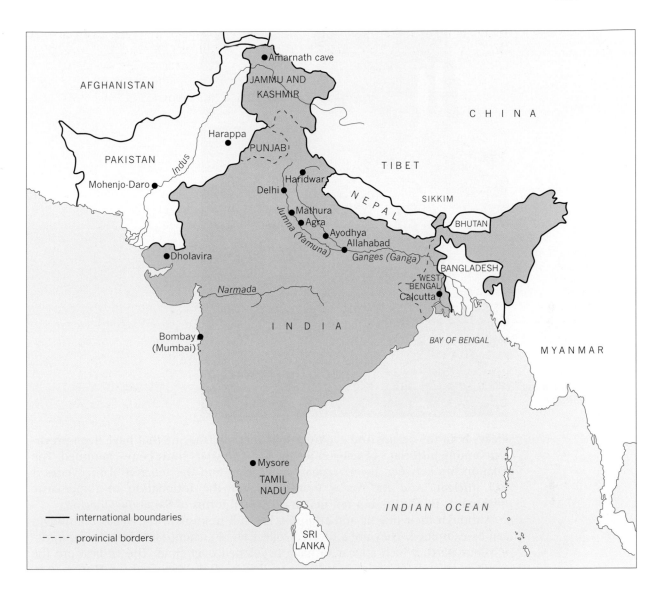

the Indo-European tribes thought to have migrated outward from the steppes of southern Russia during the second millennium BCE. The material culture of these patriarchal tribes was relatively simple—although they had powerful means of making war, such as horse-drawn chariots, composite bows, and a warrior class—and they were probably illiterate. The Vedas sing the praises of the Indian subcontinent, and do not refer to any other homeland. The Harappan urban centers do seem to have declined, but there is no clear evidence why they should have done so.

Today the Aryan Invasion Theory is contested by some scholars and by Hindu nationalists who refuse to believe that their religion is foreign-born. There may have been considerable mixing between indigenous Dravidian people and those who composed the Vedas in **Sanskrit**, the ancient language whose origins are also not definitely established. If the Aryan Invasion Theory is not true, many

The Indian subcontinent includes areas that are now politically separate from India. The Indus Valley, for instance, lies in what is now the Muslim state of Pakistan. Another Muslim state was carved out of the eastern portion of India in 1947, becoming the independent state of Bangladesh in 1972.

The Vedas include hymns praising the cow, which is still beloved and treated as sacred by Hindus: "The cow is our Mother, for she gives us her milk." The traditional diet is vegetarian; cows are raised for dairy products rather than killed for their flesh.

ideas about the origins and evolution of Sanatana Dharma that have been prevalent among historians of religion for the last 150 years must be re-examined. The relationship between the Harappan civilization and the religion of the Vedas is still unclear. And the Vedas themselves are the foundation of upper-caste Brahmanic Hinduism, but not necessarily of all forms of Sanatana Dharma.

Although their origins and antiquity are still unknown, the Vedas themselves can be examined. They are a revered collection of ancient sacred hymns comprising four parts, which appear to have developed over time. The earliest are the *Samhitas*, hymns of praise in worship of deities. Then appeared the **Brahmanas**, directions about performances of the ritual sacrifices to the deities. The *Brahmanas* explain the symbolic correspondences between the microcosm of the ritual process and the "real world" in which rituals are performed. Some people went to the forests to meditate as recluses; their writings form the third part of the Vedas—the *Aranyakas*, or "forest treatises." The last of the Vedas are the **Upanishads**, consisting of teaching from highly realized spiritual masters. They explain the personal transformation that results from psychic participation in the ritual process.

These sacred teachings seem to have been written down by the middle of the first millennium BCE, though the Indian people and some scholars feel that they are far older. We know that the Vedas are much older than their earliest written forms. After being revealed to sages, they were transmitted orally from teacher to student and may then have been written down over a period of eight or nine hundred years.

According to orthodox Hindus, the Vedas are not the work of any humans.

HINDUISM

BCE	
8000	c.8000–6000 According to Indian tradition, Vedas heard by rishis, carried orally
3000	c.3102 According to Indian tradition, beginning of Kali Yuga; Vishnu incarnates as Vyasa, who writes down the Vedas c.2500–1500 Harappan civilization
2000	c.2000–900 Aryan invasions of northern India c.1500 Early Vedas first written down
1000	c.900–700 *Brahmanas* written down c.600–400 *Upanishads* recorded
500	c.400 BCE–200 CE *Ramayana* (present form) c.400 BCE–400 CE *Mahabharata* (present form) by 200 Patanjali systematizes Yoga Sutras [Indian tradition, yoga practices are ancient, indigenous]
CE	
500	before 100 Code of Manu compiled c.300 Tantras written down [Indian tradition, Tantras are as old as the *Upanishads*] c.600–1800 Bhakti movement flourishes 711 Muslim invasions begin c.788–820 or earlier, Shankara reorganizes Vedanta c.800–900 *Bhagavata Purana* written down
1000	
1500	
	1556–1707 Mogul Empire
1800	
	1828 Brahmo Samaj revitalization 1836–1886 Life of Ramakrishna 1857–1947 British rule of India 1869–1948 Life of Mahatma Gandhi 1875 Arya Samaj reform
1900	
	1947 Independence, partition of India and Pakistan 1992 Demolition of Babri mosque
2000	2002 Violence erupts again over attempts to build Ram Temple at Ayodhya

They are the breath of the eternal, as "heard" by the ancient sages, or *rishis*, and later compiled by Vyasa (see page 56). The scriptures are thought to transcend human time and are thus as relevant today as they were thousands of years ago. The *Gayatrimantra*, a verse in a Vedic hymn, is still chanted daily by the devout as the most sacred of prayers:

> *Aum [the primordial creative sound],*
> *Bhu Bhuvah Svah [the three worlds: earth, atmosphere, and heaven],*
> *Tat Savitur Varenyum,*
> *Bhargo Devasya Dheemahe [adoration of the glory, splendor, and grace that radiate*
>   *from the Divine Light that illuminates the three worlds],*
> *Dhiyo Yo Nah Prachodayat [a prayer for liberation through awakening of the light*
>   *of the universal intelligence].*[2]

The oldest of the known Vedic scriptures—and among the oldest of the world's existing scriptures—is the **Rig Veda**. This praises and implores the blessings of the **devas**—the controlling forces in the cosmos, deities who consecrate every part of life. The major *devas* included **Indra** (god of thunder and bringer of welcome rains), Agni (god of fire), Soma (associated with a sacred drink), and Ushas (goddess of dawn). The devas included both opaque earth gods and transparent deities of the sky and celestial realms. But behind all the myriad aspects of divinity, the sages perceived one unseen reality. This reality, beyond human understanding, ceaselessly creates and sustains everything that exists, encompassing all time, space, and causation.

Vedic worship with fire is still significant in contemporary rituals.

Fire sacrifices and the cosmic order

Vedic worship centered around the fire sacrifice. Communities seem to have gathered around a fire placing offerings in it to be conveyed to the gods by **Agni**, the god of fire. The Vedic hymns sung to Agni are spiritually complex invocations of the power of truth against darkness. Metaphysically, fire represents the "forceful heat, flaming will, . . . and burning brightness" of the divine, according to the twentieth-century seer, Sri Aurobindo.[3]

Over time elaborate fire sacrifice rituals were created, controlled by **brahmins** (priests). Specified verbal formulas, sacred chants, and sacred actions were to be used by the priests to invoke the breath behind all of existence. This universal breath was later called **Brahman**, the Absolute, the Supreme Reality. The verbal formulas were called **mantras**; their sound was believed to evoke the reality they named. The language used was Sanskrit. It was considered a re-creation of the actual sound-forms of objects, actions, and qualities, as heard by ancient sages in deep meditation.

The fire rituals were apparently held in the open air. The most auspicious places for their performance were at the confluence of two rivers. The junction at Allahabad of the sacred Ganges (Ganga) and Jumna (Yamuna) rivers was considered extremely holy. A third river, the Saraswati, is believed to have gone underground but to join the other two rivers invisibly at the most auspicious point in Allahabad. The feeling that special blessings are available there continues today; the confluence of the three rivers is still a major pilgrimage spot for worshippers.

Offerings to Agni usually consisted of clarified butter oil (ghee), grains, **soma**, and sometimes animals. Soma was a drink apparently made of a specific plant that grew in mountainous, windy places; its juice seemed to confer great vigor. Despite considerable contemporary interest in recreating this drink, the soma plant has not been securely identified.

The Vedic principle of sacrifice was based on the idea that generous offerings to a deity will be rewarded by some specific result. This attitude toward giving has remained in Indian culture. Ritual fire offerings are still central to Hindu worship. Hospitality to human guests is also a duty. To turn someone away from your door without feeding him is considered a great sin, for every person is the deity incarnate. Even today, there are huge ceremonies for making offerings to a deity and feeding the public. The head of the household may, toward the end of his life, engage the services of a number of brahmins to help complete the requisite 24,000,000 repetitions of the *Gayatrimantra* during his lifetime. Professional beggars take advantage of belief in sacrifice by suggesting that those who give to them will be blessed. But the most important sacrifices are considered to be inner sacrifices—giving one's entire self over to the Supreme Reality.

In the *Rig Veda*, the sacrifical aspects of Vedic religion are linked metaphorically with the original personal sacrifice by which the universe was created. **Purusha**, the primal Being, was dismembered by the gods. His mind became the moon, his eyes the sun, his breath the wind, and so forth. The power that preserves the unity of all these parts of the cosmos, maintains harmony in society, and keeps human personalities well integrated is called *ṛta*. Earthly sacrifices were designed to preserve this order. If the sacrifices were offered correctly, the gods would be appeased.

Philosophy of the Upanishads

Of the four parts of the Vedas, the *Upanishads* are thought to have developed last, around 600 to 400 BCE. They represent the mystical insights of *rishis* who sought ultimate reality through their meditations in the forest. Many people consider these philosophical and metaphysical reflections on Vedic religion the cream of Indian thought, among the highest spiritual literature ever written. They were not taught to the masses but rather were reserved for advanced seekers of spiritual truth.

CONTEMPLATION OF THE LUMINOUS SELF The word *Upanishad* embraces the idea of the devoted disciple sitting down by the teacher to receive private spiritual instruction about the highest reality, loosening all doubts and destroying all ignorance. Emphasis is placed not on outward ritual performances, as in the earlier Vedic religion, but on inner experience as the path to realization and immortality.

The *rishis* explain that the bodily senses are made for looking outward; the eyes, ears, nose, tongue, and skin are enticed by sensory pleasures. But ultimately these are fleeting, impermanent. They pass away and then one dies, never having experienced what is of greater value because it is infinite, everlasting. What is real and lasting, they found, can be discovered only by turning away from transient worldly things. They taught their pupils to turn their attention inward and thus discover a transcendent reality from within. This unseen but all-pervading reality they called Brahman, the Unknowable: "Him the eye does not see, nor the tongue express, nor the mind grasp."[4]

From Brahman spring the multiplicity of forms, including humans. The joyous discovery of the *rishis* was that they could find Brahman as the subtle self or soul (**atman**) within themselves. One of the *rishis* explained this relationship thus:

In the beginning there was Existence alone—One only, without a second. He, the One, thought to himself: Let me be many, let me grow forth. Thus out of himself he projected the universe, and having projected out of himself the universe, he entered into every being. All that is has its self in him alone. Of all things he is the subtle essence. He is the truth. He is the Self. And that, ... THAT ART THOU.

Chandogya Upanishad[5]

The *rishis* declared that when one discovers the inner self, *atman*, and thus also its source, Brahman, the self merges into its transcendent source, and one experiences unspeakable peace and bliss.

REINCARNATION In addition to these profound descriptions of contemplation of the Absolute, the Upanishads express several doctrines that are central to all forms of Sanatana Dharma. One is the idea of **reincarnation**. In answer to the universal question, "What happens after we die?" the *rishis* taught that the soul leaves the dead body and enters a new one. One takes birth again and again in countless bodies—perhaps as an animal or some other life form—but the self remains the same. Birth as a human being is a precious and rare opportunity for the soul to advance toward its ultimate goal of liberation from rebirth and merging with the Absolute Reality.

KARMA   An important related concept is that of **karma**. It means action, and also the consequences of action. Every act we make, and even every thought and every desire we have, shape our future experiences. Our life is what we have made it. And we ourselves are shaped by what we have done: "As a man acts, so does he become. . . . A man becomes pure through pure deeds, impure through impure deeds."[6] Not only do we reap in this life the good or evil we have sown; they also follow us after physical death, affecting our next incarnation. Ethically, this is a strong teaching, for our every move has far-reaching consequences.

The ultimate goal, however, is not creation of good lives by good deeds, but a clean escape from the *karma*-run wheel of birth, death, and rebirth, which is called **samsara**. To escape from *samsara* is to achieve **moksha**, or liberation from the limitations of space, time, and matter through realization of the immortal Absolute. Many lifetimes of upward-striving incarnations are required to reach this transcendence of earthly miseries. This desire for liberation from earthly existence is one of the underpinnings of classical Hinduism, and of Buddhism as well.

Castes and social duties

Because the Vedic sacrifices were a reciprocal communion with the gods, priests who performed the public sacrifices had to be carefully trained and maintain high standards of ritual purity. Those so trained—the brahmins—comprised a special occupational group. According to Vedic religion, the orderly working of society included a clear division of labor among four major occupational groups, which later became entrenched as **castes**. The brahmins were the priests and philosophers, specialists in the life of the spirit. They had even higher status than the next group, later called **kshatriyas**. These were the nobility of feudal India: kings, warriors, and vassals. Their general function was to guard and preserve the society; they were expected to be courageous and majestic. **Vaishyas** were the economic specialists: farmers and merchants. The **shudra** caste were the manual laborers and artisans. Even lower than these original four castes were those "outcastes" who came to be considered **untouchables**. They carried on work such as removing human wastes and corpses, sweeping streets, and working with leather from the skins of dead cows—occupations that made their bodies and clothing abhorrent to others.

Over time, Vedic religion was increasingly controlled by the brahmins, and contact between castes was limited. Caste membership became hereditary. The caste system became as important as the Vedas themselves in defining Hinduism

A Hindu statue conveys the compassion of the divine.

until its social injustices were attacked in the nineteenth century. One of its opponents was the courageous leader Mahatma Gandhi, who renamed the lowest caste *harijans*, "the children of God." In 1948 the stigma of "untouchability" was legally abolished, though many caste distinctions still linger in modern India. Marriage across caste lines, for instance, is still often disapproved in India. If a boy and girl—one of whom is from the lowest caste—fall in love, sometimes the families from both sides will kill them rather than allow their marriage, to prevent disgrace or retribution.

Despite its abuses, the division of labor represented by the caste system is part of Sanatana Dharma's strong emphasis on social duties and sacrifice of individual desires for the sake of social order. Its purpose is to uplift people from worldly concerns and to encourage them to behave according to higher laws. The Vedas, other scriptures, and historical customs have all conditioned the Indian people to accept their social roles. These were set out in a major document known as the Code of Manu, compiled by 100 CE. In it are laws governing all aspects of life, including the proper conduct of rulers, dietary restrictions, marriage laws, daily rituals, purification rites, social laws, and ethical guidance. It prescribes hospitality to guests and the cultivation of such virtues as contemplation, truthfulness, compassion, non-attachment, generosity, pleasant dealings with people, and self-control. It condemns untouchables to living outside villages, eating only from broken dishes, and wearing only clothes removed from corpses. On the other hand, the code proposed charitable giving as the sacred duty of the upper castes, and thus provided a safety net for those at the bottom of this hierarchical system: "A householder must give as he is able and to those who do not cook for themselves, and to all beings one must distribute without detriment."[7]

The Code of Manu also specifies the reciprocal duties of men and women. Women are expected to be dependent on men at all times. They have no independent identity of their own. A woman is forever either the daughter, wife or mother of a man; men are to revere women in their household settings. Of ancient origin, such dharmic laws still have a strong impact in Indian culture.

Bhakti in the epics and Puranas

In addition to pre-Vedic traditions, Vedic influences, and social systems codified by Manu, other paths now also known as Hinduism have an intensely devotional quality. It is difficult to pray to the impersonal Absolute referred to in the *Upanishads*, for it is formless and is not totally distinct from oneself. More personal worship of a Divine Being can be inferred from the goddess and Siva-like low reliefs of ancient India. It probably persisted during the Vedic period and was later given written expression. Eventually **bhakti**—intense devotion to a personal manifestation of Brahman—became the heart of Hinduism as the majority of people now experience it.

Although there are many devotional passages in the *Upanishads*, personal love for a deity flowered in the spiritual literature that followed the Vedas. Two major classes of scriptures that arose after 500 BCE (according to Western scholarship) were the **epics** and the **Puranas**. These long heroic narratives and poems popularized spiritual knowledge and devotion through national myths and legends. They were particularly useful in spreading Hindu teachings to the masses at times when Buddhism and Jainism—movements born in India but not recognizing the authority of the Vedas—were winning converts.

In contrast to the rather abstract depictions of the Divine Principle in the *Upanishads*, the epics and Puranas represent the Supreme as a person, or rather as various human-like deities. As T. M. P. Mahadevan explains:

> *The Hindu mind is averse to assigning an unalterable or rigidly fixed form or name to the deity. Hence it is that in Hinduism we have innumerable god-forms and countless divine names. And, it is a truth that is recognized by all Hindus that obeisance offered to any of these forms and names reaches the one supreme God.*[8]

Two great epics, the **Ramayana** and the **Mahabharata**, present the Supreme usually as **Vishnu**, who intervenes on earth during critical periods in the cosmic cycles. In the inconceivable vastness of time as reckoned by Hindu thought, each world cycle lasts 4,320,000 years. Two thousand of these world cycles are the equivalent of one day and night in the life of Brahma, the Creator god. Each world cycle is divided into four ages, or **yugas**.

Dharma—moral order in the world—is natural in the first age. The second age is like a cow standing on three legs; people must be taught their proper roles in society. During the darker third age, revealed values are no longer recognized, people lose their altruism and willingness for self-denial, and there are no more saints. The final age, **Kali Yuga**, is as imbalanced as a cow trying to stand on one leg. The world is at its worst, with egotism, ignorance, recklessness, and war rampant. According to Hindu time reckoning, we are now living in a Kali Yuga period that began in 3102 BCE. Such an age is described thus:

> *When society reaches a stage where property confers rank, wealth becomes the only source of virtue, passion the sole bond of union between husband and wife, falsehood the source of success in life, sex the only means of enjoyment, and when outer trappings are confused with inner religion . . .*[9]

Each of these lengthy cycles witnesses the same turns of events. The balance inexorably shifts from the true *dharma* to dissolution and then back to the *dharma* as the gods are again victorious over the anti-gods. The Puranas list the many ways that Vishnu has incarnated in the world when *dharma* is decaying, to help restore virtue and defeat evil. For instance, Vishnu is said to have incarnated great **avatars** such as Krishna and Rama to help uplift humanity. It is considered inevitable that Vishnu will continually return in answer to the pleas of suffering humans. It is equally inevitable that he will meet with resistance from "demonic forces," which are also part of the cosmic cycles.

During the northern Indian festival Ram-lila, giant effigies of Ravana and the demons from the epic Ramayana *are dramatically burned to the delight of the crowds.*

Hanuman, the Monkey Chief

Hanuman was of divine origin and legendary powers, but he was embodied as a monkey, serving as a chief in the monkey army. When Rama needed to find his wife Sita after Ravana abducted her, he turned to the monkey king for help. The monkey king dispatched Hanuman to search to the south.

When the monkeys reached the sea dividing India from Sri Lanka, they were dismayed because monkeys do not swim. A vulture brought word that Sita was indeed on the other side of the water, a captive of Ravana. What to do? An old monkey reminded Hanuman of the powers he had displayed as an infant and told him that he could easily jump to Lanka and back if only he remembered his power and his divine origin.

Hanuman sat in meditation until he became strong and confident. Then he climbed a mountain, shook himself, and began to grow in size and strength. When at last he felt ready, he set off with a roar, hurling himself through the sky with eyes blazing like forest fires.

When Hanuman landed in Lanka, he shrunk himself to the size of a cat so that he could explore Ravana's forts. After many dangerous adventures, he gave Sita the message that Rama was preparing to do battle to win her back, and then he jumped back over the sea to the Indian mainland.

During the subsequent battle of Lanka, Rama and his half-brother Lakshman were mortally wounded. Nothing would save them except a certain herb that grew only in the Himalayas. In his devotion to Rama, Hanuman flew to the mountains, again skirting danger all the way. But once he got there, he could not tell precisely which herb to pick, so he uprooted the whole mountain and carried it back to Lanka. The herb would be effective only before the moon rose. From the air, Hanuman saw the moon about to clear the horizon so he swallowed the moon and reached Lanka in time to heal Rama and Lakshman.

After the victory, Rama rewarded Hanuman with a bracelet of pearls and gold. Hanuman chewed it up and threw it away. When a bear asked why he had rejected the gift from God, Hanuman explained that it was useless to him since it did not have Rama's name on it. The bear said, "Well, if you feel that way, why do you keep your body?" At that, Hanuman ripped open his chest, and there were Rama and Sita seated in his heart, and all of his bones and muscles had "Ram, Ram, Ram" written all over them.

RAMAYANA   The epics deal with the eternal play of good and evil, symbolized by battles involving the human incarnations of Vishnu. Along the way, they teach examples of the virtuous life, which is a life of responsibilities to others as defined by one's social roles. One is first a daughter, son, sister, brother, wife, husband, mother, father, or friend in relationship to others, and only secondarily an individual.

The *Ramayana*, a long poetic narrative in the Sanskrit language thought to have been compiled between approximately 400 BCE and 200 CE, is attributed to the bard Valmiki. Probably based on old ballads, it is much beloved and is acted out with great pageantry throughout India every year. It depicts the duties of relationships, portraying ideal characters, such as the ideal servant, the ideal brother, the ideal wife, the ideal king. In the story, Vishnu incarnates as the virtuous prince Rama in order to kill Ravana, the ten-headed demon king of Sri Lanka. Rama is heir to his father's throne, but the mother of his step-brother compels the king to banish Rama into the forest for fourteen years. Rama, a model of morality, goes willingly, observing that a son's duty is always to

Rama and Lakshman shoot arrows into the breast of the demon Ravana, with Hanuman and the monkeys in the background. Sita waits within Ravana's compound, guarded by his demons. (North India, c. 19th century.)

Lord Krishna and Arjuna discuss profound philosophical questions in a battle chariot, as represented in this archway above the sacred Ganges River in Rishikesh.

obey his parents implicitly, even when their commands seem wrong. He is accompanied into the ascetic life by his wife Sita, the model of wifely devotion in a patriarchal society, who refuses his offer to remain behind in comfort.

Eventually Sita is kidnapped by Ravana, who woos her unsuccessfully in his island kingdom and guards her with all manner of terrible demons. Although Rama is powerful, he and his half-brother Lakshman need the help of the monkeys and bears in the battle to get Sita back. Hanuman the monkey becomes the hero of the story. He symbolizes the power of faith and devotion to overcome our human frailties. In his love for the Lord he can do anything.

The bloody battle ends in single-handed combat between Ravana and Rama. Rama blesses a sacred arrow with Vedic mantras and sends it straight into Ravana's heart. In what may be a later addition to Valmiki's epic poem, when Rama and Sita are reunited, he accuses her of possible infidelity, so, to prove her innocence, she successfully undergoes an ordeal by fire in which Agni protects her.

Another version of the *Ramayana*, perhaps as elaborated by later ballad-singers, has Rama ordering Sita into the forest because his subjects are suspicious of what may have happened while she was in Ravana's captivity. She is abandoned near the **ashram** of Valmiki. There she takes shelter and gives birth to twin boys. Years later, Valmiki and the sons attend a great ritual conducted by King Rama, and the boys sing the *Ramayana*. There is a painful reunion of the children with their father. Thereupon, Sita, a daughter of the earth, begs the earth to receive her if she has been faithful to Rama. With these words, she becomes a field of radiance and disappears into the ground:

> *O Lord of my being, I realize you in me and me in you. Our relationship is eternal. Through this body assumed by me, my service to you and your progeny is complete now. I dissolve this body to its original state.*

Mother Earth, you gave form to me. I have made use of it as I ought to. In recognition of its purity may you kindly absorb it into your womb.[10]

MAHABHARATA   The other famous Hindu epic is the *Mahabharata*, a Sanskrit poem of more than 100,000 verses. Perhaps partly historical, it may have been composed between 400 BCE and 400 CE. The plot concerns the struggle between the sons of a royal family for control of a kingdom near what is now Delhi. The story teaches the importance of sons, the duties of kingship, the benefits of ascetic practice and righteous action, and the qualities of the gods. In contrast to the idealized characters in the *Ramayana*, the *Mahabharata* shows all sides of human nature, including greed, lust, intrigue, and the desire for power. It is thought to be relevant for all times and all peoples. A serial dramatization of the *Mahabharata* has drawn huge television audiences in contemporary India, and many people replay the episodes on home videotape. Throughout its episodes, the *Mahabharata* teaches one primary ethic: that the happiness of others is essential to one's own happiness. This consideration of others before oneself is the basis of *dharma*.

The eighteenth book of the *Mahabharata*, which may have originally been an independent mystical poem, is the **Bhagavad-Gita** ("Song of the Supreme Exalted One"). Krishna, revered as a glorious manifestation of the Supreme, appears as the charioteer of Arjuna, who is preparing to fight on the virtuous side of a battle that will pit brothers against brothers. The battle provides the occasion for a treatise about the conflict that may arise between our earthly duties and our spiritual aspirations.

Before they plunge into battle, Krishna instructs Arjuna in the arts of self-transcendence and realization of the eternal. The eternal instructions are still central to Hindu spiritual practice. Arjuna is enjoined to withdraw his attention from

Krishna is often pictured as drawing humans to the divine by the power of love, symbolized by the lure of his flute.

the impetuous demands of the senses, ignoring all feelings of attraction or aversion. This will give him a steady, peaceful mind. He is instructed to offer devotional service and to perform the prescribed Vedic sacrifices, but for the sake of discipline, duty, and example alone rather than reward—to "abandon all attachment to success or failure . . . renouncing the fruits of action in the material world."[11]

Actually, Lord Krishna says those who do everything for love of the Supreme transcend the notion of duty. Everything they do is offered to the Supreme, "without desire for gain and free from egoism and lethargy."[12] Thus they feel peace, freedom from earthly entanglements, and unassailable happiness.

This yogic science of transcending the "lower self" by the "higher self" is so ancient that Krishna says it was originally given to the sun god and, through his agents, to humans. But in time it was lost, and Krishna is now renewing his instructions pertaining to "that very ancient science of the relationship with the Supreme."[13] He has taken human form again and again to teach the true religion:

> Whenever and wherever there is a decline in religious practice . . .
> and a predominant rise of irreligion—at that time I descend Myself.
>   To deliver the pious and to annihilate the miscreants, as well as to re-establish
> the principles of religion, I advent Myself millennium after millennium.[14]

Krishna says that everything springs from his Being:

> There is no truth superior to Me. Everything rests upon Me, as pearls are strung
> on a thread. . . .
>   I am the taste of water, the light of the sun and the moon, the syllable om
> in Vedic mantras; I am the sound in ether and ability in man. . . .
>   All states of being—goodness, passion or ignorance—are manifested by My
> energy. I am, in one sense, everything—but I am independent. I am not under
> the modes of this material nature.[15]

This supreme Godhead is not apparent to most mortals. The deity can be known only by those who love him, and for them it is easy, for they remember him at all times: "Whatever you do, whatever you eat, whatever you offer or give away, and whatever austerities you perform—do that . . . as an offering to Me." Any small act of devotion offered in love becomes a way to him: "If one offers Me with love and devotion a leaf, a flower, fruit, or water, I will accept it."[16]

KRISHNA OF THE PURANAS   The Puranas, poetic Sanskrit texts that narrate the myths of ancient times, were probably compiled between 500 and 1500 CE. *Bhakti*—the way of devotion so beloved by the masses in India, and said to be the best path for Kali Yuga—is evident in the *Bhagavata Purana* ("Tales of the Lord") to an even greater extent than in the *Mahabharata*. Most Western Indologists think it was written about the ninth or tenth century CE, but according to Indian tradition it was one of the works written down at the beginning of Kali Yuga by Vyasa ("collector"), traditionally considered to be one person but more likely many people acting as compilers. It is said that once Vyasa had written down all the Vedas, Puranas, and the *Mahabharata*, he still felt dissatisfied, as though something were missing. When he asked his spiritual master why this was so, his master said that the missing element was love of the divine. What Vyasa then wrote describes the Supreme as a person to be adored.

The supreme personality of Godhead is portrayed first in its vast dimensions: the Being whose body animates the material universe. For instance:

> His eyes are the generating centers of all kinds of forms, and they glitter and illuminate. His eyeballs are like the sun and the heavenly planets. His ears hear from all sides and are receptacles for all the Vedas, and His sense of hearing is the generating center of the sky and of all kinds of sound.[17]

This material universe we know is only one of millions of material universes. Each is like a bubble in the eternal spiritual sky, arising from the pores of the body of Vishnu, and these bubbles are created and destroyed as Vishnu breathes out and in. This cosmic conception is so vast that it is impossible for the mind to grasp it. It is much easier to comprehend and adore Krishna in his incarnation as a cowherding boy. Whereas he was a wise teacher in the *Bhagavad-Gita*, Krishna of the Puranas is a much-loved child, raised by cowherds in an area called Vrindavan near Mathura on the Jumna River.

The mythology is rich in earthly pleasures. The boy Krishna mischievously steals balls of butter from the neighbors and wanders garlanded with flowers through the forest, happily playing his flute. Between episodes of carefree bravery in vanquishing demons that threaten the people, he playfully steals the hearts of the *gopis*, the cowherd girls, many of them married. His favorite is the lovely Radha, but through his magical ways, each thinks that he dances with her alone. He is physically beautiful.

Eventually Krishna is called away on a heroic mission, never returning to the *gopis*. Their grief at his leaving, their loving remembrances of his graceful presence, and their intense longing for him serve as models for the *bhakti* path—the way of extreme devotion. In Hindu thought, the emotional longing of the lover for the beloved is one of the most powerful vehicles for concentration on the Supreme Lord.

Spiritual disciplines

Another ancient and persistent thread of Sanatana Dharma is spiritual discipline. The process of attaining spiritual realization or liberation is thought to take at least a lifetime, and probably many lifetimes. Birth as a human being is prized as a chance to advance toward spiritual perfection.

In the past, spiritual training was usually available to upper-caste males only; women and *shudras* were excluded. It was preceded by an initiation ceremony in which the boy received the **sacred thread**, a cord of three threads to be worn across the chest from the left shoulder.

A Hindu male's lifespan was traditionally divided into four periods of approximately twenty-five years each. For the first twenty-five years he is a chaste student at the feet of a teacher. Next comes the householder stage, in which he is expected to marry, raise a family, and contribute productively to society. After this period, he begins to withdraw into semi-retirement, starting to detach himself from worldly pursuits and to turn to meditation and scriptural study. By the age of seventy-five, he is able to withdraw totally from society and become a ***sannyasin***.

Many gurus migrated to the West to spread Sanatana Dharma there. Paramahansa Yogananda's book Autobiography of a Yogi *continues to attract Western followers to Indian religious traditions.*

Living as a renunciate, the *sannyasin* is a contemplative who ritually cuts himself off from wife and family, declaring, "No one belongs to me and I belong to no one." Some *sannyasins* take up residence in comfortable temples; others wander alone with only a water jar, a walking staff, and a begging bowl as possessions. Some wandering *sannyasins* wear no clothes. In silence, the *sannyasin* is supposed to concentrate on practices that will finally release him from *samsara* into cosmic consciousness.

The majority of contemporary Hindu males do not follow this path to its *sannyasin* conclusion in old age, but many Hindus still become *sannyasins*. Some of them have renounced the world at a younger age and joined a monastic order, living in an ashram, a retreat community that has developed around a **guru**.

The guru

Those who choose the path of study and renunciation often place themselves at the feet of a spiritual teacher, or guru. The title "guru" is applied to venerable spiritual guides. Gurus do not declare themselves as teachers; people are drawn to them because they have achieved spiritual status to which the seekers aspire. Gurus are often regarded as enlightened or "fully realized" individuals. A guru does not provide academic instruction. Rather, he or she gives advice, example, and encouragement to those seeking enlightenment or realization.

> *Anyone and everyone cannot be a guru. A huge timber floats on the water and can carry animals as well. But a piece of worthless wood sinks, if a man sits on it, and drowns him.*
>
> *Ramakrishna[18]*

For instance, Ramana Maharshi (1879–1951) lived on a holy mountain in southern India, Arunachala, so absorbed in Ultimate Consciousness that he neither talked nor ate and had to be force-fed by another holy man. But the needs of those who gathered around him drew out his compassion and wisdom, and he spontaneously counseled them in their spiritual needs. His glance alone was said to have illuminated many who visited him.

The Siddha tradition of southern India specializes in "teaching" by **shaktipat**—the power of a glance, word, touch, or thought. A disciple of the late Swami Muktananda describes the effect, referring to him as "Baba" (Father):

> *When a seeker receives* shaktipat, *he experiences an overflowing of bliss within and becomes ecstatic. In Baba's presence, all doubts and misgivings vanish, and one experiences inner contentment and a sense of fulfillment.[19]*

When seekers find their guru, they love and honor him or her as their spiritual parent. The guru does not always behave as a loving parent; often disciples are treated harshly, to test their faith and devotion or to strip away the ego. True devotees are nevertheless grateful for opportunities to serve their guru, out of love. They often bend to touch the feet or hem of the robe of the guru, partly out of humility and partly because great power is thought to emanate from the guru's feet. Humbling oneself before the guru is considered necessary in order to receive the teaching. A metaphor commonly used is that of a cup and a pitcher of water. If the cup (the disciple, or *chela*) is already full, no water (spiritual wisdom) can be poured into it from the pitcher (the guru). Likewise, if the cup is on the same level as the pitcher, there can be no pouring. What is necessary is for the cup to be empty and below the pitcher; then the water can be freely poured into the cup.

Yogic practices

Spiritual seekers are generally encouraged to engage in disciplines that clear the mind and support a state of serene, detached awareness. This desired state of balance, purity, wisdom, and peacefulness of mind is described as *sattvic*, in contrast with active, restless states or lethargic, dull states. The practices for increasing *sattvic* qualities are known collectively as **yoga**. There are four main yogic paths, suited to different kinds of human personalities—*raja, jnana, karma,* and *bhakti.*

RAJA YOGA The physical and psychic practices of *raja yoga* are those with which non-Hindus are most familiar, as they have been popularized in the West. They are thought to be extremely ancient. Some believe that the **sadhanas**, or practices, were known as long ago as the Neolithic Age and were practiced in the great Indus Valley culture. By 200 BCE, a yogi named Patanjali (or perhaps a series of people taking the same name) had described a coherent system for attaining the highest consciousness. Patanjali's *Yoga Sutras* is a book of 196 terse sayings called **sutras**. These include observations such as these:

> *"From contentment comes the attainment of the highest happiness."*
> *"From penance comes destruction of impurities, thence the perfection of the body and the senses."*
> *"From study, comes communion with the desired deity."*
> *"From the profound meditation upon Isvara [God], comes success in spiritual absorption."*[20]

Yogis say that it is easier to calm a wild tiger than it is to quiet the mind, which is like a drunken monkey that has been bitten by a scorpion. The problem is that the mind is our vehicle for knowing the Self. If the mirror of the mind is disturbed, it reflects the disturbance rather than the pure light within. The goal of yogic practices is to make the mind absolutely calm and clear.

Patanjali distinguishes eight "limbs" of the yogic path: moral codes (*yama-niyama*), physical conditioning (*asana*), breath control (*pranayama*), sense control (*pratyahara*), concentration (*dharana*), meditation (*dhyana*), and the state of peaceful spiritual absorption (*samadhi*).

The moral and ethical principles that form the first limb of yogic practice are truth, non-violence, non-stealing, continence, and non-covetousness, plus cleanliness, contentment, burning zeal, self-study, and devotion to God. The **asanas** are physical postures used to cleanse the body and develop the mind's ability to concentrate. Regulated breathing exercises are also used to calm the nerves and increase the body's supply of **prana**, or invisible life energy. Breath is thought to be the key to controlling the flow of this energy within the subtle energy field surrounding and permeating the physical body. Its major pathway is through a series

Yogic adepts have developed extreme control of their bodies to amplify meditation efforts.

In kundalini yoga, the body is thought to exist within a field of energy, which is most concentrated at the major chakras—subtle centers along the vertical axis of the body.

The OM symbol, representing the original sound of creation, is topped by the sun and the moon, harmonized opposites. To chant OM is to commune with this cosmic sound vibration.

of **chakras**, or subtle energy centers along the spine. To raise the energy from the lowest, least subtle chakra at the base of the spine to the highest, most subtle energy center at the crown of the head is the goal of *kundalini* yoga practices, with **kundalini** referring to the latent energy at the base of the spine. Ideally, the opening of the highest chakra leads to the bliss of union with the Sublime. In its fully open state, the crown chakra is depicted as a thousand-petaled lotus, effulgent with light.

In addition to these practices using the body and breath, Indian thought has long embraced the idea that repetition of certain sounds has sacred effects. It is said that some ancient yogic adepts could discern subtle sounds and that mantras (sacred formulas) express an aspect of the divine in the form of sound vibration.

Chanting sacred syllables is thought to allow the consciousness to ride over the sea of the mind, calming and raising the vibration of the devotee, stilling the mind and attuning him or her to the Divine Ground of Existence. Indians liken the mind to the trunk of an elephant, always straying restlessly here and there. If an elephant is given a small stick to hold in its trunk, it will hold it steadily, losing interest in other objects. In the same way, the mantra gives the restless mind something to hold, quieting it by focusing awareness in one place. If chanted with devoted concentration, the mantra may also invoke the presence and blessings of the deity.

Many forms of music have also been developed in India to elevate a person's attunement. Concerts may go on for hours if the musicians are spiritually absorbed. The most cherished sound vibrations are the "unheard, unstruck" divine sounds that cannot be heard with our outer ears.

Another way of steadying and elevating the mind is concentration on some visual form—a candle flame, the picture of a saint or guru, the **OM** symbol, or **yantras**. A *yantra* is a linear image with complex cosmic symbolism. Large *yantras* are also created as designs of colorful seeds for ritual invocations of specific deities.

Many forms of music and dance have evolved within Sanatana Dharma as ways of communicating with and about the divine.

One-pointed concentration ideally leads to a state of meditation. In meditation, all worldly thoughts have dissipated. Instead of ordinary thinking, the clear light of awareness allows insights to arise spontaneously as flashes of illumination. There may also be phenomena, such as colored lights, visions, waves of ecstasy, or visits from supernatural beings. The mind, heart, and body may gradually be transformed.

The ultimate goal of yogic meditation is **samadhi**: a super-conscious state of union with the Absolute. Swami Sivananda attempts to describe it:

Words and language are imperfect to describe this exalted state. . . . Mind, intellect and the senses cease functioning. . . . It is a state of eternal Bliss and eternal Wisdom. All dualities vanish in toto. . . . All visible merge in the invisible or the Unseen. The individual soul becomes that which he contemplates.[21]

JNANA YOGA   Another yogic path employs the rational mind rather than trying to transcend it by concentration practices. This is **jnana yoga**—"the way of wisdom." In this path, ignorance is considered the root of all problems. Our basic ignorance is our idea of our selves as being separate from the Absolute. One method is continually to ask, "Who am I?" The seeker discovers that the one who asks the question is not the body, not the senses, not the pranic body, not the mind, but something eternal beyond all these. The guru Ramana Maharshi explains:

After negating all of the above-mentioned as "not this," "not this," that Awareness which alone remains—that I am. . . . The thought "Who am I?" will destroy all other thoughts, and, like the stick used for stirring the burning pyre, it will itself in the end get destroyed. Then, there will arise Self-realization.[22]

In the *jnana* path, the seeker must also develop spiritual virtues (calmness, restraint, renunciation, resignation, concentration, and faith) and have an intense longing for liberation. Finally one graduates from theoretical knowledge of the self to direct experience of it. The ultimate wisdom is spiritual insight rather than intellectual knowledge.

Spiritual knowledge is the only thing that can destroy our miseries for ever; any other knowledge removes wants only for a time.

Swami Vivekananda[23]

KARMA YOGA   In contrast to these ascetic and contemplative practices, another way is that of helpful action in the world. **Karma yoga** is service rendered without any interest in its fruits and without any personal sense of giving. The yogi knows that it is the Absolute who performs all actions, and that all actions are gifts to the Absolute. This consciousness leads to liberation from the self in the very midst of work. Krishna explains these principles in the *Bhagavad-Gita*:

The steadily devoted soul attains unadulterated peace because he offers the results of all activities to Me; whereas a person who is not in harmony with the divine, who is greedy for the fruits of his labor, becomes entangled.[24]

BHAKTI YOGA   The final type of spiritual path is the one embraced by most Indian followers of Sanatana Dharma. It is the path of devotion, **bhakti yoga**.

Preparation for worship of the goddess by brahmin priests.

Bhakti means "to share," to share a relationship with the Supreme. For the **bhakta** (devotee), the relationship is that of intense love. Bhakta Nam Dev described this deep love in sweet metaphors:

> *Thy Name is beautiful, Thy form is beautiful, and very beautiful is Thy love, Oh my Omnipresent Lord.*
> *As rain is dear to the earth, as the fragrance of flowers is dear to the black bee, and as the mango is dear to the cuckoo, so is the Lord to my soul.*
> *As the sun is dear to the sheldrake, and the lake of Man Sarowar to the swan, and as the husband is dear to the wife, so is God to my soul.*
> *As milk is dear to the baby and as the torrent of rain to the mouth of the sparrowhawk who drinks nothing but raindrops, and as water is dear to the fish, so is the Lord to my soul.*[25]

Bhaktas' devotion is thought to be more dear to the Supreme than ritualistic piety. The story is told that a pious brahmin came daily to offer ritual worship to a stone statue of Siva. One day he was horrified to see wild flowers and partly eaten pork decorating the shrine. These had been left by a hunter who stopped to worship Siva in his own fashion. Hoping to teach the brahmin a lesson, Siva appeared to him in a dream commanding that he watch from hiding while the hunter expressed his devotion. When the hunter then came to worship, he saw blood oozing from the eye of the statue. Without hesitation, he plucked out his own eye to place it on that of the idol. The bleeding stopped, but then the statue's other eye started bleeding. The hunter prepared to pull out his other eye when Siva manifested himself, healed the hunter, and took him as one of his chosen devotees, thenceforth called "the beloved of the eye."

The love between Radha and Krishna is a model for bhaktas' *devotion to the supreme person.*

A vision of a deity like that in the story is what the *bhakta* hopes for. Bhakta Ravi Das, a shoemaker who became a highly regarded spiritual teacher because of his intense devotion, implored his beloved: "I am a sacrifice unto You, my Omnipresent Lord. Why are you silent? For many births I have been separated from you. This life I dedicate to You. I live only with the hope of you. It is so long since I have seen You."[26]

Mirabai, a fifteenth-century Rajput princess, was married to a ruler at a young age, but from her childhood she had been utterly devoted to Krishna. Her poetry expresses her single-minded love for her beloved:

Everything perishes,
sun, moon, earth, sky, water, wind,
everything.
Only the One Indestructible remains.
Others get drunk on distilled wine,
in love's still I distil mine;
day and night I'm drunk on it
in my Lover's love, ever sunk . . .
I'll not remain in my mother's home,
I'll stay with Krishna alone;
   He's my Husband
   and my Lover,
   and my mind is
   at his feet forever.[27]

When Mirabai continued to spend all her time in devotions to Krishna, an infuriated in-law tried to poison her. It is said that Mirabai drank the poison while laughingly dancing in ecstasy before Krishna; in Krishna's presence the poison seemed like nectar to her and did her no harm. Such is the devotion of the fully devoted *bhakta* that the Beloved One is said to respond and to be a real presence in the *bhakta*'s life.

In the *bhakti* path, even though the devotee may not transcend the ego in *samadhi*, the devotee's whole being is surrendered to the deity in love. Ramakrishna explains why the *bhakti* way is more appropriate for most people:

As long as the I-sense lasts, so long are true knowledge and Liberation impossible. . . . [But] how very few can obtain this Union [Samadhi] and free themselves from this "I"? It is very rarely possible. Talk as much as you want, isolate yourself continuously, still this "I" will always return to you. Cut down the poplar tree today, and you will find tomorrow it forms new shoots. When you ultimately find that this "I" cannot be destroyed, let it remain as "I" the servant.[28]

Major theistic cults

After a period when Brahmanic ritual and philosophy dominated Sanatana Dharma, the *bhakti* approach came to prominence around 600 CE. It opened spiritual expression to both *shudras* and women, and has been the primary path of the masses ever since. It may also have been the initial way of the people, for

AN INTERVIEW WITH SARALA CHAKRABARTY

Living Hinduism

Sarala Chakrabarty, a Calcutta grandmother, has undertaken spiritual studies with a guru in the Ramakrishna tradition. Her love for the Supreme, in many forms, is highly personal.

"In our Hindu religion, we worship God in some form. God is infinite, but we cannot imagine the infinite. We must have some finite person—whom I love like friend, like father, like son, like lover. We make a relation with God like this. When I think he is my lover, I can always think of him. When I think he is my father, when I am in trouble, I pray to him, ask him to save me.

"And I always pray to the Holy Mother [Ramakrishna's spiritual bride and successor, Sarada Devi]. When I have a problem, Mother will save me. She has given word when she was leaving her body (you say 'dying')—she said, 'I am blessing all who have come, who are coming, who have not come yet but are coming, blessings for all.' Only Mother can say this—so big heart, so much affection for us.

"I feel something. Somebody is standing behind me. I feel always the hands on my shoulders, guarding me. Everybody is protected by God, everyone. I am not his only child. But I think God is only mine.

"I want everything from God. God does not want anything from me. He wants *bhakti*—devotion. A mother wants nothing from a child but love. She says only, 'Pray to me, call me, and I will do everything for you.' When I am traveling I say to Her, 'I am talking to you,' and this is done.

"As we love God, God loves us. Our Lord Krishna says Love is the rope. It ties God and pulls him down to you.

"I have a very powerful guru, a swami of the Ramakrishna Mission, who has passed on. He gave me a mantra, and it gives me very much peace. When I chant, I cannot leave it. Time is over, somebody is calling, I have to cook, I have to work—then I get up and still I am chanting in my mind. After bedding, I worship and chant. After that I realize I am pleased, I am quiet. There is no trouble in body and mind. I am very happy, very blissful. Whatever that problem is, all goes away."

devotion to personal deities is thought to predate Vedic religion.

Of all the deities worshipped by Hindus, there are three major groupings: **Vaishnavites**, who worship the god Vishnu, **Saivites** who worship the god Siva, and **Saktas** who worship a Mother Goddess. Each devotee has his or her own "chosen deity," but will honor others as well.

Ultimately, many Hindus rest their faith in one genderless deity with three basic aspects: creating, preserving, and destroying. The latter activity is seen as a merciful act that allows the continuation of the cosmic cycles.

Saktas

An estimated 50 million Hindus worship some form of the goddess. Some of these Saktas follow a Vedic path; some are more independent of Vedic tradition. As we have seen, worship of the feminine aspect of the divine probably dates back to the pre-Vedic ancient peoples of the Indian subcontinent. Her power is called *sakti* and is often linked with the *kundalini* energy. Lushly erotic, sensual imagery is frequently used to symbolize her abundant creativity.

The feminine principle is worshipped in many forms. At the village level, especially in southern India, local deities are most typically worshipped as goddesses. They may not be perceived as taking human-like forms; rather, their presence may be represented by round stones, trees, *yantras*, or small shrines without images. These local goddesses are intimately concerned with village affairs, unlike the more distant great goddesses of the upper class, access to whose temples was traditionally forbidden to those of low caste.

The great goddesses have been worshipped both in the plural and in the singular, in which case one goddess is seen as representing the totality of deity—eternal creator, preserver, and destroyer. The great goddess **Durga** is often represented as a beautiful woman with a gentle face but ten arms holding weapons with which she vanquishes the demons who threaten the *dharma*; she rides a lion (see page 35). She is the blazing splendor of God incarnate, the ultimate light and power in benevolent female form.

Kali, by contrast, is the divine in its fierce form. She may be portrayed dripping with blood, carrying a sword and a severed head, and wearing a girdle of severed hands and a necklace of skulls symbolizing her aspect as the destroyer of evil. What appears as destruction is actually a means of transformation. With her merciful sword she cuts away all personal impediments to realization of truth, for those who sincerely desire to serve the Supreme. At the same time, she opens her arms to those who love her. Some of them worship her with blood offerings.

Folk representation of the goddess Kali. It is said that when Kali threatened to destroy the whole world in her battle against evil, Lord Siva placed himself in her path to calm and stop her.

Fearsome to evil-doers, but loving and compassionate as a mother to devotees, Kali wears a mask of ugliness. The divine reality is a wholeness encompassing both the pleasant and the unpleasant, creation and destruction. In Hindu thought, death and birth are linked, each giving way to the other in eternal cycles. All beings, all phenomena, are interrelated parts of the same divine essence. Sanskrit scholar Leela Arjunwadkar observes that there is a deeply sensed unity among all beings in classical Indian literature:

> That is why we find all types of characters in Sanskrit literature—human beings, gods and goddesses, rivers, demons, trees, serpents, celestial nymphs, etc., and their share in the same emotional life is the umbilical cord that binds all to Mother Nature.[29]

From ancient times, worship of the divine female has been associated with worship of nature, particularly great trees and rivers. The Ganges River is considered especially sacred, an extremely powerful female presence, and her waters, which flow down from the Himalayas, are thought to be extraordinarily purifying. Pilgrims reverently bathe in Mother Ganga's waters, facing the sun at sunrise, and corpses or the cremated ashes of the dead are placed in the river so that their sins will be washed away.

Sacred texts called **Tantras** instruct worshippers how to honor the feminine divine. Ways of worship include concentration on *yantras*, meditation with the hands in *mudras* (positions that reflect and invoke a particular spiritual reality), *kundalini* practices, and use of mantras. One such text gives a thousand different "names" or attributes of the Divine Mother as mantras for recitation, such as these: "*Sri mata* (She who is the auspicious Mother), *Sri maha rajni* (She who is the Empress of the Universe) ... *Raga svarupa pasadhya* (She who is holding the rope of love in Her hand) ... *Nirmada* (She who is without pride), *Mada nasini* (She who destroys pride), *Niscinta* (She who has no anxiety about anything), *Nir ahankara* (She who is without egoism) ... *Mahaisvarya* (She who has supreme sovereignty), *Maha virya* (She who is supreme in valor), *Maha bala* (She who is supreme in might), *Maha buddhih* (She who is supreme in intelligence).[30] Praising and invoking one deity by many divine names is also a common way of worshipping deities other than the goddess.

Sakti worship has also been incorporated into worship of the gods. Each is thought to have a female consort, often portrayed in close physical embrace signifying the eternal unity of male and female principles in the oneness of the divine. Here the female is often conceived as the life-animating force; the transcendent male aspect is inactive until joined with the productive female energy.

Worship of the goddess in India and Nepal continues to exist side by side with social attempts to limit and confine women's power. This ambivalence is ancient. On the one hand, the female is highly venerated in Hinduism, compared to many other religions. Traditionally, women are thought to make major contributions to the good earthly life, consisting of *dharma* (order in society), marital wealth (by bearing sons in a patriarchal society), and the aesthetics of sensual pleasure. Women are auspicious beings, mythologically associated with wealth, beauty, splendor, and grace. As sexual partners to men, they help to activate the spiritualizing life-force. No ceremonial sacrifice is complete unless the wife participates as well as the husband.

In the ideal marriage, husband and wife are spiritual partners. Marriage is a vehicle for spiritual discipline, service, and advancement toward a spiritual goal, rather than a means of self-gratification. Men and women are thought to complement each other, although the ideal of liberation has traditionally been intended largely for the male.

Women were not traditionally encouraged to seek liberation through their own spiritual practices. A woman's role is usually linked to that of her husband, who takes the position of her god and their guru. For many centuries, there was even the hope that a widow would choose to be cremated alive with her dead husband in order to remain united with him after death.

In early Vedic times, women were relatively free and honored members of Indian society, participating equally in important spiritual rituals. By the nineteenth century, however, wives had become virtual slaves of the husband's family. With expectations that the girl will take a large dowry to the boy's family in a marriage arrangement, having girls is such an economic burden that many female babies are intentionally aborted or killed at birth. There are also cases today of women being beaten or killed by the husband's family after their dowry has been handed over. Nevertheless many women in contemporary India have been well educated, and many have attained high political positions.

Siva as Lord of the
Dance, trampling the
demon of evil and
bearing both the flame
of destruction and the
drum of creation. One
of his two free hands
gestures "Fear not";
the other points to his
upraised foot, denoting
bliss.

Saivites

Siva is a personal, many-faceted manifestation of the attributeless supreme deity. In older systems he is one of the three major aspects of deity: Brahma (Creator), Vishnu (Preserver), and Siva (Destroyer). Saivites nevertheless worship him as the totality, with many aspects. As Swami Sivasiva Palani, Saivite editor of *Hinduism Today*, explains: "Siva is the unmanifest; he is creator, preserver, destroyer, personal Lord, friend, primal Soul"; and he is the "all-pervasive underlying energy, the more or less impersonal love and light that flows through all things."[31] Siva is sometimes depicted dancing above the body of the demon he has killed, reconciling darkness and light, good and evil, creation and destruction, rest and activity in the eternal dance of life.

Siva is also the god of yogis, for he symbolizes asceticism. He is often shown in austere meditation on Mount Kailas, clad only in a tiger skin, with a snake around his neck. The latter signifies his conquest of the ego. In one prominent story, it is Siva who swallows the poison that threatens the whole world with darkness, neutralizing the poison by the power of his meditation.

Siva has various saktis or feminine consorts, including Durga. He is often shown with his devoted spouse **Parvati**. Through their union, cosmic energy flows freely, seeding and liberating the universe. Nevertheless, they are seen mystically as eternally chaste. Siva and his sakti are also expressed as two aspects of a single being. Some sculptors portray Siva as androgynous, with both masculine and feminine physical traits. Tantric belief incorporates an ideal of balance of male and female qualities within a person, hopefully leading to enlightenment, bliss, and worldly success as well. This unity of male and female is often expressed abstractly, as a lingam within a **yoni**, a symbol of the female vulva.

Lingams are naturally occurring or sculpted cylindrical forms honored since antiquity in India (and apparently in other cultures as well, as far away as Hawaii). Those shaped by nature, such as stones polished by certain rivers, are most highly valued, with rare natural crystal lingams considered especially precious. Tens of thousands of devotees each year undergo dangerous pilgrimages to certain high mountain caves to venerate large lingams naturally formed of ice. While the lingam sometimes resembles an erect phallus, most Siva-worshippers focus on its symbolic meaning, which is abstract and asexual. They see the lingam as a nearly amorphous, "formless" symbol for the unmanifest, transcendent nature of Siva—that which is beyond time, space, cause, and form—whereas the yoni represents the manifest aspect of Sivaness.

Saivism encompasses traditions that have developed outside Vedic-based Brahmanism. These include sects such as the Lingayats, who wear a stone lingam in remembrance of Siva as the One Undivided Being. Their ancient ways of Siva worship underwent a strong reform movement in the twelfth century, refusing caste divisions, brahminical authority, and consideration of menstruating women as polluted. They practice strict vegetarianism and regard men and women as equals.

Another branch is represented by the sixty-three great Saivite saints of Tamil Nadu in southern India, who from the seventh century onward expressed great love for Siva. They experienced him as the Luminous One, present everywhere in subtle form but apparent only to those who love him. For this realization,

A large lingam from the 6th century CE honors Siva as the unmanifest creative force beyond time and space.

knowledge of the scriptures and ascetic practices are useless. Only direct personal devotion will do. The Tamil saint Appar sang,

Above left *Milk slowly drains from a spoon held to the trunk of a Ganesh statue, on one miraculous day in 1995.* **Above right** *The auspicious blessings of Ganesh are invoked for all occasions. Here his image has been painted on a wall before a marriage celebration.*

> *Why chant the Vedas, hear the shastras' lore? ...*
> *Release is theirs, and theirs alone,*
> *Whose heart from thinking of its Lord shall never depart.*[32]

Siva's son is Ganesh, a deity with the head of an elephant, who guards the threshold of space and time and who is, therefore, invoked for his auspicious blessings at the beginning of any new venture or worship ceremony. Ganesh was the subject of an extraordinary event that happened in temples in many parts of India, as well as in Hindu temples in other parts of the world. On September 21, 1995, statues devoted to Ganesh began drinking milk from spoons, cups, and even buckets of milk offered by devotees. Crowds queued up at temples to see if the divine would accept their offering. Scientists suggested explanations such as mass hysteria or capillary action in the stone, but the phenomenon, which lasted only one day, was fully convincing to many who experienced it. Contrary to caste expectations, the statues accepted milk from members of the lowest castes.

Vaishnavites

In contrast to Sakti and Siva, Vishnu is beloved as the tender, merciful deity. In one myth, a sage was sent to determine who was the greatest of the gods by trying their tempers. The first two, Brahma and Siva, he insulted and was soundly abused in return. When he found Vishnu, the god was sleeping. Knowing of Vishnu's good-naturedness, the sage increased the insult by kicking him awake. Instead of reacting angrily, Vishnu tenderly massaged the sage's foot, concerned

Lakshmi is often pictured standing gloriously upon a lotus flower, bestowing coins of prosperity and flanked by elephants signifying her royal power.

that he might have hurt it. The sage exclaimed, "This god is the mightiest, since he overpowers all by goodness and generosity!"

Vishnu has been worshipped since Vedic times and came to be regarded as the Supreme as a person. According to ideas appearing by the fourth century CE, Vishnu is considered to have appeared in many earthly incarnations, some of them animal forms. Worship of many deities in their own right has been drawn into this complex, in which they are interpreted as incarnations of Vishnu. Most beloved of his purported incarnations have been Rama, subject of the *Ramayana* (see page 90), and Krishna (see page 93). However, many people still revere Krishna without reference to Vishnu.

Popular devotion to Krishna takes many forms, depending on the relationship the devotee feels toward Krishna. If Krishna is regarded as the transcendent Supreme Lord, the worshipper humbly lowers himself or herself. If Krishna is seen as master, the devotee is his servant. If Krishna is loved as a child, the devotee takes the role of loving parent. If Krishna is the divine friend, the devotee is his friend. And if Krishna is the beloved, the devotee is his lover. The latter relationship was popularized by the ecstatic sixteenth-century Bengali saint and sage Sri Caitanya, who adored Krishna as the flute-playing lover. Following Sri Caitanya, the devotee makes himself (if a male) like a loving female in order to experience the bliss of Lord Krishna's presence. It is this form of Hindu devotion that was carried to America in 1965, organized as the International Society for Krishna Consciousness, and then spread to other countries. Its followers are known as Hare Krishnas.

Vishnu is often associated with his consort, **Lakshmi**, who is also an ancient goddess worshipped in her own right. She is associated with the presence of prosperity and glorious regal power. Lakshmi is often depicted as a radiant woman sitting on a water-borne lotus flower. The lotus floats pristine on the water but has its roots in the mud, thus representing the refined spiritual energy that rises above worldly contamination. The lotus also symbolizes the fertile growth of organic life, as over the eons the world is continually reborn on a lotus growing out of Vishnu's navel.

Major philosophical systems

Although the majority of followers of Sanatana Dharma are *bhaktas*, the spiritual wisdom of India has also expressed itself in elaborate intellectual systems of philosophy. Many distinct systems have evolved, but they all have certain features in common:

1 All have deep roots in the Vedas and other scriptures but also in direct personal experiences of the truth through meditation;
2 All hold ethics to be central to orderly social life. They attribute suffering to the law of *karma*, thereby suggesting incentives to more ethical behavior;
3 All hold that the ultimate cause of suffering is people's ignorance of their true nature, the Self, whch is omniscient, omnipotent, omnipresent, perfect, and eternal.

Two of the major philosophical systems born in India do not acknowledge the authority of the Vedas but nevertheless draw on many of the same currents as Sanatana Dharma. These two, Jainism and Buddhism, will be considered in the following two chapters. Prominent among the others are **Samkhya** and **Advaita Vedanta**.

Samkhya

The Samkhya system, though undatable, is thought to be the oldest in India. Its founder, the semi-mythical sage Kapila, was mentioned in the *Mahabharata*. But both Buddhism and Jainism, which developed simultaneously in the sixth century BCE, include Samkhya principles, so the system probably preceded them and may be of pre-Vedic origin.

Samkhya philosophy holds that there are two states of reality. One is the Purusha, the Self, which is eternally wise, pure, and free, beyond change, beyond cause. The other is **Prakriti**, the cause of the material universe. All our suffering stems from our false confusion of Prakriti with Purusha, the eternal Self. A **dualistic** understanding of life is essential, according to this system, if we are to distinguish the ultimate transcendent reality of Purusha from the temporal appearances of Prakriti, which bring us happiness but also misery and delusion.

An illuminating story is told about Indra, who was once king of the gods. He was forced by the other *devas* to descend to earth in the body of a boar. Once there, he began to enjoy the life, wallowing in the mud, mating, and siring baby pigs. The *devas* were aghast; they came down to try to convince him to return, but Indra had forgotten his kingly state and insisted on remaining as a boar. Unable to talk him out of his delusion, the *devas* tried killing his babies; he was distraught but simply mated to have more piglets. Then the *devas* killed his mate. Indra grieved his loss but stayed in the mud. They finally had to kill him as well to bring him back to his senses. His soul could then see the body of the boar it had been inhabiting and was glad to return to heaven. The moral is that we, too, are like gods who forget the heights from which we came, so intent are we on the joys and sorrows of earthly life.

Advaita Vedanta

Whereas Samkhya is a dualistic system, Advaita ("non-dualist") Vedanta is generally **monistic**, positing a single reality. It is based on the *Upanishads*: its founder is said to be Vyasa, systematizer of the *Upanishads*. Shankara reorganized the teachings many centuries later, probably between the eighth and ninth centuries CE.

Whereas one view of the *Upanishads* is that the human self (*atman*) is an emanation of Brahman, Shankara insisted that the *atman* and Brahman are actually one. According to Shankara, our material life is an illusion. It is like a momentary wave arising from the ocean, which is the only reality. Ignorance consists in thinking that the waves are different from the ocean. The absolute spirit, Brahman, is the essence of everything, and it has no beginning and no end. It is the eternal ocean of bliss within which forms are born and die, giving the false appearance of being real.

That which makes us think the physical universe has its own reality is **maya**, the power by which the Absolute veils itself. *Maya* is the illusion that the world as we perceive it is real. Shankara uses the metaphor of a coil of rope that, at dusk, is mistaken for a snake. The physical world, like the rope, does actually exist but we superimpose our memories and subjective thoughts upon it. Moreover, he says, only that which never changes is truly real. Everything else is changing, impermanent. Apparent phenomenal existence is not the same thing as reality.

In ignorance we think that we exist as individuals, superimposing the notion of a separate ego-self on the underlying absolute reality of pure being, pure consciousness, pure bliss. It is a mistake to identify with the body or the mind, which exist but have no unchanging reality. When a person reaches transcendent consciousness, superimposition stops and the monistic oneness of reality is experienced.

Popular forms of worship

Having evolved in so many directions for thousands of years, Sanatana Dharma today is rich in personal and public opportunities for serving and celebrating the Supreme in many forms.

Devotions and rituals

There are sixteen rites prescribed in the ancient scriptures to purify and sanctify the person in his or her journey through life, including rites at the time of conception, the braiding of the pregnant mother's hair, birth, name-giving, beginning of solid foods, starting education, investing boys with a sacred thread, first leaving the family house, starting studies of Vedas, marriage, and death. The goal is to continually elevate the person above his or her basically animal nature.

Pilgrimages to holy places and sacred rivers are also thought to be special opportunities for personal purification and spiritual elevation. Millions of pilgrims yearly undertake strenuous climbs to remote mountain sites that are thought to be blessed by the divine. One of the major pilgrimage sites is Amarnath cave. At an altitude of 11,090 feet (3,380 m) in the Himalayas of Kashmir, ice has formed a giant stalagmite, which is highly revered as a Siva lingam. Pilgrims may have been trekking to this holy place in the high Himalayas for up to three thousand years. The 14,800-feet (45-km) footpath over a glacier is so dangerous that 250 people were killed by freak storms and landslides in 1996, but in subsequent years, tens of thousands of devotees continue to undertake the pilgrimage. Similarly, Saktas trek up to Saktipithas, fifty-one pilgrimage spots in the Indian subcontinent that are thought to mark abodes of the goddess or places where parts of Her body now rest.

Nearly every home in India has a shrine with pictures or small statues of various deities, and many have a special prayer room set aside for their worship. For **puja**, or worship, ritual purity is emphasized; the time for prayer and offerings to the deities is after the morning bath or after one has washed in the evening. *Puja* is an everyday observance, although among orthodox families, women are considered unclean when menstruating and are not allowed to approach the shrines at that time. Typically, a small oil lamp and a smoldering stick of incense are waved in a circle before the deities' images. If the devotee or family has a guru, a picture of him or her is usually part of the shrine.

Public worship is usually performed by *pujaris*, or brahmin priests, who are trained in Vedic practices and in proper recitation of Sanskrit texts. They conduct worship ceremonies in which the sacred presence is made tangible through devotions employing all the senses. Siva-lingams may be anointed with precious substances, such as ghee (clarified butter), honey, or sandalwood paste, with offerings of rose water and flowers. In a temple, devotees may have the great blessing of receiving **darsan** (visual contact with the divine) through the eyes of the images. One hears the sounds of mantras and ringing bells. Incense and flowers fill the area with uplifting fragrances. **Prasad**, food that has been sanctified by being offered to the deities and/or one's guru, is passed around to be eaten by devotees, who experience it as sacred and spiritually charged.

Millions of Hindus undertake difficult pilgrimages to worship at mountain shrines each year.

In temples, the deity image is treated as if it were a living king or queen. Fine-haired whisks may be waved before it, purifying the area for its presence. Aesthetically pleasing meals are presented on the deity's own dishes at appropriate intervals; fruits must be perfect, without any blemishes. During visiting hours, the deity holds court, giving audience to devotees. In the morning, the image is ritually bathed and dressed in sumptuous clothes for the day; at night, it may be put to rest in bedclothes. If it is hot, the deity takes a nap in the afternoon, so arrangements are made for its privacy. For festivals, the deity is carefully paraded through the streets. The great Jagganath festival, held only once every twelve years in Puri, was attended by some one and a half million devotees in 1996, all clambering for *darsan* of the deity, pulled in a massive sixteen-wheeled chariot (mispelled long ago as "juggernaut" in English).

For the devout, loving service to the divine makes it real and present. To many Hindus the statue is not just a symbol of the deity; the deity may be experienced through the statue, reciprocating the devotee's attentions. According to Swami Sivasiva Palani:

> *It is thought that the subtle essences of these things given in devotion are actually absorbed by the divine, in an invisible and rather mystical process. It's as though we are feeding our God in an inner kind of way. It's thought that if this is done properly, with the right spirit, the right heartfulness, the right mantras, that we capture the attention of the personal Lord and that he actually communes with us through that process, and we with him. Of course, when I say "us" and "him" I connote a dualism that is meant to be transcended in this process.*[33]

In addition to worshipping the divine through services to images, orthodox brahmins observe many days of fasting and prayer, corresponding to auspicious points in the lunar and solar cycles or times of danger, such as the four months of the monsoon season. The ancient practice of astrology is so highly regarded that many couples are now choosing birth by Caesarean section for the purpose of selecting the most auspicious moment for their children's birth.

Many expressions of Indian spirituality, particularly in rural areas, are not encapsulated within Brahmanic traditions but rather have a timeless existence of their own. Such, for instance, are the home-made designs daily laid out before homes at dawn. They are created by women with the intention of protecting their household by inviting a deity such as the goddess Lakshmi. Typically made of edible substances, such as rice flour, the designs are soon dismantled by insects and birds, but this is of no concern, for they help to fulfill the dharmic requirement that one should feed a thousand souls every day.

Practices such as worship under large trees stretches back into pre-history and is apparent in archaeological evidence from the Harappan civilization. Such worship continues at countless small shrines today. There is a strong taboo against cutting certain sacred tree species, such as the peepul tree, which sprouts wherever it can gain the slightest foothold, often in stone or brick walls, even on the sides of buildings. Whole tracts of virgin forest are kept intact by villagers in some parts of India. There they reverently protect both animal and plant life with the understanding that the area is the home of a deity. These sacred groves are now viewed by environmentalists as important islands of biological diversity.

Even the poorest Hindu families have a special room or place for puja *to their favorite deities.*

Not only forests but also hilltops, mountains, and river sources are often viewed as sacred and their natural environment thus protected to a certain extent. The Narmada River, one of India's most sacred, is regarded by millions of people as a goddess (as are most Indian rivers). Its banks are lined with thousands of temples devoted to Mother Narmada and Lord Shiva. Pilgrims reverently circumambulate the entire 815-mile (1,312-km) length of the river, from its source in central India to its mouth in the Gulf of Khambhat, and back again. However, the river and its huge watershed are the subjects of the world's largest water development scheme, with a project including thirty major dams, 135 medium dams, and 3,000 minor dams. The highest of the dams is under construction, creating a reservoir with a final proposed height of 448 feet (136.5 m). When the reservoir is filled, some 245 villages will be submerged, temples and all. The idea is to capture the water and divert it to drought-ridden areas to benefit people there. However, the inhabitants of the watershed that will be inundated are closely linked to their local sacred landscape. One of them explains, "Our gods cannot move from this place. How can we move without them?"[34] Fierce conflicts have been raging since 1990 between environmentalists and social activists who are fighting the high dams, claiming they will adversely affect at least one million people in the watershed for the sake of vested interests elsewhere, and modernists who regard such high dams, as Nehru said, as "the secular temples of modern India."[35]

High dams are not the only threat to sacred rivers. Religious practices themselves may lead to high levels of water pollution. Mass bathing on auspicious occasions is accompanied by wastes, such as butter oil, flowers, and human excreta (contrary to scriptural injunctions about proper behavior in sacred rivers). The remains of dead bodies reverently immersed in the sacred rivers may be incompletely cremated. Immersion of idols of Ganesh or Durga on holy days as a symbol of purification (as explained in the next section) has become a major source of water pollution because of the quantities of idols and the toxicity of their materials. In one year alone, ritual immersion of idols in Calcutta added to the Hoogli River an estimated 17 tons of varnish and 32 tons of paints, including manganese, lead, mercury, and chromium.[36]

An Indian woman prepares a protective rice flour pattern on the earth outside her home, honoring the ancient tradition by which her female ancestors created intuitive designs to bring spiritual protection for their families.

Festivals

Sanatana Dharma honors the divine in so many forms that almost every day a religious celebration is being held in some part of India. Sixteen religious holidays are honored by the central government so that everyone can leave work to join in the throngs of worshippers. These are calculated partially on a lunar calendar, so dates vary from year to year. Most Hindu festivals express spirituality in its happiest aspects. Group energy attracts the gods to overcome evils, and humorous abandon helps merry-makers transform their fears.

Pilgrims to Benares take a purifying bath and offer prayers at sunrise in the sacred Ganges River.

On a midwinter night in northern India, people happily celebrate Lohari by building a bonfire and throwing popcorn, peanuts, and sesame candies into it. The feeling is that one is symbolically throwing away one's evils, and at the same time invoking blessings for the year to come. In particular, families who have given birth to a male child during the past year perform this ceremony for his auspicious future.

Holi is the riotously joyful celebration of the death of winter and the return of colorful spring. In northern Indian areas where Vaishnavism is strong, the

Youths fling paint upon each other with gay abandon at Holi.

holiday is associated with Krishna, for as an infant he is said to have killed a demon employed by the king of winter. Pilgrims flock to Mathura, purported birthplace of Krishna, for re-enactments of Krishna's playful exploits with the *gopis*. The festivities are probably of ancient indigenous origin, and in some areas, the two-day craziness is dedicated to Kama, the god of sexual love. Whatever the excuse, bands of people take to the streets throwing brightly colored powder or paint on anyone they meet. At the end of this uninhibited gaiety, everyone hugs and old grudges are dropped as the new year begins.

Legends about Krishna as a child are often re-enacted by children as part of a holiday honoring Krishna's birthday, Janmashtami.

In July or August a special day, Naga Panchami, is devoted to the **nagas**, or snakes. Snakes were considered powerful gods by the indigenous peoples, and the tradition persists. In southern Indian villages, where they are especially honored, thousands of live snakes are caught and exhibited by brave handlers. Worshippers sprinkle vermilion and rice on the hoods of cobras, considered especially sacred. On Naga Panchami, farmers abstain from ploughing to avoid disrupting any snake-holes.

In August or September, Vaishnavites celebrate Krishna's birthday (Janmashtami). Devotees fast and keep a vigil until midnight, retelling stories of Krishna's life or reading his enlightened wisdom from the *Bhagavad-Gita*. In some places Krishna's image is placed in a cradle and lovingly rocked by devotees. Elsewhere,

On Janmashtami, devotees lovingly rock an image of the child Krishna in a cradle.

pots of milk, curds, and butter are strung high above the ground to be seized by young men who form human pyramids to get to their prize. They romp about with the pots, drinking and spilling their contents like Krishna, playful stealer of these milk products he loved.

At the end of the summer, it is Ganesh who is honored, especially in western and southern India, during Ganesh Chaturti. Special potters make elaborate clay images of the jovial elephant-headed remover of obstacles, son of Parvati who formed him from her own body's dirt and sweat, and set him to stand guard while she bathed. Since he wouldn't let Siva in, her angry spouse smashed the boy's head into a thousand pieces. Parvati demanded that the boy be restored to life with a new head, but the first one found was that of a baby elephant. To soothe Parvati's distress at the peculiarity of the transplant, Siva granted Ganesh the power of removing obstacles. The elephant-headed god is now the first to be invoked in all rituals. After days of being sung to and offered sweets, the Ganesh images are carried to a body of water and bidden farewell with prayers for an easy year until Ganesh Chaturti comes around again.

In different parts of India, the first nine or ten days of Asvina, the lunar month corresponding to September or October, are dedicated either to the Durga Puja (in which elaborate images of the many-armed goddess celebrate her powers to vanquish the demonic forces) or to Dussehra, which marks Rama's nine nights of worshipping Durga before killing Ravana on the tenth day). For Dussehra, huge effigies of the wicked Ravana and his helpers may be burned, re-enacting the climax of the *Ramayana* and the triumph of Rama, his half-brother Lakshman, and the beloved monkey Hanuman. The theme of both Durga Puja and Dussehra is the triumph of good over evil.

Twenty days later, on the night of the new moon, is Divali, the happy four-day

At the end of the Durga Puja, images of the ten-armed vanquisher of evil are carried to the river and consigned to the deep, so that she may return to her mate Siva, who awaits her in the Himalayas.

festival of lights. Variously explained as the return of Rama after his exile, the *puja* of Lakshmi (goddess of wealth, who visits only clean homes), and the New Year of those following one of the Indian calendars, it is a time for tidying business establishments and financial records, cleaning and illuminating houses with oil lamps, wearing new clothes, gambling, feasting, honoring clay images of Lakshmi and Ganesh, and setting off fireworks.

Initially more solemn is Mahashivaratri, a day of fasting and a night of keeping vigil to earn merit with Siva. During the ascetic part of the observance, many pilgrims go to sacred rivers or special tanks of water for ritual bathing. Siva lingams and statues are venerated, and the faithful stay awake throughout the night, chanting and telling stories of their Lord. In one of the stories, a discussion among Brahma, Vishnu, and Siva leads to Siva's manifesting as a pillar of fire and challenging the others to touch the ends, which they will not. A reformist group, Arya Samaj, decries what it considers superstition and idolatry and honors the day as the end of a week-long celebration of their reform. They carry out Vedic fire sacrifices and hold spiritual talks, throwing personal offerings into the fire on the last day.

Every few years, millions of Hindus of all persuasions gather for the immense Kumbha Mela. It is held alternately at four sacred spots where drops of the holy nectar of immortality are said to have fallen. On one day in 2001, in what has been recorded as the largest ever gathering of human beings for a single purpose, over twenty-five million people amassed at the point near Allahabad where the Jumna River meets the sacred Ganges and the invisible Saraswati. There they took a purifying bath in the frigid waters on the most auspicious date, as determined by astrologers. Among the Kumbha Mela pilgrims are huge processions of ascetic **sadhus** from various orders, many of whom leave their retreats only for this festival. The *sadhus* gather to discuss religious matters and also social problems, sometimes leading to revisions of the codes of conduct governing Hindu society. Many of the lay pilgrims are poor people who undergo great hardships to reach the site. A typical pilgrim, an illiterate woman from West Bengal, traveled to Haridwar with her family in a crowded bus, slept in the open in the cold, and was fed free meals at immense tents set up by philanthropical groups and families. She explained, "We are poor, but we have enough. I asked God not for money but for peace and salvation."[37]

Hinduism in the modern world

Hinduism did not develop in India in isolation from other religions and national influences. Groups continually flowed into the subcontinent from outside. Muslims began taking over certain areas beginning in the eighth century CE; during the sixteenth and seventeenth centuries a large area was ruled by the Muslim Mogul emperors. Islam and Hinduism generally co-existed, despite periods of intolerance, along with Buddhism and Jainism, which had also grown up within India. Indian traders carried some aspects of Sanatana Dharma to Java and Bali, where Hinduism survives today with a unique Balinese flavor.

When the Mogul Empire collapsed, European colonialists moved in. Ultimately the British dominated, and in 1857 India was placed under direct British rule. Christian missionaries set about to correct abuses they perceived in certain Hindu practices, such as widow-burning and the caste system. But they

Haridwar is one of the four sites where huge Kumbha Mela celebrations are held on the banks of the Ganges.

also taught those who were being educated in their schools that Hinduism was "intellectually incoherent and ethically unsound."[38] Some Indians believed them and drifted away from their ancient tradition.

To counteract Western influences, Mahatma ("Great Soul") Gandhi (1869–1948) encouraged grassroots nationalism, emphasizing that the people's strength lay in awareness of spiritual truth and in non-violent resistance to military-industrial oppression. He claimed that these qualities were the essence of all religions, including Hinduism, which he considered the universal religion.

In addition to being made a focus for political unity, Hinduism itself was revitalized by a number of spiritual leaders. One of these was Ramakrishna (1836–1886) who was a devotee of the Divine Mother in the form of Kali. Eschewing ritual, he communicated with her through intense love. He practiced Tantric disciplines and the *bhavanas* (types of loving relationships). These brought him spiritual powers, spiritual insight, and reportedly a visible brilliance, but he longed only to be a vehicle for pure devotion:

> *I seek not, good Mother, the pleasures of the senses! I seek not fame! Nor do I long for those powers which enable one to do miracles! What I pray for, O good Mother, is pure love for Thee—love for Thee untainted by desires, love without alloy, love that seeketh not the things of the world, love for Thee that welleth up unbidden out of the depths of the immortal soul!*[39]

Ramakrishna worshipped the divine through many Hindu paths, as well as Islam and Christianity, and found the same One in them all. Intoxicated with the One, he had continual visions of the Divine Mother and ecstatically worshipped her in unorthodox, uninhibited ways. For instance, once he fed a cat some food that was supposed to be a temple offering for the Divine Mother, for she revealed herself to him in everything, including the cat. He also placed his spiritual bride, Sarada Devi, in the chair reserved for the deity, honoring her as the Great Goddess.

The pure devotion and universal spiritual wisdom Ramakrishna embodied inspired what is now known as the Ramakrishna Movement, or the Vedanta Society. A famous disciple, named Vivekananda (1863–1902), carried the eternal message of Sanatana Dharma to the world beyond India and excited so much interest in the West that Hinduism became a global religion. He also reintroduced Indians to the profundities of their great traditions.

Within India Hinduism was also influenced by reform movements such as Brahmo Samaj and Arya Samaj. The former defended Hindu mysticism and *bhakti* devotion to an immanent deity. The latter advocated a return to what it saw as the purity of the Vedas, rejecting image worship, devotion to a multiplicity of deities, priestly privileges, and popular rituals. Though different, both movements were designed to convince intellectuals of the validity of "true" Hinduism.

Ramakrishna, the great nineteenth-century mystic, recognized the divine as being both formless and manifested in many forms, and also as transcending both form and formlessness.

> *Do not care for doctrines, do not care for dogmas, or sects, or churches, or temples; they count for little compared with the essence of existence in each [person], which is spirituality. . . . Earn that first, acquire that, and criticise no one, for all doctrines and creeds have some good in them.*
>
> *Ramakrishna*[40]

Global Hinduism

Hinduism is also experiencing vibrant growth beyond the Indian subcontinent, partly among expatriates and partly among converts from other faiths. For the past hundred years, many self-proclaimed gurus have left India to develop followings in other countries. Some were discovered to be fraudulent, with scandalous private behavior or motives of wealth and power. Despite increased Western wariness of gurus, some of the exported movements have continued to grow.

Many non-Indians discovered Sanatana Dharma by reading *Autobiography of a Yogi*, by Paramahansa Yogananda (1893–1952). The book, which has been translated into eighteen languages, describes his intriguing spiritual experiences with Indian gurus and also explains principles of Sanatana Dharma in loving fashion. Yogananda travelled to the United States and began a movement, the California-based Self-Realization Fellowship, which has survived his death and is still growing under the supervision of Western disciples, with centers, temples, and living communities in forty-six countries.

Another still-flourishing example is the Netherlands-based Transcendental Meditation (TM) movement, which was begun by Maharishi Mahesh Yogi in the 1960s. For a fee, he and his disciples teach people secret mantras and assert that repeating the mantra for twenty minutes twice each day will bring great personal benefits. These range from enhanced athletic prowess to increased satisfaction with life. By paying more money, advanced practitioners can also learn how to "fly." That is, they take short hops into the air while sitting cross-legged. The organization claims a success rate of sixty-five percent in ending drug and alcohol addiction. Its "flying" practitioners are sent to cities to meditate intensely and thus lower the crime rates in the area, according to research published by the TM organization. TM has now entered politics as well, with its Natural Law Party promoting its own candidates in fifty countries. TM now commands a vast global organization, complete with luxurious health spas in Europe, a Vedic "theme park" near Niagara Falls in Canada, Vedic-based development projects in Africa, colleges, universities, and Maharishi Schools of Management in many countries, and an ashram for 10,000 people in India.

Another rather unlikely success story is found in ISKCON, the International Society for Krishna Consciousness. In 1965, the Indian guru A. C. Bhaktivedanta Swami Prabhupada arrived in the United States, carrying the asceticism and *bhakti* devotion of Sri Caitanya's tradition of Krishna worship from India to the heart of Western materialistic culture. Adopting the dress and diet of Hindu monks and nuns, his initiates lived in temple communities. Their days began at 4 a.m. with meditation, worship, chanting of the names of Krishna and Ram, and scriptural study, with the aim of turning from a material life of sense gratification to one of transcendent spiritual happiness. During the day, they chanted and danced in the streets to introduce others to the bliss of Krishna, distributed literature (especially Swami Prabhupada's illustrated and esteemed translation of the *Bhagavad-Gita*), attracted new devotees, and raised funds.

Despite schisms and scandals, the movement has continued since Swami Prabhupada's death in 1977, and is growing in strength in various countries, particularly in India and eastern Europe. In England, followers have turned a great mansion into a huge ISKCON temple, which also serves Indian immigrants as a place

Dharmic Principles: The Swadhyaya Movement

Today there are said to be 20 million people in 100,000 villages in India who are beneficiaries of a silent social revolution based on the principles of the ancient Hindu scriptures, especially the *Bhagavad-Gita*. The movement is called Swadhyaya. The term means self-study, using traditional scriptural teachings as a means for critically analyzing oneself in order to improve. On this basis, villagers and village life have profoundly improved.

The work began in the 1950s, as scriptural scholar Pandurang Shastri Athavale, known by his followers as "Dada" (elder brother), determined that the Gita was "capable of resolving the dilemmas of modern man and solving the problems of material life, individual and social."[41] He founded a school near Bombay, refusing until today to accept any financial help from the government or outside funding agency, insisting that "those institutions which depend upon others' favors are never able to achieve anything worthwhile or carry out divine work."[42] He named the buildings for the ancient sages who have inspired people to live according to Vedic principles. It was they who recognized that within each person is a divine spark whose realization gives them the energy and guidance with which to uplift themselves. As Dada once observed, the sage who wrote the *Ramayana* is

virtually urging us to take Ram—the awareness that the Lord is with us and within us all the time—to every home and every heart, as this alone will provide the confidence and the strength to the weakest of the weak and will bring joy and fragrance into the life of every human being.[43]

Realization of the divine within themselves also leads to realization of the divine within others, which is the beginning of social harmony and cooperation.

The principle upon which Dada's social development work is centered is *bhakti*, or selfless devotion. He inspired his students to pay devotional visits to towns and villages in Gujarat state. They carried their own food and asked for nothing from the people. They simply met the inhabitants one to one and spoke of the divine love which made them reach out to distant places. After years of regular visits and assurance that gratefulness to God and brotherly love was developing among the villagers, they allowed the villagers to build simple hut temples of local materials, devotional places for villagers of all castes and creeds.

In gratitude toward the in-dwelling God for being present when they go to their farms, giving them energy to work, *swadhyayees* feel that God is entitled t o a share in the produce. They therefore bring a portion of their income to the hut temples to be distributed among the most needy, as the benevolence of God.

Believing in work as worship, the villagers were also inspired to set aside a portion of land to be farmed in common, as "God's farm." All give a certain number of days of volunteer service on the farm, in grateful service to God. The harvests are treated as "impersonal wealth." One-third of the money is distributed directly to the needy; two-thirds are put into a community trust for long-term needs to help people stand on their own feet.

The movement spreads from village to village, as missionaries who have seen the positive results of the program voluntarily go to other areas to tell the people there about it. When Swadhyaya volunteers first appeared in fishing villages on India's west coast, they found the people were spending what income they had on gambling and liquor. Now, the same people place a portion of their earnings from fishing and navigation at the feet of God, as it were. Since they no longer waste money on gambling and liquor, they have created such a surplus that they have been able to purchase community fishing boats. These are manned by volunteers on a rotation basis, with everyone eager to take a turn, and the income is distributed impersonally as God's graceful beneficence to those in need.

In addition, *swadhyayees* have also created "tree temples," in which trees are planted in formerly barren lands and cared for in a spirit of devotion to God. *Swadhyayees* have also developed cultural programs, sports clubs, family stores, dairy produce centers, children's centers, centers for domestic skills, and discussion centers for intellectuals and professionals. Through waterharvesting by recharging of over ninety thousand wells and construction of over five hundred percolation tanks, *swadhyayees* by their own skill and labor are generating additional annual farm produce worth some 300 million US dollars for small and medium-sized farmers. They have also introduced soakpit systems for disposal of household drainwater and refuse, thus improving village hygiene and health.

Throughout the growing network of *swadhyayees*, there is no hierarchy and no paid staff. Those whose lives have been improved by inner study and devotional service become enthusiastic volunteers and living demonstrations that people are happiest when dharmic principles are placed ahead of self-interest.

to celebrate major festivals. Exposure of scandals, such as the physical, emotional, and sexual abuse of children in ISKCON schools, has prompted new reform efforts within the movement. At present there are approximately one million ISKCON followers worldwide.

Some contemporary gurus are also enjoying great global popularity. One of the most famous at present is Mata Amritanandamayi, a seemingly tireless, motherly saint from South India who takes people from all walks of life into her arms. She encourages her "children" to find personal solace and compassion for others through worship of the divine in any form. Many of her followers regard "Amma" herself as the personification of the Divine Mother.

Hindu exclusivism vs. universalism

There is a highly ecumenical spirit of tolerance in many of the ways that Sanatana Dharma is being shared with the world. The international Vedanta Society and the Ramakrishna Movement, for instance, emphasize these central principles:

> *Truth or God is One.*
> *Our real nature is divine.*
> *The purpose of our life is to realize the One in our own soul.*
> *There are innumerable spiritual paths, all leading to this realization of divinity.*[44]

At the same time, inter-religious disharmony is being fanned into violent hatreds in India by those using the name of religion for divisive, power-amassing political purposes. Late in 1992, Hindu mobs stormed and destroyed the Babri Masjid, a Muslim mosque built in the sixteenth century by the Muslim emperor Babar in Ayodhya on the site where his army had torn down a temple thought to mark Lord Rama's birthplace. The extensive Hindu–Muslim violence that ensued throughout India revealed deep communal antipathies that have been

Mata Amrityanandamayi comforts a man after his operation for a brain tumor and also embraces his father with her left arm.

strengthened by fundamentalist organizations. One of these is the RSS—Rashtriya Svayamsevak Sangh—which arose early in the twentieth century, espousing Hindu cultural renewal. It gave organized expression to the ideals of V. D. Savarkar, who wrote of an ancient Hindu nation and "Hindu-ness," excluding Muslims and Christians as aliens, in contrast to the historical evidence that Sanatana Dharma is a noncentralized, evolving composite of variegated ways of worship, with as many ways to the Ultimate as there are people.

History professor Romila Thapar of Jawaharlal Nehru University in Delhi describes the newly absolutist version of Sanatana Dharma as "Syndicated Hinduism," with the *Bhagavad-Gita* and *Ramayana* used as its central texts, Ram portrayed as its historical founder, TV serials of the Hindu epics presented as actual history to promote a sense of nationalism, and Hindu *sadhus* becoming the authority figures and wielding political power. She claims:

> *The creation of this Syndicated Hinduism for purposes more political than religious and mainly supportive of the ambitions of an emerging social class, has been a long process during this century and has now come more clearly into focus. . . . Syndicated Hinduism claims to be re-establishing the Hinduism of pre-modern times: in fact it is only establishing itself and in the process distorting the historical and cultural dimensions of the indigenous religions and divesting them of the nuances and variety which were major sources of their enrichment.*[45]

The RSS maintains tens of thousands of branches in Indian villages and cities where Hindu men and boys meet for group games, martial arts training, songs, lectures, and prayers to the Hindu nation, conceived as the Divine Mother. The leader of the RSS has publicly urged throwing all Christian missionaries out of India and has encouraged Indian Christians and Muslims to recognize their "Hindu" roots. There are estimated to be 12,000 RSS schools in India in which children are, according to the National Steering Committee for Textbook Evaluation, being taught from texts "designed to promote bigotry and religious fanaticism in the name of inculcating knowledge of culture in the young generation."[46]

Political affiliates of the RSS with a "Hindu agenda"—particularly the BJP (Bharatiya Janata Party)—have become very powerful in Indian politics. Its religious affiliate—the Vishva Hindu Parishad (VHP)—has sponsored Hindu unity processions throughout India. Without official government approval, the VHP is pushing ahead controversial plans to build a new temple to Lord Ram in Ayodhya as a symbol of restoration of the rule of Ram, a legendary time when Hindu virtues were maintained by a perfect ruler. In 2002, a train carrying volunteers to construct the temple was set on fire by a mob. Hindus responded with terrible violence against Muslims.

Extremist Hindu groups are also trying to woo Christian converts back to Hinduism and are actively opposing Christianity in India. In recent years, Christian nuns in India have been raped, priests killed, Bibles burned, and churches and Christian schools destroyed, apparently by Hindu extremists. Some "untouchable" Hindus have converted to Christianity, Buddhism, or Islam because those religions do not make caste distinctions. Christians have instead offered social services for the poor such as schools and hospitals. An estimated fifty percent of all Christians in India were formerly of scheduled caste origin. Statements by certain Christians from outside India have exacerbated Hindu complaints against conversions of

A family visit a temple together, seeking spiritual blessings for the family members.

Indian poor and tribal people to Christianity. Pope John Paul II, for instance, in his 1999 tour of India, said, "Just as in the first millennium the Cross was planted in the soil of Europe, and in the second one that of the Americas and Africa, we can pray that in the third Christian millennium a great harvest of faith will be reaped in this vast and vital continent."[47] And a Southern Baptist book published in the United States angered Hindus with a reference to "more than 900 million people lost in the hopeless darkness of Hinduism."[48]

Tensions are also running high between Hindus and Muslims along political lines. In Kashmir, particularly, violence around efforts to bring Kashmiri independence from India often pits Hindus and Muslims against each other. Serious concerns on both sides are often lost in political flagwaving, such as a statement by the leader of the Hindu nationalist party Shiv Sena that Muslims should be denied the right to vote.

Despite the sometimes exclusivist nature of the current "Hindu renaissance," there is a growing interest in the spiritual foundations of Sanatana Dharma, both in India and abroad. Many large new temples are being built around the world, encouraging Indian expatriates to return to public forms of worship. The BJP is trying to encourage interest in Sanskrit, the ancient language of the scriptures, no longer spoken.

The Indian Supreme court has formally defined Hindu beliefs in a way that affirms universality rather than exclusiveness. According to the Court's definition, to be a Hindu means:

1 Acceptance and reverence for the Vedas as the foundation of Hindu philosophy;
2 A spirit of tolerance, and willingness to understand and appreciate others' points of view, recognizing that truth has many sides;
3 Acceptance of the belief that vast cosmic periods of creation, maintenance, and dissolution continuously recur;

Dr. Karan Singh

Globally active in an extraordinary number of public posts and projects, Dr. Karan Singh is also one of the world's most respected spokesmen for Hinduism. He was born wealthy, as heir to the Maharaja of Jammu and Kashmir, but has never retired from a life of intense public service. In fact, he turned over his entire princely inheritance to the service of the people of India and converted his palace into a museum and library, which houses his priceless collection of artworks and his personal library of over twenty thousand books.

Dr. Karan Singh's political life began in 1949 when he was only eighteen years old, for his father appointed him Regent of Jammu and Kashmir, as requested by Prime Minister Jawaharlal Nehru. Eventually he was elected to the Governorship of the area, thus becoming both the last representative of the old hereditary lineage and the first of the new democratic era. In 1967, he became the youngest person ever to become a Central Cabinet Minister in India, in the Cabinet of Prime Minister Indira Gandhi. Over the years, he has held three ministerial posts, as well as many other posts, including being the Chancellor of Jammu and Kashmir University, Founder of the International Centre of Science, Culture and Consciousness, President of the People's Commission on Environment and Development, Chairman of the Temple of Understanding, and a member of the international steering committee of the Global Forum of Parliamentarians and Spiritual Leaders on Human Survival.

A brilliant orator, Dr. Karan Singh quotes extensively and effectively from the Vedas in his talks and says he has been deeply influenced by them—in particular, the *Upanishads*. He states:

The Upanishads *are the high-water mark of Hindu philosophy. They are texts of tremendous wisdom and power. They represent some of the deepest truths with regard to the all-pervasiveness of the divine. One is the concept that every individual encapsulates a spark of the divine, the atman. There is also the concept of the human race as an extended family. Then there is the concept that "The truth is one; the wise call it by many names." That is the ultimate unity of all religions. We also have the concept of the welfare of the many, the happiness of the many. Thus, there are universal concepts in the Vedanta which have been of tremendous inspiration to me in all the work that I do in interfaith.*

Busy though he is, Dr. Karan Singh always takes time daily to perform his private *puja* (worship ceremonies). He is a worshipper of Lord Siva. Before Lord Siva, he also worships the goddess, as is common in Hindu tradition. He feels that acknowledging the feminine aspect of the divine is a very important part of Hindu worship, as is the freedom of choice of one's favorite deity.

My personal devotion is to Lord Siva; my philosophical background is the Vedanta. As part of my daily routine, I have my own puja. *I do it in the morning, again at night before going to bed, and in the course of the day. Ours is not a religion where you go once a week to a church and that's it. Hinduism is supposed to be something which permeates your entire consciousness. Therefore these* puja *sessions are supposed to be ways of reminding yourself of the Divinity.*

Despite his personal devotion to Lord Siva, Dr. Karan Singh emphasizes that Hinduism supports acceptance of all manifestations of the divine, and therefore all religions. He asserts,

The exclusivism or monopolistic tendencies in religions who claim that they have the sole agency in the sphere of the divine is not acceptable in this day and age. We have got to accept the fact that there are multiple paths to the divine. We have to not only accept them—we have to respect whoever is traveling on his or her path. That has come to me particularly from the Vedanta tradition.

Although Dr. Karan Singh has often been deeply involved in government, he is free from the taint of corruption and scandal that mars so many political careers. He attributes his clear reputation partly to the fact that the was born into "favourable financial circumstances," and also to his religious upbringing:

Not being corrupt is part of the basic religious teachings around the world. We are brought up on the stories of Raja Harish Chandra, who gave up everything for the sake of truth, and Sri Rama, who gave up everything for the sake of his father's word, and so on. Those sort of mythological stories based on truth and the quest for truth are very strong in wisdom. And if you are pursuing the path of truth, then I presume that automatically rules out your being corrupt.[49]

4 Acceptance of belief in reincarnation;

5 Recognition that paths to truth and salvation are many;

6 Recognition that there may be numerous gods and goddesses to worship, without necessarily believing in worship through idols;

7 Unlike other religions, absence of belief in a specific set of philosophic concepts.[50]

Finally, Hindu scholar and statesman Karan Singh observes that the vast understandings of the ancient Vedas will always make them relevant to the human condition:

> *We, who are children of the past and the future, of earth and heaven, of light and darkness, of the human and the divine, at once evanescent and eternal, of the world and beyond it, within time and in eternity, yet have the capacity to comprehend our condition, to rise above our terrestrial limitations, and, finally, to transcend the throbbing abyss of space and time itself. This, in essence, is the message of Hinduism.*[51]

Suggested reading

The Bhagavad-Gita, available in numerous translations. Central teachings about how to realize the immortal soul.

Chapple, Christopher Key and Tucker, Mary Evelyn, eds., *Hinduism and Ecology*, Cambridge, Massachusetts: Harvard University Press, 2000. Perceptive contemporary essays about the relationship between various Hindu paths and environmental protection.

Eck, Diana, *Darsan: Seeing the Divine Image in India*, second edition, Chambersburg, Pennsylvania: Anima Books, 1985. A lively explanation of deity images and how the people of India respond to them.

Jayakar, Pupul, *The Earth Mother*, New Delhi: Penguin Books, 1989. Explorations of ways of worshipping the goddess in rural India.

Lopez, Donald S., Jr., ed., *Religions of India in Practice*, Princeton, New Jersey: Princeton University Press, 1995. An interesting anthology of popular texts with contemporary rather than stereotypical understandings, primarily from Hinduism but also including Buddhist, Jain, and Sikh material.

Sahi, Jyoti, *The Child and the Serpent*, London: Routledge & Kegan Paul, 1980. An artist's attempt to rediscover the inner meanings of traditional visual symbols by living in the villages of southern India.

Sastri, *The Cultural Heritage of India*, Calcutta, 1962. A classic survey of the social aspects of Sanatana Dharma.

Singh, Karan, *Essays on Hinduism*, New Delhi: Ratna Sagar, 1987 and 1990. An excellent and concise introduction of the many facets of Hinduism, interpreted in modern terms.

Sondhi, Madhuri Santanam, *Modernity, Morality and the Mahatma*, New Delhi: Haranand Publications, 1997. A brilliant analysis of Indian responses to the challenges of modernity, including the contribution of many religious figures.

Sontheimer, Gunther-Dietz, and Hermann Kulke, *Hinduism Reconsidered*, New Delhi: Manohar, 1997. Provocative articles by Indian and Western scholars on controversial new ways of interpreting many facets of Sanatana Dharma.

CHAPTER 3
JAINISM

"Be careful all the while!"

Although the majority of Indians who are religious continue to follow the Hindu paths, Mother India has given birth to several other religions which are not based on the Vedas. One of them is Jainism. Until recently, it has been little known outside India. Even within India it is practiced by only a small minority. Yet its ascetic teachings offer valuable clues to our global survival.

Interest in Jainism is reviving, for it is becoming recognized as a complete and fruitful path with the potential for uplifting human awareness and inculcating high standards of personal ethics. For example, it has never condoned war or the killing of animals for any reason. Jain teachings recognize that we humans are imperfect, but hold out the promise that through strict control of our senses and thoughts we can attain perfection, freedom, and happiness.

Mahavira is said to have become so detached from worldly concerns that he shed his clothes as well as his royal status.

The Tirthankaras and ascetic orders

Jainism's major teacher for this age is Mahavira ("The Great Hero"). He was a contemporary of the Buddha and died approximately 527 BCE. Like the Buddha, he was the prince of a **kshatriya** clan and renounced his position and his wealth at the age of thirty to wander as a spiritual seeker. The austerities he tolerated while meditating without clothes in the intense summer heat and winter cold are legendary. Villagers are said to have treated him miserably to make him leave:

Once when he [sat in meditation], his body unmoving, they cut his flesh, tore his hair, and covered him with dirt. They picked him up and then dropped him, disturbing his meditational postures. Abandoning concern for his body, free from desire, the Venerable One humbled himself and bore the pain.[1]

Finally after twelve years of meditation, silence, and extreme fasting, Mahavira achieved liberation and perfection. For thirty years until his death at Pava, he spread his teachings. His community is said to have consisted of 14,100 monks, 36,000 nuns, and 310,000 female and 150,000 male lay followers. They came from all castes, as Jainism does not officially acknowledge the caste system.

The Jain teachings are not thought to have originated with Mahavira, however. He is considered the last of twenty-four

Tirthankaras ("Fordmakers") of the current cosmic cycle. In Jain cosmology, the universe is without beginning or end. Eternally, it passes through long cycles of progress and decline. At the beginning of each downward cycle, humans are happy, long-lived, and virtuous; they have no need for religion. As these qualities decline, humans look at first to elders for guidance, but as things get worse Tirthankaras must create religion in order to steer people away from the growing evil in the world.

The first Tirthankara is said to have been the ancient Lord Rishabha. He introduced civilizing social institutions, such as marriage, family, law, justice, and government, taught the arts of agriculture, crafts, reading, writing, and mathematics, and built villages, towns, and cities. Twenty-three more Tirthankaras followed over a vast expanse of time. The twenty-second is generally acknowledged by scholars as an historic figure, Lord Krishna's cousin, renowned for his compassion toward animals. During his wedding procession, it is said that he heard the groans of animals who were to be slaughtered and immediately decided not to marry since so many innocent animals would be killed to feed the wedding guests. He became an ascetic who preached religion for many years. His betrothed princess became an ascetic nun. The twenty-third Tirthankara, a prince who became an extreme ascetic and a great preacher of Jain principles, lived from 877 to 777 BCE.

The extreme antiquity of Jainism as a non-Vedic, indigenous Indian religion is well documented. Ancient Hindu and Buddhist scriptures refer to Jainism as an existing tradition that began long before Mahavira.

After Mahavira's death, his teachings were not written down at first because the monks lived as ascetics without possessions; they were initially carried orally. In the third century BCE, the great Jain saint Bhadrabahu predicted that there would be a prolonged famine where Mahavira had lived, in what is now Bihar in northeast India. He led some 12,000 monks to southern India to avoid the famine, which lasted for twelve years. When they returned to their original home, they discovered that two major changes had been introduced by the monks who had remained in the area. One was relaxation of the requirement of nudity for monks; the other was the convening of a council to edit the existing Jain texts into an established canon of forty-five books.

Eventually the two groups split over their differences into the **Digambaras**, who had left and did not accept the changes as authentic to Mahavira, and the **Svetambaras**, who had stayed near his original location. Two major differences remain between the ascetic orders today. Digambara ("sky clad") monks wear nothing at all, symbolizing their innocence of shame and their non-attachment to material goods. They do not consider themselves "nude"; rather, they have taken the environment as their clothing, thus damaging it as little as possible by stoically enduring all kinds of weather. They have only two possessions: a broom of feathers dropped by peacocks and a gourd for drinking water. The Svetambara ("white-clad") monks feel that wearing a piece of white cloth does not prevent them from attaining liberation.

The two orders also differ over the subject of women's abilities. Digambaras believe that women cannot become so pure that they could rise to the highest heaven or so impure that they would be reborn in the lowest hell; they cannot renounce clothes and be naked; they cannot be such skillful debaters as men; they are of inferior status in society and in the monastic order. They can be liberated only if they are reborn in a man's body.

Rishabhadeva, the first Tirthankara of the present cosmic cycle. The Tirthankaras are always depicted either in cross-legged lotus position or standing up, a form of deep meditation for enlightened beings who are said never to sleep. (Northeast India, 12th–13th century.)

Jain nuns wearing mouth-cloths to prevent injury to inhaled minute beings; they are carrying all their worldly possessions.

Svetambaras feel that women are capable of the same spiritual achievements as men, and that the nineteenth Tirthankara was a woman. In truth, even Svetambara nuns are of lower status than monks, but they still comprise the great majority of Jain nuns. Of today's approximately 6,000 Jain nuns, fewer than one hundred are Digambaras, and most of these are widows, compared to the many young Svetambara nuns, many of whom come from wealthy families. The existence of this thriving order of female ascetics—which includes many skillful teachers and counselors and outnumbers the approximately 2,500 Jain monks—is unique in India, where no other native religion provides a monastic option for women; in Brahmanic Hindu tradition, women were never allowed to be mendicants and marriage was obligatory.

Freeing the soul: the ethical pillars

In the midst of a world of decline, as they see it, Jains are given great room for hope. The *jiva*—the individual's higher consciousness, or soul—can save itself by discovering its own perfect, unchanging nature and thus transcend the miseries of earthly life. This process may require many incarnations. Jains, like Hindus and Buddhists, believe that we are reborn again and again until we finally free ourselves from **samsara**, the wheel of birth and death and of life's ups and downs.

The gradual process by which the soul learns to extricate itself from the lower self and its attachments to the material world involves purifying one's ethical life until nothing remains but the purity of the *jiva*. In its true state, it is fully omniscient, shining, potent, peaceful, self-contained, and blissful. One who has thus brought forth the highest in his or her being is called a **Jina** (a "winner" over the passions), from which the term Jain is derived. The Tirthankaras were Jinas who helped others find their way, regenerating the community by teaching inspiring spiritual principles.

Karma

Like Hindus and Buddhists, Jains believe that our actions influence the future course of our current life, and of our lives to come. But in Jain belief, **karma** is actually subtle matter—minute particles that we accumulate as we act and think. Mahavira likened *karma* to coats of clay that weigh down the soul.

Jains are very careful to avoid accumulating *karma*. Three of the chief principles to which they adapt their lives are **ahimsa** (non-violence), **aparigraha** (non-attachment), and **anekantwad** (non-absolutism).

Ahimsa

The principle of non-violence—*ahimsa*—is very strong in Jain teachings, and through Jainism it also influenced Mahatma Gandhi. Jains believe that every centimeter of the universe is filled with living beings, some of them minute. A single drop of water contains 3,000 living beings. All of them want to live. Humans have no special right to supremacy; all things deserve to live and evolve as they can. To kill any living being has negative karmic effects.

It is difficult not to do violence to other creatures. As we walk, we squash insects unknowingly. Even in breathing, Jains feel, we inhale tiny organisms and kill them. Jains avoid eating after sunset, so as not to inadvertently eat unseen insects that might have landed on the food, and some Jain ascetics wear a cloth over their mouth to avoid inhaling any living organisms.

The higher the life-form, the heavier the karmic burden of its destruction. Levels of life are determined by their degree of sensitivity. The highest group of beings are those with many senses, such as humans, gods, and higher animals. Lower forms have fewer senses. The "one-sensed" beings have only the sense of touch. They include plants and the earth-bodies in soil, minerals, and stones, the water-bodies in rivers and lakes, fire-bodies in fires and lightning, and wind-bodies in winds and gases. The Jain *sutras* describe the suffering of even these one-sensed beings: their agony at being wounded is like that of a blind and mute person who cannot see who is hurting him or express the pain.

The new Jain symbol: ahimsa is inscribed on the open palm. The swastika is an ancient Indian symbol representing the wheel of samsara. The three dots symbolize insight, knowledge, and conduct. The crescent and dot above symbolize the liberated soul in the highest region of the universe.

> *All breathing, existing, living, sentient creatures should not be slain, nor treated with violence, nor abused, nor tormented, nor driven away. This is the pure, unchangeable, eternal law ... Correctly understanding the law, one should arrive at indifference for the impressions of the senses, and not act on the motives of the world.*
> *Akaranga Sutra, IV: Lesson 1*[2]

Jains are therefore strict vegetarians, and they treat everything with great care. In Delhi, Jain benefactors have established a unique hospital for sick and wounded birds. Great attention is paid to their every need, and their living quarters are air-conditioned in the summer. Jains also go to markets where live animals are usually bound with wire, packed into hot trucks, and driven long distances without water, to be killed for meat. Jains buy the animals at any price and raise them in comfort. Even to kick a stone while walking is to injure a living being.

Ahimsa also extends to care in speaking and thinking, for abusive words and negative thoughts can injure another. The revered ascetic Acharya Tulsi (1914–1997) explained,

> *A non-violent man is he who does not in the least discriminate between rich and poor or between friend and foe. . . . Non-violence is the best guarantee of humanity's survival and progress. A truly non-violent man is ever awake and is incapable of harbouring any ill will.*[3]

One's profession must also not injure beings, so most Jains work at jobs considered harmless, such as banking, clerical occupations, education, law, and publishing. Agriculture is considered harmful, for in digging into the soil one harms minute organisms in the earth; in harnessing bullocks to plows or water buffalos to carts, one would harm not only the bullock or buffalo but also the tiny life-forms on its body. Monks and nuns must move slowly with eyes downward, to avoid stepping on any being. In general, they will do the least harm if they devote their time to sitting or standing in meditation rather than moving around.

According to Jain teachings, when we injure others, we also do violence to our own true spiritual nature. Layman R. P. Jain tells a story of how he felt when he learned how silk is made:

> *I used to wear silk. On my eighteenth birthday I was telling one of my distant relatives not to eat chocolate because it had egg powder in it. He said, "Turn around—you're wearing silk. What are you preaching? Do you know that to make one yard of silk, nearly fifty thousand to one hundred thousand silkworms are boiled alive? To wear silk is a sin!" When I learned that is the way natural silk is made, I said, "R. P. Jain, what are you doing to your own soul? Shame on you!" From that day, I took a vow never in my life to wear natural silk.*[4]

In society and on a global level, Acharya Mahapragya asserts that all the peace conferences in the world will not lead to peace until people are trained in non-violence, on as massive a scale as training in violence is now going on. He says,

> *The human mind has seeds of both violence and non-violence. Training in violence sprouts its seeds. It means that the seeds of non-violence can sprout too only if there is training in non-violence. . . . Non-violence cannot gain a permanent and broad base without a transformation of consciousness.*[5]

Aparigraha

Another central Jain ideal is non-attachment to things and people. One should cut one's living requirements to a bare minimum. Possessions possess us; their acquisition and loss drive our emotions. Some Jain monks wear no clothes; the Tirthankaras are always depicted as naked, and therefore free. Even attachments to our friends and relatives bind us to *samsara*. We are to live helpfully and consciously within the world but not be drawn into its snares.

Aparigraha, or non-acquisitiveness, is considered the way to inner peace. If we can let go of things and situations, moment by moment, we can be free. The story is told of a **muni** (Jain monk) who saw twelve stray dogs chasing another dog who was racing away with a bone he had found. When they caught the dog, they attacked him to wrest it from his jaws. Wounded and bleeding, he let go of it. The others immediately abandoned him to chase the one that picked it up. The monk saw the scene as a moral lesson: So long as we cling to things, we have to bleed for them. When we let them go, we will be left in peace.

A Jain nun of the Rajasthan desert, Samani Sanmati Pragya, belongs to an order in which the nuns' clothing and bedding is limited to four white saris, one white shawl, and one woolen cloth. She explains:

In the winter we do not have a quilt for warmth at night, for it would be too bulky to carry. In the summer we use no fan. It is so hot that we cannot sleep at night. We bear any kind of circumstances. In fact, we remain very happy. Our happiness comes from inside.[6]

Aparigraha is of value to the world community as well. Contemporary Jains point out that their principle of limiting consumption offers a way out of the global poverty, hunger, and environmental degradation that result from unequal grasping of resources by the wealthy. As His Holiness Acharya Sushil Kumar explained:

If we live simply, limit our needs and do not try to fulfill every desire, collecting more and more, automatically we will protect the environment. Because we will not need so many things, we will not need big industries to produce unnecessary things. . . . If we live simply, automatically the environment will stay clean.[7]

RELIGION IN PRACTICE

Jain Purification

A central Jain practice undertaken both by laypeople and by ascetics has for thousands of years been used for freeing the soul from internal impurities. Anger, pride, deceit, and greed are lasting stains that must be completely eradicated if the soul is to realize its true nature: pure consciousness, infinite knowledge, and bliss. Even a momentary realization of this state brings a feeling of great inner purity and calmness and a longing to return to it permanently. The ritual for achieving this inner purification is known as *samayika*.

Jain laypeople usually undertake this practice in the evening, after work and meal. They sit in a quiet and solitary place, remove excess clothing, sit cross-legged on a mat, and chant formulas to cleanse and pacify their mind. These begin with a pledge to renounce all harmful activities, followed by requesting forgiveness:

I ask forgiveness of all beings
may all beings forgive me.
I have friendship with all beings,
and I have hostility with none.[8]

They reach out mentally to all life forms, saying

Friendship toward all beings,
Delight in the qualities of virtuous ones,
Utmost compassion for affected beings,
Equanimity towards those who are not well-
*   disposed towards me,*
May my soul have such dispositions forever![9]

Then follow verses that commit the person to renouncing food, bodily desires, and passions for the period of the meditation, persisting in equanimity, come what may. The meditation ends with the universal Jain prayer:

Cessation of sorrow
Cessation of karmas
Death while in meditation,
Attainment of enlightenment.
O holy Jina! friend of the entire universe, let these
*   be mine, for*
I have taken refuge at your feet.

Anekantwad

The third central principle is *anekantwad*, roughly translated as "relativity." Jains try to avoid anger and judgmentalism, remaining open-minded by remembering that any issue can be seen from many angles, all partially true. They tell the story of the blind people who are asked to describe an elephant. The one who feels the trunk says an elephant is like a tree branch. The one grasping a leg argues that an elephant is like a pillar. The one feeling the ear asserts that an elephant is like a fan. The one grasping the tail insists that an elephant is like a rope. And the one who encounters the side of the elephant argues that the others are wrong; an elephant is like a wall. Each has a partial grasp of the truth.

In the Jain way of thinking, the fullness of truth has many facets. There is no point in finding fault with others; our attention must be directed to cleansing and opening our own vision. Shree Chitrabhanu describes the results of eliminating false impressions and allowing the pure consciousness to flow in:

> *Once you have closed the open gates, dried up the polluted water, and cleaned out all the debris, then you can open them again to receive the fresh, clean rainfall. What is that rainfall? It is the flow of* maitri—*pure love, compassion, and communication. You feel free. . . . See how easily you meet people when there is no feeling of greater or lesser, no scar or bitterness, no faultfinding or criticism.*[10]

Spiritual practices

Jainism is an ascetic path and thus is practiced in its fullest by monks and nuns. In addition to practicing meditation, monks and nuns adopt a life of celibacy, physical penance and fasting, and material simplicity. They may sleep on the bare ground or wooden slabs, and are expected to endure any kind of weather with indifference. At initiation, they may pull their hair out by the roots rather than be shaved. They must learn to accept social disapproval, to depend on others for their food, and to feel no pride at being more spiritually advanced than others.

Jain monks and nuns carry *ahimsa* to great extremes in their wariness of injuring one-sensed beings. Among the many activities they must avoid are digging in the ground (because of the earth-bodies there), bathing, swimming, or walking in the rain (because of the water-bodies they might injure), extinguishing or lighting fires (because even to light a fire means that a fire-body will eventually be destroyed), fanning themselves (to avoid sudden changes in air temperature that would injure air-bodies), and walking on vegetation or touching living plants.

In New Delhi, a wealthy sixty-year-old Jain businessman, head of a large construction company, astounded the populace in 1992 by advancing from lay austerities, such as eating and drinking only once in twenty-four hours, to the utterly renunciate life of a naked Digambara monk. Before a huge celebration in which he shed his clothes and his possessions, Lala Sulekh Chand announced:

> *I have no interest in life. I have found that life just means one remains agitated for twenty-four hours and there is no peace of mind. I have fulfilled all my responsibilities and obligations in life and handed over my business to my son and family. I am not taking this path due to some problem.*[11]

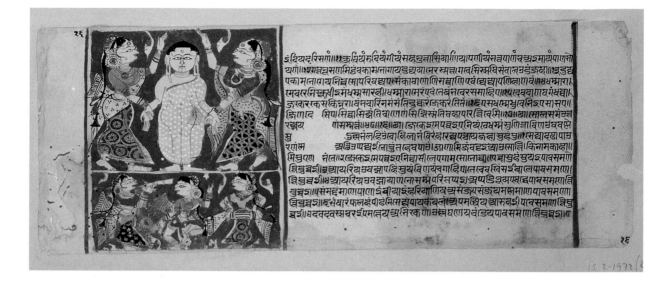

He then sat unflinching as his mentor, Muni Amit Sagar, pulled all the hairs from his head, a process that took an hour and a half. Afterward, Muni Amit Sagar admonished the crowd that the way to spiritual liberation lies in non-attachment and patient, indifferent forbearance of all difficulties. "We cannot change anything, but we can change our attitude of expectation," he said. "The peace one gets from renunciation cannot be gained by reading a lot of religious books."[12]

Jain monks and nuns are celibate ascetics. This 15th-century illustrated text of Mahavira's last teachings shows a monk resisting the attractions of women.

> *Difficult to conquer is oneself; but when that is conquered, everything is conquered.*
> *Uttaradhyayana Sutra 9.34–36*

Most householders cannot carry renunciation as far as monks and nuns, but they can nonetheless purify and perfect themselves. This effort includes great attention to purity in food, body, and environment. Jain homes and temples are typically scrupulously clean, their diets carefully vegetarian, and the medicines they use are prepared without cruel testing on animals. The mind and passions are also to be held under strict control. Jains believe that the universe is without beginning and that it has no creator or destroyer. Our lives are therefore the results of our own deeds; only by our own efforts can we be saved. Padma Agrawal explains:

In Jainism, unlike Christianity and many Hindu cults, there is no such thing as a heavenly father watching over us. To the contrary, love for a personal God would be an attachment that could only bind Jainas more securely to the cycle of rebirth. It is a thing that must be rooted out.[13]

The world operates by the power of nature, according to natural principles. Jains do believe in gods and demons, but the former are subject to the same ignoble passions as humans. In fact, one can only achieve liberation if one is in the human state, because only humans can clear away karmic accumulations on the soul. Until it frees itself from *karmas*, the mundane soul wanders about through the universe in an endless cycle of deaths and rebirths, instantly trans-migrating into another kind of being upon death of its previous body. Acharya Shri Kund Kund asserts, "Nowhere throughout the space in the entire universe is there any place in its course where the mundane soul has not taken birth in many forms, big and small."[14]

Birth as a human is prized by Jains as the highest stage of life short of liberation. One should therefore lose no time in this precious, brief period in human incarnation, for within it lies the potential for perfection. Householders can journey toward the final state by passing through fourteen stages of ascent of the soul, or *gunasthana*. The first four are efforts to remove false mental impressions. Moral effort to purify oneself begins with the fifth stage. Jains attempt to plumb the depths of their negative tendencies in order to free themselves from emotional problems. Then, as spiritual inertia is overcome, self-control and relinquishing of the passions follow. Throughout this process, the veils of karma are lifting and the soul experiences more and more of its natural luminosity. In the highest state of perfection, known as **kevala**, all gross activities have come to an end, and the liberated being has "boundless vision, infinite righteousness, strength, perfect bliss, existence without form, and a body that is neither light nor heavy."[15]

Although severe vows of renunciation can be taken by householders, lay spiritual life is more likely to consist of six duties: the practice of equanimity through meditation, praise of the Tirthankaras, veneration of teachers (who live as mendicants), making amends for moral transgressions, indifference to the body (often by holding a particular position for a length of time), and renunciation of certain foods or activities for specific periods. Laypeople as well as ascetics often undertake total fasts lasting for days—or for the ascetics, weeks or even months. This is done to help weaken the bonds of karma. There are many scriptural exortations to control the desire for food, because to eat anything has karmic repercussions since no food can be consumed without harming some life-form. If one can uproot the craving for food, the most primary of instincts, one can eliminate all passions.

Practicing strict ethics and self-control, Jains are often quite successful and trusted in their professions. Many Jains have thus become wealthy. Because of the religion's emphasis on non-possessiveness, wealthy Jains are often philanthropists. Their charitable works include the construction of very ornate Jain temples, which are kept immaculately clean.

Within the temples, the Tirthankaras are honored through images. They all look alike, for the perfect soul is non-particularized; symbols such as the bull, always shown with the first Tirthankara, are used to help worshippers identify each of the twenty-four.

The worshipper's feeling is one of reverence rather than supplication; the Tirthankaras are elevated beyond the human plane and are not available as helpers. They are instead models for one's own life, and since there can be no divine intervention, there is not a great emphasis on priesthood. Laypeople can carry out worship services themselves, either alone or in groups. People pay their respects before images of the Tirthankaras with offerings and waved lamps, but do not expect any reciprocation from them. Liberation from *samsara* is a result of personal effort, often portrayed by a symbolic diagram laid out with rice grains. Acharya Tulsi expressed the Jain point of view: "The primary aim of *dharma* is to purify character. Its ritualistic practices are secondary."[16]

TEACHING STORY

The Story of Bahubali

Rishabha, the first Tirthankara of the current cosmic cycle, had one hundred sons from one wife and one son, Bahubali, from the other. He gave his eldest son, Bharat, the lion's share. Bharat was eager to be the supreme king, and he wanted his other brothers, who had been given smaller portions of land, to come under his subjugation. All the people surrendered to his sovereignty, except for Bahubali, who refused to surrender his kingdom. He said to Bharat, "You are independent, I am independent. Why should I come under your rule?"

The armies of the two sides were drawn up on the battleground. The wise men from the two sides came forth and said, "In the clash of two brothers, millions of people will be killed. Millions of innocent people will be killed to satisfy the egos of two brothers. Why should this happen?" So it was decided that the two would fight it out between themselves. They would fight in three ways to see who was defeated.

First, they looked into each other's eyes, concentrating until one looked away. Bahubali knocked out Bharat in this combat. Then they fought underwater, and again Bahubali was victorious. Thirdly, Bahubali picked up Bharat physically and held him overhead, ready to dash him to the ground. That is how he got the name Bahubali—"He whose arms are very powerful."

As Bahubali was holding Bharat aloft, a thought crossed his mind: "Whom am I throwing? My own brother. For what? For this parcel of land? For this kingdom? Only for that, I would kill my brother?" He put Bharat down.

At that point, Bahubali felt like renouncing the world. He ceased to make war, and he went standing into meditation. For twelve years he meditated, standing. Vines grew on his legs. Snakes made their homes around his body. Many people tried to convince him to come out of his meditation, but he was unmoved. Nevertheless, he could not attain ultimate liberation.

Rishabha, his father, was asked why Bahubali was not attaining liberation. From his omniscient knowledge, Rishabha said that just before Bahubali started his meditation, he had a thought left in his mind: "I am standing on my brother's soil." So Bharat went and prayed to him: "This soil is universal, not yours or mine." The moment that thought entered Bahubali's mind, he was liberated.

> *Just as a fire quickly reduces decayed wood to ashes, so does an aspirant who is totally absorbed in the inner self and completely unattached to all external objects shake to the roots, attenuate, and wither away his karma-body.*
>
> *Samantabhadra, Aptamimamsa 24–7*

World Jainism

Through the centuries, Jainism managed to survive as a small heterodox (non-orthodox) minority within largely Hindu India. Today there are approximately 6 million Jains. Since the twentieth century, Jainism has been carried to the outside world by several teachers. One of them, Shree Chitrabhanu, was for twenty-

Living Jainism

In addition to monastic orders of monks and nuns, there is now another order of "semi-monks" and "semi-nuns" developed by Acharya Tulsi in 1980. The main difference between them and traditional monks and nuns is that they are allowed to travel and thus teach their religion in other countries. The women who have taken vows in this order are called *samanis*. Samani Charitra Prajna took initiation into this order ten years ago, and has traveled to the United States with groups from her organization to teach meditation and Jain principles there. She explains her lifestyle:

"Basically, our lifestyle is very similar to the monks and nuns. The rules are the same. We have given up our family. We don't keep money or property or anything in our name. We have dedicated our whole life for this institution, for our Acharya, for our organization. The main purpose for us is to learn ourselves and teach others, too, what we have got.

"Basically, the main restrictions are that we have to follow the principles of non-violence, truth, celibacy, non-acquisition, and non-stealing. Just like monks and nuns, every morning and evening we repeat the vows we have taken and ask forgiveness for whatever mistakes we have made. It means, 'I am a monk now, so I have to follow these principles and lead a very peaceful life.'

"We sleep on the floor on a piece of cardboard, over which we spread our blanket. No pillow, nothing. We do not switch on lights or fans with our own hands. If some other people come and sit with us, for their convenience they may turn on the light. Instead of fans, we just open the windows and take the fresh air.

"We have three pairs of clothes. We use only two pairs a day—one for the morning, one for the night. And then two or three handkerchiefs and one or two small napkins. We keep our wooden bowls in which we eat our food. These are made by our own hands, and we polish them every year.

"Normally we get up at 3 or 4 a.m. Then we repeat the scriptures which we have learned, without looking at the books. And then before sunrise we do meditation, prayer, and our repetition of vows and asking forgiveness for any mistakes. And after sunrise, we do our yoga exercise. Then we go to collect our alms, because we don't cook food ourselves. We go to different houses and take a little portion from each house. I go to ten to fifteen houses every day, in the morning, in the lunchtime, and in the dinnertime. It is not like we are begging from them. They give us full respect, appreciating that someone has come into their home so that they can give them food."

After receiving the breakfast offerings in their wooden bowls, the *samanis* listen to a lecture for an hour and a half, followed by a short interval, and then again going from house to house to receive their lunch offerings. After a rest of half an hour, they learn scriptures, sometimes accompanied by lay followers. After the evening round of food collection, there is another lecture, followed at 10 o'clock by sleeping on the floor. Having followed this life for ten years, Samani Charitra Prajna says:

"I am really enjoying it. I feel myself more happy and tension-free, because I need not worry for myself. Our Acharya looks after each and everybody with full care and attention—what she has to do next, what is the planning for her. Before taking this initiation, I took training for six years in an institution for people who come from all over India, because ultimately they are dedicating their whole life. For monks and nuns, and *samans* and *samanis*, it is not that 'I am taking vows for one month or six months or two years and then I can go back.' It is for the whole life long. After doing graduation, post-graduation, master's degree, and PhD research work, we can be initiated only when Acharya Ji has given permission that we are capable of doing this practice. Ultimately it depends on our willpower. If I am not fully completed and dedicated, maybe my mind can wander and I can go back. But when my mind is steady and I have dedicated myself, then Acharya gives us permission and we start this life.

"Families usually object because they do not want their daughters and sons to lead such a hard life. They think we should live a normal life like they are living. In the beginning, they don't give us permission. But afterwards when they see that he or she is very committed and that they are going in their right path, ultimately they give their permission.

"My family belongs to the Jain religion. My father and mother are very religious, and I had a good environment from them. And especially I can say that some of my previous imprints—which we call *sanskars*, a kind of memories from previous births—taught me a lesson. Then such feelings can arise in your mind: 'I have to do this lifestyle.'

"Religion says that our life should be self-disciplined, having some restraint. If you have no discipline, no vows in your life, ultimately this materialistic stuff can give you more pressure instead of peace of mind. But if you are limiting your desire, if you are satisfied with what you have, it means that you get the ultimate peace of mind, tranquillity of mind, and you can think, 'I have gained something in my life.'

"We have seen persons who are very rich, but even at the time of dying, they feel that their mind is empty. They have not gained in their life. But for those who have practiced religion, in a true sense, in life as well as at the time of death they are more satisfied and happy, having bliss and actually enjoying their life. So we think that religion is the basic part of our life. We have to practice according to our faculty, according to our extent of time, according to our interest. At least we have to do it every day."

In Jain worship, images of the Tirthankara are ideally to be venerated without expectation of a personal response to their prayers or help for the worshippers.

nine years a monk who walked barefoot over 30,000 miles (48,279 km) of Indian soil to teach Jain principles to the populace. When he was invited to address the Temple of Spiritual Understanding Summit Conferences in Switzerland and the United States in 1970 and 1971, his controversial decision to attend in person marked the first time in Jain history that a Jain monk had traveled outside India. He then established Jain meditation centers in the United States, Brazil, Canada, Kenya, the United Kingdom, and India.

Acharya Shri Sushil Kumar likewise established Jain centers in the United Kingdom and the United States as well as in India. He pointed out that the Jain scriptures consider as "Jains" all those who practice Jain principles:

> *If somebody is a real symbol of non-violence, love, compassion, peace, harmony, oneness, then he is the perfect Jain. We can't convert any Jains, but you can convert your habits, your mind.*[17]

The revered Acharya Tulsi initiated new orders of *samans (*semi-monks) and *samanis* (semi-nuns) who are allowed to travel abroad in order to spread Jain teachings. He also began the Anuvrat Movement in 1949, to enlist people of all faiths and nationalities to commit themselves to *anuvrats* (small vows). He developed these to help people rejuvenate strong moral standards of self-restraint in the midst of ethically unhealthy society. The small vows include these: to avoid willful killing of any innocent creature, to refrain from attacks and aggression and to work instead for world peace and disarmament, to avoid discrimination on the basis of caste or race, to eschew religious intolerance, to avoid false business and political practices, to limit acquisition of possessions, to eschew addictive substances, and to avoid wasting water or cutting down trees.

In 1995, Acharya Tulsi renounced even his own position as the leader of his order by installing Acharya Mahapragya as his successor. The latter's self-description is an indication of the internal qualities which keep Jain faith alive:

I am an ascetic. My asceticism is not bound by inert rituals. . . . I follow a tradition, but do not treat its dynamic elements as static. I derive benefit from the scriptures, but do not believe in carrying them as a burden. . . . In my consciousness there is no bondage of "yours and mine." It is free from it. My spiritual practice is not to "worship" truth, but to subject it to minute surgery. The only mission of my life is boundless curiosity to discover truth. . . . It is not an external accoutrement. Like a seed it is sprouting out of my being.[18]

Suggested reading

Chitrabhanu, Gurudev Shree, *Twelve Facets of Reality: The Jain Path to Freedom*, New York: Jain Meditation International Center/Dodd, Mead & Company, 1980. Classic Jain reflections on the realities of life, with many teaching tales.

Fischer, Eberhard, and Jain, Jyotindra, *Jaina Iconography*, parts 1 and 2, Leiden: E. J. Brill, 1978. An inside look at Jainism through the visual representations of its beliefs.

Jaini, Padmanabh S., *The Jaina Path of Purification*, Berkeley: University of California Press, 1979. An appreciative, scholarly analysis of the Jaina path.

Jaini, Padmanabh S., ed., *Collected Papers on Jaina Studies*, Delhi: Motilal Banarsidass Publishers, 2000.
In-depth examination of many contemporary issues in Jain scholarship and practice.

Kumar, Acharya Sushil, *Song of the Soul*, Blairstown, New Jersey: Siddhachalam Publishers, 1987. Insights into Jain mantra practice, as taught by a twentieth-century monk.

Muller, F. Max, ed., *Jaina Sutras*, vols. XLV and XXII of *Sacred Books of the East*, Oxford: Clarendon Press, 1884 and 1895. Engaging translations of various sorts of *sutras*, including both philosophical treatises and rules of conduct for Jain ascetics.

Nyayavijayaji, Munisri, trans. by Nagin J. Shah, *Jaina Philosophy and Religion*, Delhi: Motilal Banarsidass Publishers, 1998. A renowned twentieth-century monk's comprehensive tome describing the major aspects of Jain philosophy, liberation practices, logics, metaphysics, and ethics in contemporary terms.

Sangave, Vilas A., *Aspects of Jaina Religion*, New Delhi: Bharatiya Jnanpith, 1990. Concise, accurate discussions of Jain antiquity, principles, practice, relationships to other religions, and cultural contributions.

Tobias, Michael, *Life Force: The World of Jainism*, Berkeley, California: Asian Humanities Press, 1991. A highly appreciative and readable account of Jain practices and philosophy by a Western observer.

CHAPTER 4
BUDDHISM

*"He will deliver by the boat of knowledge
the distressed world"*

At the same time that Mahavira was teaching the way of Jainism, the man who came to be known as the Buddha preached another alternative to the ritual-bound Brahmanism of India in the sixth century BCE. The Buddha taught about earthly suffering and its cure. Many religions offer comforting supernatural solutions to the difficulties of earthly life. In its early forms, Buddhism was quite different: it held that our salvation from suffering lies only in our own efforts. The Buddha taught that in understanding how we create suffering for ourselves we can become free.

We might imagine that the discomfort of having to face ourselves and take responsibility for our own liberation would be an unappealing path that would attract few followers. But the way of the Buddha spread from his native India throughout East Asia, becoming the dominant religion in many Eastern countries. In the process, it took on devotional and mystical qualities from earlier local traditions, with various deity-like buddhas to whom one could appeal for help. And now, more than two and a half thousand years after the Buddha's death, the religion that he founded is also attracting considerable interest in the West.

The life of the Buddha

What we know about the Buddha himself is sketchy. His prolific teachings were probably not collected in written form until at least four hundred years after his death. In the meantime they were apparently held, and added to, as an oral tradition, chanted from memory by monks, groups of whom were responsible for remembering specific parts of the teachings. Only a few factual details of the Buddha's own life have been retained. While stories from the life of the Buddha are abundant in authorized Buddhist texts, these stories were never organized into a single canonical biography. Most of what is usually taught about the life of the Buddha is rich in symbolic meanings but not verifiable as historical fact.

The one who became the Buddha (a title that means "Enlightened One") was born about 563 BCE. His father was apparently a wealthy landowner serving as one of the chiefs of a ***kshatriya*** clan, the Shakyas. They lived in the foothills of the Himalayas and could probably see these great mountains looming in the distance.

The birth legends describe a miraculous conception in which the future Buddha came to his mother in the form of a white elephant and entered her right side. He had been born many times before and was drawn to earth once again by

The Buddha gives his first sermon, using the mudra *(sacred gesture) representing the karmic wheel of birth, death, and rebirth.*

The region where Siddhartha grew up is in full view of the high peaks of the Himalayas.

his compassion for all suffering beings. Stories also tell of the brahmins' interpretation of his mother's dream (and of marks on the baby himself): a son would be born whose greatness would lead to his either becoming king of all India or one who retires from earthly life to become an enlightened being, sharing his own awakening with the world.

The heralded birth occurred in Lumbini, a garden retreat, which is now in Nepal. The boy was named Siddhartha*, "wish-fulfiller," or "he who has reached his goal." His family name, Gautama, honored an ancient Hindu sage whom the family claimed as ancestor or spiritual guide. It is said that Siddhartha's father, wanting his son to succeed him as a king, tried to make the boy's earthly life so pleasant that he would not choose to retire from it. Siddhartha later described a life of fine clothes, white umbrellas for shade, perfumes, cosmetics, a mansion for each season, the company of female musicians, and a harem of dancing girls. He was also trained in martial arts and married to at least one wife, who bore a son.

In the midst of this life of ease, Siddhartha was apparently unconvinced of its value. An early indication of his future direction occurred during his youth. While sitting beneath a rose-apple tree, he spontaneously entered an extremely blissful state of meditation. By contrast, he was struck by the stark fact that despite its temporary pleasures, life always leads to decay and death. According to the legend, the gods arranged for him to see the "four sights" that his father had carefully tried to hide from him: a bent old man, a sick person, a dead person, and a monk seeking eternal rather than temporal pleasure. Seeing the first three sights, he was reportedly dismayed by the impermanence of life and the existence of suffering, old age, and death; the sight of the monk suggested the possibility of a life of renunciation. Increasingly dissatisfied with the futility of sensual delights, at the age of twenty-nine Prince Siddhartha renounced his wealth and position as heir to the throne, left his wife and baby, shaved his head, and donned the coarse robe of a wandering ascetic.

Many Indian *sannyasins* were already leading the homeless life of poverty considered appropriate for seekers of spiritual truth. Although the future Buddha would later develop a new religion that departed significantly from Brahmanic Hindu beliefs, he initially tried the traditional methods. He headed southeast to study with a famous brahmin teacher who had many followers. Although Siddhartha is said to have achieved the mental state of No-thing-ness under his teachings, he resumed his search, apparently feeling that a still higher state of realization lay beyond. His next brahmin teacher helped him to realize an even higher level, the mental state of Neither-perception-nor-non-perception. But again he moved on, not satisfied that he had reached his ultimate goal: the way of total liberation from suffering. He sought out temple priests but was disturbed by their animal sacrifices to the gods, which Siddhartha considered cruel. Before leaving them, he tried to teach them that it was hypocritical and futile to try to atone for misdeeds by destroying life.

---

* Buddhist terms have come to us both in **Pali**, an Indian dialect first used for preserving the Buddha's teachings (the Buddha himself probably spoke a different ancient dialect), and in Sanskrit, the language of Indian sacred literature. For instance, the Pali *sutta* (aphorism) is equivalent to the Sanskrit **sutra**. In this chapter Sanskrit will be used, as it is more familiar to Westerners, except in the section on Theravada, which uses Pali.

BUDDHISM

BCE	
600	c.563–483 Life of Gautama Buddha
300	
	c.258 King Asoka begins spreading Buddhism outward from India
200	c.200 BCE–200 CE Development of Theravada Buddhism
100	c.100 BCE–300 CE Perfection of Wisdom scriptures originally developed
	c.80 Pali Canon written down in Sri Lanka

CE	
	c.50 Buddhism transmitted to China and then East Asia
	1st century Development of Mahayana Buddhism
100	
	c.150–250 Life of Nagarjuna
500	
	c.550 Buddhism enters Japan
	589–845 Peak of Chinese Buddhism
600	c.609–650 Life of Songtsan, who declares Buddhism the national religion of Tibet
	845 Persecution of Buddhism begins in China
1000	1079–1153 Life of Milarepa
1200	1200–1253 Life of Dogen, who spread Zen Buddhism in Japan
	1222–1282 Life of Nichiren
	c.1200–1500 Buddhism declines in northern India, then southern India
1500	
1900	1905 Zen Buddhism carried to the USA
	1959 Communist Chinese repress Buddhism in Tibet, Dalai Lama escapes to India
2000	1998 Full ordination of 135 nuns from 23 countries

Still searching, Siddhartha found five pupils of his second teacher living as ascetics in the forest. Admiring their efforts to subdue the senses, he decided to try their practices himself as an experiment in liberation. For six years he outdid them in extreme self-denial techniques: nakedness, exposure to great heat and cold, breath retention, a bed of brambles, severe fasting. Finally he acknowledged that this extreme ascetic path had not led to enlightenment. He described his appearance after his long and strenuous fasting:

> Because I ate so little, all my limbs became like the knotted joints of withered creepers; because I ate so little, my protruding backbone became like a string of balls; because I ate so little, my buttocks became like a bullock's hoof; because I ate so little, my gaunt ribs became like the crazy rafters of a tumbledown shed; because I ate so little, the pupils of my eyes appeared lying low and deep in their sockets as sparkles of water in a deep well appear lying low and deep.[1]

Siddhartha then shifted his practice to a Middle Way of neither self-indulgence nor self-denial. To the disillusionment of the five ascetics, who left him, he revived his failing health by accepting food once more and taking reasonable care of his body. Placing his faith in clarity of mind, he began a period of reflection. On the night of the full moon in the sixth lunar month, as he sat in deep meditation beneath a sacred fig tree at Gaya, he finally experienced Supreme Enlightenment.

After passing through four states of serene contemplation, he first recalled all his previous lives. Then he had a realization of the wheel of deaths and rebirths, in which past good or bad deeds are reflected in the next life. Finally, he realized the cause of suffering and the means for ending it. After this supreme experience, it is said that he radiated light. The realization made Siddhartha an enlightened being, a "Buddha". According to the legend, he was tempted by Mara, the personification of evil, to keep his insights to himself, for they were too complex and profound for ordinary people to understand. But the Buddha, as he now knew himself, compassionately determined to set the wheel of teaching in motion, even if only for the sake of a few who would understand: those with "only a little dust" in their eyes.

The first people with whom the Buddha shared the essence of his insights were the five ascetics who had abandoned him, thinking he had given up. In his famous Deer Park sermon at Sarnath, "The First Turning of the Wheel of Dharma," he taught them what became the essence of Buddhism: the Four Noble Truths about suffering and the Eightfold Path for liberation from suffering. Soon convinced, they became the first disciples of the new path.

The Buddha continued to teach the **dharma** (**Pali**: dhamma)—which in his system means the truths of reality, and the right conduct for each person's state of evolution—for forty-five years. As he walked through the northern Indian countryside, still as a voluntarily poor teacher with a begging bowl, he gave sermons to people of all sects and classes. Some, including his son, became a **bhikshu** (Pali: bhikkhu), monks emulating his life of poverty and spiritual dedication; others adopted his teachings but continued as householders.

The **sangha**—the order of Buddha's disciples—was free from the caste system; people from all levels of society became Buddhists. His stepmother and his wife became bhikshunis (Pali: bhikkhunis), members of the order of nuns that the

The Buddha's first disciples, to whom he is shown preaching his first sermon, were the five ascetics with whom he had lived in the forest.

Buddha founded. After the death of his father the king, the Buddha's stepmother had requested permission to start an order of Buddhist nuns. The Buddha refused. Then she and five hundred women from the court reportedly shaved their heads, put on yellow robes, and followed him on foot, making the same request. At last he agreed. His reluctance is today a matter of much speculation. In patriarchal Indian society, for women to leave their homes and become itinerant mendicants would likely have been perceived as socially disruptive, as well as being difficult for women of the court. According to Hindu social codes, a woman could not lead a religious life and could achieve spiritual salvation only through devotion to her husband. By contrast, the Buddha asserted that women were as capable as men of achieving enlightenment. In his compassion, the Buddha also forbade animal sacrifice and admonished his followers to be kind to all living beings.

The circumstances of the Buddha's death at the age of eighty bespeak his selfless desire to spare humankind from suffering. His last meal, served by a blacksmith, inadvertently included some poisonous mushrooms or perhaps spoiled pork. Severely ill and recognizing his impending death, the Buddha nevertheless pushed on to his next teaching stop at Kusinara, converting a young man along the way. He sent word back to the blacksmith that he must not feel remorse or blame himself for the meal, for his offering of food brought him great merit.

When he reached his destination, he lay down on a stone couch, at which point, it is said, the trees above rained blossoms down upon him. As his monks came to pay their last respects, he urged them to tend to their own spiritual development:

You must be your own lamps, be your own refuges. . . . A monk becomes his own lamp and refuge by continually looking on his body, feelings, perceptions, moods, and ideas in such a manner that he conquers the cravings and depressions of ordinary men and is always strenuous, self-possessed, and collected in mind.[2]

He designated no successor, no one to lead the order. But it survived and spread because, as his closest helper, Ananda, explained, before his passing away, the Buddha had made it clear that his followers should take the *dharma* and discipline as their support. They should study the *dharma*, put it into practice, and if outsiders criticized it, they should be able to defend it.

The dharma

Buddhism is often described as a non-theistic religion. There is no personal God who creates everything and to whom prayers can be directed. The Buddhists at the 1993 Chicago Parliament of the World's Religions found it necessary to explain to people of other religions that they do not worship Buddha:

Shakyamuni Buddha, the founder of Buddhism, was not God or a god. He was a human being who attained full Enlightenment through meditation and showed us the path of spiritual awakening and freedom. Therefore, Buddhism is not a religion of God. Buddhism is a religion of wisdom, enlightenment and compassion. Like the worshippers of God who believe that salvation is available to all through confession

The Buddha's final liberation into nirvana when he physically died is symbolized by this enormous Sri Lankan statue in which he is serenely lying down with eyes closed to the world.

of sin and a life of prayer, we Buddhists believe that salvation and enlightenment are available to all through removal of defilements and delusion and a life of meditation. However, unlike those who believe in God who is separate from us, Buddhists believe that Buddha which means "one who is awake and enlightened" is inherent in us all as Buddhanature or Buddhamind.[3]

Unlike other Indian sages, the Buddha did not focus on descriptions of ultimate reality, the nature of the soul, life after death, or the origin of the universe. He said that curiosity about such matters was like a man who, upon being wounded by a poisoned arrow, refused to have it pulled out until he was told the caste and origin of his assailant, his name, his height, the color of his skin, and all details about the bow and arrow. In the meantime, he died.

Being religious and following dhamma *has nothing to do with the dogma that the world is eternal; and it has nothing to do with the other dogma that the world is not eternal. For whether the world is eternal or otherwise, birth, old age, death, sorrow, pain, misery, grief, and despair exist. I am concerned with the extinction of these.[4]*

The Buddha spoke of his teachings as a raft to take us to the farther shore, rather than a description of the shore or something to be carried around once we get there. The basic planks of this raft are insights into the truths of existence and the path to liberation; **nirvana** (Pali: *nibbana*) is the farther shore, the goal of spiritual effort.

The basic facts of existence

In his very first sermon, the Deer Park sermon preached to the five ascetics, the Buddha set forth the "Four Noble Truths" around which all his later teachings revolved. These were:

1 Life inevitably involves suffering, is imperfect and unsatisfactory.
2 Suffering originates in our desires.
3 Suffering will cease if all desires cease.
4 There is a way to realize this state: the Noble Eightfold Path.

The Buddha is therefore neither pessimistic nor optimistic about our human condition. Sri Lankan monk and scholar Walpola Rahula speaks of the Buddha as "the wise and scientific doctor for the ills of the world."[5] To look at the diagnosis and treatment of our human condition one step at a time, the Buddha's First Noble Truth is the existence of *dukkha*, which means suffering or frustration. We all experience grief, unfulfilled desires, sickness, old age, physical pain, mental anguish, and death. We may be happy for a while, but happiness is not permanent. Even our identity is impermanent. There is no continual "I." What we regard as our self is simply an ever-changing bundle of fleeting feelings, sense impressions, ideas, and evanescent physical matter. One moment's identity leads to the next like one candle being lit from another.

The Second Noble Truth is that *dukkha* has its origin in desire—desire for sensory pleasures, for fame and fortune, for things to stay as they are or become different than they are—and in attachment to ideas. The reason that desire leads us to suffering, the Buddha taught, is that we do not understand the nature of things, of that which we desire. Everything is actually impermanent, changing all the time. We seek to grasp and hold life as we want it to be, but we cannot, since everything is in constant flux.

In Buddhism, unhappiness is understood as the inevitable companion of happiness. The sun will give way to rain; a lovely flower will decay; beloved friends will die; our bodies will surely age. As the contemporary monk Ajahn Sumedho points out, "trying to arrange, control and manipulate conditions so as to always get what we want, always hear what we want to hear, always see what we want to see, so that we never have to experience unhappiness or despair, is a hopeless task."[6]

The Buddha taught skillful means of freeing oneself from the delusions and desires of worldly life.

What a Buddhist strives for instead is the recognition of *dukkha*, **anicca** (impermanence), and **anatta** (the revolutionary and unique doctrine that there is no separate, permanent, or immortal self; rather, a human being is an energy process composed of momentary energy flashes, interconnected with all other beings and with the universe as energy processes). This realization of *anatta* is spiritually valuable because it reduces attachment to one's mind, body, and selfish desires. Suffering is also useful to us because it helps us to see things as they really are. When our attention is drawn to the fact that everything changes and passes away, moment by moment, we can become aware that nothing in this world has an independent, solid character. There are only momentary configurations within a continual process of change. Once we have grasped these basic facts of life, we can be free in this life, and free from another rebirth. Ajahn Sumedho explains:

> *When you open the mind to the truth, then you realize there is nothing to fear. What arises passes away, what is born dies, and is not self—so that our sense of being caught in an identity with this human body fades out. We don't see ourselves as some isolated, alienated entity lost in a mysterious and frightening universe. We don't feel overwhelmed by it, trying to find a little piece of it that we can grasp and feel safe with, because we feel at peace with it. Then we have merged with the Truth.*[7]

The Third Noble Truth is that *dukkha* can cease if desire ceases. Thus illusion ends, and ultimate reality, or nirvana, is revealed. One lives happily and fully in the present moment, free from self-centeredness and full of compassion for others. One can serve them purely, for in this state there is no thought of oneself.

The Fourth Noble Truth is that only through a life of morality, concentration, and wisdom—which the Buddha set forth as the Noble Eightfold Path—can desire and therefore suffering be extinguished.

The Eightfold Path of liberation

The Buddha set forth a systematic approach by which dedicated humans could pull themselves out of suffering and achieve the final goal of liberation. The Eightfold Path offers ways to burn up all past demerits, avoid accumulating new demerits, and build up merit for a favorable rebirth. Perfection of the path means final escape from the cycle of death and rebirth, into the peace of nirvana.

One factor is right understanding—comprehending reality correctly through deep realization of the Four Noble Truths. Initially, this means seeing through illusions, such as the idea that a little more wealth could bring happiness. Gradually one learns to question old assumptions in the light of the Four Noble Truths. Everything we do and say is governed by the mind. The Buddha said that if our mind is defiled and untrained, suffering will follow us just as a chariot follows the horse. If we think and act from a purified, trained mind, happiness will always follow us.

A second aspect of the Eightfold Path is right thought or motives. The Buddha encourages us to uncover any "unwholesome" emotional roots behind our thinking, such as a desire to hide our imperfections or avoid contact with others. As we discover and weed out such emotional blocks, our thought becomes free from the limitations of self-centeredness—relaxed, clear, and open.

A third factor is right speech. The Buddha cautions us to relinquish our propensity to vain talk, gossip, tale-bearing, harsh words, and lying, and to use communication instead in the service of truth and harmony. He also advises us to speak in a positive manner to our own minds—to say to ourselves, "May you be well and happy today."

A fourth factor, right action, begins for the layperson with observing the five basic precepts for moral conduct: avoid destroying life, stealing, sexual misconduct, lying, and intoxicants. Beyond these, we are to base our actions on clear understanding. "Evil deeds," said the Buddha, are those "done from motives of partiality, enmity, stupidity, and fear."[8]

Fifth is right livelihood—being sure that one's way of making a living does not violate the five precepts. One's trade should not harm others or disrupt social harmony.

Right effort, a sixth factor in the Eightfold Path, bespeaks continual striving to cut off "unwholesome states," past, present, and future. This is not a way for the lazy.

A seventh factor, right mindfulness, is particularly characteristic of Buddhism, for the way to liberation is said to be through the mind. We are urged to be aware

TEACHING STORY

The Monkeys Take Care of the Trees

The king's park-keeper wanted to celebrate a festival in the city. Therefore he wanted to find some people to water the trees so that he could take a leave for a week or so. He wondered to himself, "How can I find some people to look after the trees?" Then he thought of the monkeys in the park.

He summoned the chief monkey. "Can you water the trees for me during my leave?"

The chief monkey said, "Oh, sure."

The park-keeper said to him, "Here are the watering pots. Please tell the monkeys in this park to water the trees while I am gone." Then he went away.

When the time came for watering the trees, the chief monkey said to the other monkeys who had gathered to take the watering pots, "One moment, please. We have to use water economically. How can we do so? We have to water the trees according to their needs. How can we know the needs of the trees? The tree with long roots needs much water; the tree with short roots needs less water. We should make a division of labor by dividing the monkeys into groups. Two monkeys to a group: one monkey pulls up the tree to see if it has long or short roots; the other monkey, when he sees—'Oh, this one has short roots'— waters it less. If it has long roots, he should water it more."

The monkeys divided their labor in this way. They watered all the trees in the garden park, and all the trees died.

Then a wise man came and saw what the monkeys were doing. The chief monkey, who considered himself very wise, explained his orders. Then the wise man uttered this stanza:

A foolish person, even when he wants to do something good, may instead do something that leads to destruction.

(A tale from one of the Buddha's previous lives, as retold by Phra Depvedi.)

in every moment. In the **Dhammapada**, short verses about the way of truth, said to have been uttered by the Buddha, there appears this pithy injunction:

Check your mind.
Be on your guard.
Pull yourself out
as an elephant from mud.[9]

The eighth factor, right meditation, applies mental discipline to the quieting of the mind itself. "It is subtle, invisible, treacherous,"[10] explains the Buddha. Skillful means are therefore needed to see and transcend its restless nature. When the mind is fully stilled, it becomes a quiet pool in which the true nature of everything is clearly reflected. The various schools of Buddhism that have developed over the centuries have taught different techniques of meditation, but this basic principle remains the same.

> *Try to be mindful, and let things take their natural course. Then your mind will become still in any surroundings, like a clear forest pool. All kinds of wonderful, rare animals will come to drink at the pool, and you will clearly see the nature of all things. You will see many strange and wonderful things come and go, but you will be still. This is the happiness of the Buddha.*
> *Achaan Chah, meditation master, Wat Pa Pong, Thailand*[11]

The wheel of birth and death

Buddhist teachings about rebirth are slightly different from those of Hindu orthodoxy, for there is no eternal soul to be reborn. In Buddhism, one changing state of being sets another into motion: every event depends on a cause. The central cause in this process is **karma** (Pali: *kamma*)—our acts of will. These influence the level at which that personality-developing process we think of as "me" is reborn. The impressions of our good and bad actions help to create our personality moment-by-moment. When we die, this process continues, passing on the flame to a new life on a plane that reflects our past *karma*.

There are thirty-one planes of existence, interpreted as psychological metaphors by some Buddhists. Whether metaphors or metaphysical realities, these include hells, "hungry ghosts" (beings tormented with unsatisfied desires), animals, humans, and gods. Like the lower levels, the gods are imperfect and impermanent. Round and round we go, life after life, caught in this cycle of **samsara** (worldly phenomena), repeatedly experiencing aging, decay, suffering, death, and painful rebirth, unless we are freed into nirvana, which is beyond all the cause-and-effect-run planes of existence.

Nirvana

About the goal of Buddhist practice, nirvana, the Buddha had relatively little to say. The word itself refers to the extinguishing of a flame from lack of fuel. The only way to end the cycle in which desire feeds the wheel of suffering is to end all cravings

The Wheel of Life: in the center are animals representing lust, hatred, and delusion. The next circle shows the fate of those with good karma (left) and bad karma (right). The third circle represents the six spheres of existence from the gods to the infernal regions. The outer rim shows the chain of cause and effect. Grasping the wheel is a monster representing death, impermanence.

and lead a passion-free existence that has no karmic consequences. Thence one enters a condition of what the Buddha called "quietude of heart."[12] "Where there is nothing," he said, "where naught is grasped, there is the Isle of No-beyond. Nirvana do I call it—the utter extinction of aging and dying,"[13] "the unborn, ... undying, ... unsorrowing, ... stainless, the uttermost security from bonds."[14]

A nun leaves the meditation hall in Dharamsala, India, after sunrise practices.

For the **arhant** (Pali: *arhat, arahat*), worthy one, who has found nirvana in this life:

No suffering for him
who is free from sorrow
free from the fetters of life
free in everything he does.
He has reached the end of his road. . . .

Like a bird invisibly flying in the sky,
he lives without possessions,
knowledge his food, freedom his world,
while others wonder. . . .

He has found freedom—
peaceful his thinking, peaceful his speech,
peaceful his deed, tranquil his mind.[15]

What happens when such a being dies? One enters a deathless, peaceful, unchanging state that cannot be described. Individuality disappears and one enters the realm of ultimate truth, about which the Buddha was silent. Why? At one point he picked up a handful of leaves from the forest floor and asked his disciples which were more numerous, the leaves in his hand or those in the surrounding forest. When they replied, "Very few in your hand, lord; many more in the grove," he said:

Exactly. So you see, friends, the things that I know and have not revealed are more
than the truths I know and have revealed. And why have I not revealed them?
Because, friends, there is no profit in them; because they are not helpful to holiness;
because they do not lead from disgust to cessation and peace, because they do not
lead from knowledge to wisdom and nirvana.[16]

Buddhism south and north

As soon as he had attracted a small group of disciples, the Buddha sent them out to help teach the *dharma*. This missionary effort spread in all directions. Two hundred years after the Buddha died, a great Indian king, Asoka, developed an appreciation of many religions. Under his leadership Buddhism was carried throughout the kingdom and outward to other countries as well, beginning its development as a global religion. After Asoka's death, brahmins reasserted their political influence and Buddhists were persecuted in parts of India. By the time of the twelfth-century Muslim invasions of India, Buddhism had nearly died out and never became the dominant religion in the Buddha's homeland.

Many Buddhist sects have developed as the Buddha's teachings have been expanded upon and adapted to local cultures in different areas. There are

Buddhism spread in all directions from India but nearly disappeared in India itself by the 13th century CE.

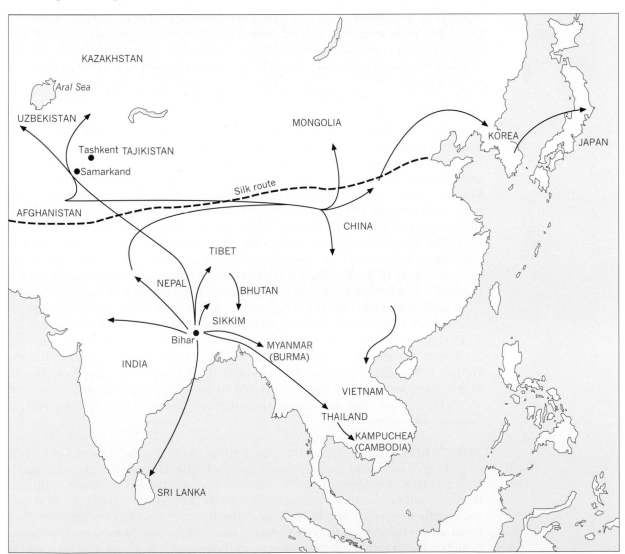

two primary divisions. The form that tries to adhere closely to what it considers the original teachings is called **Theravada**, or "Way of the Elders." It is prevalent in the Southeast Asian countries such as Sri Lanka, Myanmar (formerly Burma), Thailand, Kampuchea (formerly Cambodia), and Laos and is therefore geographically referred to as the Southern School. The other major grouping is the Northern School, dominant in Nepal, Tibet, China, Korea, Mongolia, and Japan. Those of this group call it **Mahayana**, the "Greater Vehicle," because they feel that theirs is a bigger raft that can carry more people across the sea of samsara than the stark teachings of the Theravadins, which they call the **Hinayana**, or "Lesser Vehicle." Both groups are in general agreement about the Four Noble Truths, the Eightfold Path, and the teachings about *karma* and nirvana described above.

Theravada: the path of mindfulness

Theravada is a conservative and traditional Buddhist way. Theravadin Buddhists study the early scriptures in Pali, honor the monastic life of renunciation, and follow mindfulness meditation teachings. These characteristics are more obvious among the intellectuals and monastics; the common people are more devotional in their practices.

THE PALI CANON   Buddhists who follow the Theravada tradition study a large collection of ancient scriptures preserved in the Pali language of ancient India. This ancient **canon**, or authoritative collection of writings, is called the Pali Canon. It is also referred to as the **Tipitaka** (Sanskrit: *Tripitaka*), the "Three Baskets." This label derives from the old practice of storing palm-leaf manuscripts in wicker baskets; thus, the "Three Baskets" are three collections of sacred writings: rules, teachings, and scholastic treatises. They were collected immediately after the Buddha's death by a council of five hundred elders, monks who had studied directly with him. The Venerable Ananda recited his discourses from memory, and another close disciple rehearsed the discipline of the order. Then the elders agreed on a definitive body of the Buddha's teachings, which were carried orally until the first century BCE, when they were written down on palm leaves and stored in baskets.

In addition to the Tipitaka, Theravadins also honor other non-canonical Pali works, such as later commentaries and commentaries-on-the-commentaries. The 547 lively *Jataka Tales*, such as the story of the foolish monkeys, appear in the commentaries as explanations of the context of the pithy sayings found in the discourses ("A foolish man, even when he tries to do good . . ."). These folk tales are said to have been told by the Buddha and to represent scenes from his own previous births, but they are also used to demonstrate Buddhist virtues, such as wisdom and compassion.

THE TRIPLE GEM   Like all Buddhists, those of the Southern School soften the discipline of the mind with devotion to the **Triple Gem** (or "Three Refuges"): Buddha (the Enlightened One), *dharma* (the doctrine he taught, Ultimate Reality), and *sangha* (the order of his disciples). To become a Buddhist, and then afterwards to reassert the basis of one's faith, a person "takes refuge" in these three jewels by reciting the Pali formula, *Buddham saranam gacchami* ("I go to the Buddha for refuge"), *dhammam saranam gacchami* ("I go to the *dharma* for

Training of Buddhist monks often begins at an early age.

refuge"), *Sangham saranam gacchami* ("I go to the *sangha* for refuge").

One takes refuge in the Buddha not by praying to him for help but by paying homage to him as supreme teacher and inspiring model. In a sense, taking refuge in the Buddha is honoring the Buddha-wisdom within each of us.

The *dharma* is like a medicine, but it will not cure our suffering unless we take it. In the Pali chanting, it is described as immediate, timeless, leading to calmness, and known only through our direct experience and personal effort.

The *sangha* is the order of *bhikshus* and *bhikshunis* who have renounced the world in order to follow, preserve, and share the *dharma*. The Buddha established one of the world's first monastic orders, and this core remains strong in Theravada. There are presently about half a million Theravadin monks in Southeast Asia. To simplify their worldly lives and devote themselves to studying and teaching the *dharma*, monks must shave their heads, dress in simple robes, own only a few basic material items, eat no solid foods after noon, practice celibacy, and depend on the laity for their food, clothing, and medical supplies. Early every morning they set forth with a begging bowl, and the laypeople regard it as a merit-making opportunity to offer food to them. In this interdependent system, the monks reciprocate by offering spiritual guidance, chanted blessings, and various social services, including secular advice and education. Monks offer discourses on the *dharma* in monasteries and, when invited, in private homes.

Buddhist monasteries are at the center of village life, rather than separated from it. The monasteries are open, and people come and go. The monks hold a revered social position as models of self-control, kindness, and intelligence. In Thailand it is common for young men to take temporary vows of monkhood—often for the duration of the rainy season when little farmwork can be done. They wear the saffron robes, set forth with shaven heads and begging bowls, and receive religious instruction while they practice a life of simplicity.

A twenty-year-old Buddhist nun in Dharamsala, north India.

By contrast, there has traditionally been little social support for *bhikshunis*, or Buddhist nuns, in Southeast Asia. Provisions were made during the time of the Buddha for women monastics to live in the same monasteries as men, with the same lifestyle, but the order of fully ordained nuns disappeared completely in Theravadin countries about a thousand years ago. Many of the early Buddhist scriptures take an egalitarian position toward women's capacity for wisdom and attainment of nirvana, but spiritual power was kept in the hands of monks. Nuns were by rules of the order forever subservient to the monks, seniority notwithstanding, so there was little opportunity for them to grow into positions of leadership.

Over time, some of the monks and the texts they edited apparently became actively misogynist. Even today a Thai Buddhist monk is not allowed to come into direct contact with a woman, with the idea that women are hindrances to monks' spiritual development. Feminist scholars object to this interpretation. Thai Buddhist Dr. Chatsumarn Kabilsingh, for instance, asserts:

> *Newly ordained monks who have not had much experience with practice and are very weak in their mental resolve may be easily swayed by sensual impulses, of which women are the major attraction. Even if no women are present, some monks still create problems for themselves by images of women they have in their minds. Women are not responsible for the sexual behavior or imaginings of men; the monks themselves must cope with their own sensual desires. Enlightened ones are well-fortified against such mental states and are able to transcend gender differences. The Buddha himself found no need to avoid women, because women no longer appeared to him as sexual objects. He was well-balanced and in control of his mental processes.[17]*

There are now attempts to revive fully ordained orders of nuns in Theravadin countries. In 1998 a landmark occurred: the full ordination at Bodh Gaya of 135 nuns from many countries. According to the code of discipline, ordination of nuns is possible only if both ordained monks and nuns are present. The lack of ordained nuns had been used by conservative senior monks as a way of blocking women's ordinations. But in China, Taiwan, Japan, and Korea, women's orders

Some 135 women from 23 countries received full ordination as Buddhist nuns at Bodh Gaya in 1998, helping to revive orders of bhikshunis.

had continued, and thus Master Hsing Yun, founder of a Taiwanese Buddhist order, was able to bring the requisite participants to Bodh Gaya and perform the ordinations, 980 years after the *bhikshuni* order had become extinct in India and Sri Lanka.

VIPASSANA MEDITATION   In addition to trying to preserve what are thought to be the Buddha's original teachings, Theravada is the purveyor of mindfulness meditation techniques. *Vipassana* literally means "insight," but the meditation methods used to develop insight begin by increasing one's attentiveness to every detail as a way of calming, focusing, and watching the mind. As taught by the Burmese meditation master Mahasi Sayadaw, the way to begin *vipassana* practice is simply to watch oneself breathing in and out, with the attention focused on the rise and fall of the abdomen. To keep the mind concentrated on this movement, rather than dragged this way and that by unconscious, conditioned responses, one continually makes concise mental notes of what is happening: "rising," "falling." Inevitably other mental functions will arise in the restless mind. As they do, one simply notes what they are—"imagining," "wandering," "remembering"—and then returns the attention to the rising and falling of the breath. Body sensations will appear, too, and one handles them the same way, noting "itching," "tight," "tired." Periods of sitting meditation are alternated with periods of walking meditation, in which one notes the exact movements of the body in great detail: "lifting," "moving," "placing."

This same mindfulness is carried over into every activity of the day. If ecstatic states or visions arise, the meditator is told simply to note them and let them pass away without attachment. In the same way, emotions that arise are simply observed, accepted, and allowed to pass away, rather than labeled "good" or "bad." By contrast, says *dharma* teacher Joko Beck, we usually get stuck in our emotions:

> *Everyone's fascinated by their emotions because we think that's who we are. We're afraid that if we let our attachment to them go, we'll be nobody. Which of course we are! When you wander into your ideas, your hopes, your dreams, turn back— not just once but ten thousand times if need be, a million times if need be.*[18]

The truths of existence as set forth by the Buddha—*dukkha* (suffering), *anicca* (impermanence), *anatta* (no eternal self)—will become apparent during this process, and the mind becomes calm, clear, attentive, and flexible, detached from likes and dislikes. Thus it is free.

THE LAITY   Although meditators from all over the world travel to Southeast Asia to study with the masters of meditation, their demanding discipline is embraced by relatively few Theravadins. Not all monasteries are meditation centers. Most laypeople's religious lives are more devotional than intellectual. Traditional teaching in Theravada emphasizes development of morality, concentration, and wisdom leading to freedom, but popular Buddhism as it is practiced in Southeast Asia tends to shift the emphasis to giving alms and observing the Three Refuges.

Even within the relatively austere Theravada path there have arisen a number of ways of worship. One is the veneration of relics thought to be from the

AN INTERVIEW WITH KOMKAI CHAROENSUK

Living Buddhism

In Thailand, over ninety-three percent of the population is Buddhist, and there are historically close ties between State and *sangha*. The pressures of rapid modernization, consumerism, and economic troubles are beginning to erode traditional values in this society where people had been happy and free, perhaps partly because of their Buddhist faith.

Komkai Charoensuk is a cheerful, matter-of-fact Bangkok grandmother who practices meditation and studies with monks and nuns. She says:

"I'm just beginning to become a good Buddhist. We have meditation courses every month at our center in Bangkok. The course I have been taking is a ten-day course, and I have taken it over twenty times. Now I'm going to take a thirty-day course in India. I'm going there with six other people, including a professor in engineering and a woman physician. All of them are younger than I. I hope my meditation there will be of great benefit to me because of its continuity in practice. We'll be sitting in a cell by ourself for thirty days, getting up at 4 o'clock and starting our meditation at 4:30 a.m. Most of the day we are working in our cell. Then in the evening from 7 to 8:30 p.m. we come to listen to the discourse on tapes in the hall together with other students, but no talking is encouraged at all. Noble silence all day, all the time.

"Otherwise, I practice meditation, but not continuously. It needs a lot of patience and great attention. Not time. The present moment—that's the most important thing we must know.

"When somebody else is angry and starts to curse us, it is very easy for us to feel that we are hurt by them. But we can try to find out what is the cause of their suffering, their anger. The longer you keep the pain in yourself, the worse it will become. You stay angry, angry, and angry. That's the way that you are hurting yourself. And it's foolish to hurt one's own heart or one's mind. But we need a lot of practice before we can overcome these sorts of things. From

meditation we learn to observe the sensations in the body, which are certainly related to the mind. Every sensation in the body is connected to what affects the mind. But before one learns to start to meditate, one has to learn to develop *sathi*, awareness. And we learn to develop *sathi* by observing our respiration, so that the mind becomes concentrated. If the mind is still wandering, then you can't grow *sathi*.

"If you practice a lot, then you become aware of what you are doing or thinking. Moment by moment, you try to keep aware. Buddha has been called the One who is aware, awake, happy, and conscious. To be aware is to be awake all the time.

"Besides learning to develop *sathi*, we learn to observe the truth that nothing is still, but keeps changing, so we should not hold on to things or persons. Even ourself: Today we have this idea, but tomorrow our idea may change completely or not be so firm as yesterday. To learn to understand this truth helps a lot. Everything is impermanent. Nothing really belongs to us, even our own self—our body and mind. Understanding this *anicca* ("Nothing is permanent") helps change my attitude, character, and way of thinking—though not absolutely, but bit by bit. I feel less attached to things and people. Also one learns to understand other people's doing—then one learns to stop finding other people's faults. We learn to become more generous and understanding, and to obtain more and more compassionate love. This is what happens to me, and my life becomes easier, simpler, and calmer.

"We don't want to start and end and come back and start and end again and come back and start again. We don't want to be born again and suffer, another time be happy, another time suffer. You laugh and you cry, and you laugh and you cry all your life. That's why we want to go to nirvana: no more happiness, no more unhappiness. And then when anyone scolds you, you are smiling, you understand why they are scolding you. You understand everything. Nobody can hurt you."

Buddha. These are placed in **stupas**, architectural mounds reaching into the sky, perhaps derived from the indigenous spiritual traditions. A tiny bone chip believed to be a relic from the Buddha, for instance, is enshrined at Doi Suthep temple in Chiang Mai in Thailand. To share this sacred relic with the people, the ruler was said to have placed it on the back of a sacred white elephant—legendary symbol of the Buddha—so that it would choose the best place for the temple. The elephant climbed a nearby hill until it reached the auspicious spot, where it circled three times and then went down on its knees. Today, thousands of pilgrims climb the 290 steps to the temple, praying for blessings by acts such as pressing squares of gold leaf onto an image of the Buddha, lighting three sticks of incense to honor the Triple Gem, lighting candles, and offering flowers to the images of the Buddha.

Loving images of the Buddha proliferate in the temples and roadside shrines (which are almost identical to the indigenous spirit shrines, which are still quite common in Thailand, where Buddhism is a combination of indigenous spirituality, Buddhism, and Brahmanism). These physical images of the Buddha give a sense of his protective, guiding presence, even though according to Theravadin orthodoxy the Buddha no longer exists as an individual, having entered nirvana.

In Southeast Asia, aspects of Theravada Buddhism have often been adopted by shamans for greater efficacy in healing rituals. In Sri Lanka, the *yakeduras* invoke the power of the Buddha and the *dharma* to ward off evil spirits and thus help cure supernaturally afflicted people. In the cosmic hierarchy, the Buddha and

Stupas, such as these bell-shaped monuments in Borobudur, Java, may house relics or statues of the Buddha and are sacred places for pilgrimage. The Buddha's long ears symbolize long life; elders are valued because of their experience and wisdom. The raised upper part of his head represents higher consciousness developed through years of meditation practice. The flame at the top signifies extinction of the flames of anger, hatred, and delusion.

dharma are considered the ultimate powers, and therefore useful in subduing lesser forces. During healing rituals, patients are also obliged to listen to Buddhist stories, to inspire them to free and protect themselves by the power of the mind.

Even monks are regarded as magical protectors of sorts, and the faithful can request chantings of blessings for protection. For instance, in the books of Pali chants there is a special prayer for protection from unwanted crawling creatures, such as spiders and rats. It addresses them in a spirit of **metta** (loving-kindness) and then requests, "May those beings go away!"[19]

In Theravadan areas, as in all Buddhist cultures, Buddhist temples are important centers for community identity and integration. There the monks not only teach the *dharma* but also, with the help of the laity, conduct agricultural festivals to improve the harvest, ceremonies to assist the dead to better rebirth, and ceremonies to please the deities in order to receive their blessings and to generate festive atmospheres for community joy.

Above left Among popular ways of worship, butter sculptures and other offerings are made to the Buddha by Tibetan Buddhists at New Year. *Above right* The golden feet of a 105 ft (32 m) tall Buddha at Wat Indra Viharn, Bangkok.

Mahayana: the path of compassion and metaphysics

Further Buddhist practices and teachings appeared in a wide range of scriptures dating from the first century BCE. These innovations in thought and practice beyond the Pali scriptures became grouped together and called Mahayana, the Greater Vehicle. Rather than emphasizing a distinction between monastics and the common people, these new scriptures take a more liberal approach designed to encompass everyone. They honor the scriptures in the Pali Canon but claim to be more advanced teachings of the Buddha. They are explained by Mahayanists as esoteric teachings given only to compassionate, enlightened beings.

The Mahayana **sutras** (scriptures) emphasize the importance of religious experience. The *dharma* is not embodied only in scriptures; for the Mahayanist it is the source of a conversion experience that awakens the quest for enlightenment as the greatest value in life.

Each school, and there are many branches within Mahayana, offers a special set of methods, or "skillful means," for awakening. They are quite varied, in contrast to the relative uniformity of Theravada, but most Mahayana traditions have a few characteristics in common.

Buddhist nuns from Tibet, where a distinct version of Mahayana developed. Behind them, prayer flags flutter in the wind.

Many Buddhists anticipate the coming of Maitreya, the Buddha of the future, to re-establish the purity of the dharma.

BODHISATTVAS   An early Mahayana scripture, the Lotus Sutra, defended its innovations beyond the Pali Canon by claiming that the earlier teachings were merely skillful means for those with lower capacities. They were ideally to be replaced by the true *dharma* of the Lotus. The idea is that the Buddha geared his teaching to his audience, and that his teachings were at different levels of completeness depending on the readiness of his audience to hear the full truth. This is explained by some researchers as a way to give credit to earlier teachings while going beyond them, and also a way to include helpful popular practices, mythology, and local customs.

In contrast to the earlier goal of individual liberation from suffering by those who were capable, the Lotus Sutra claimed that a higher goal was to become like the Buddha by seeking enlightenment for the sake of saving others. In fact, it asserted that we are called not just to individual liberation but to Buddhahood itself. The Lotus Sutra says that all beings have the capacity for Buddhahood and are destined to attain it eventually. Members of the new Mahayana communities called themselves **Bodhisattvas**, beings dedicated to attaining enlightenment. Both monastics and laity took the Bodhisattva vow to become enlightened.

Today Mahayana Buddhists often express this commitment in the Four Great Bodhisattva Vows compiled in China in the sixth century CE by Tien-t'ai Chih-i (founder of the Tendai School of Mahayana Buddhism):

Beings are infinite in number, I vow to save them all;
The obstructive passions are endless in number, I vow to end them all;
The teachings for saving others are countless, I vow to learn them all;
Buddhahood is the supreme achievement, I vow to attain it.

As His Holiness the fourteenth Dalai Lama says:

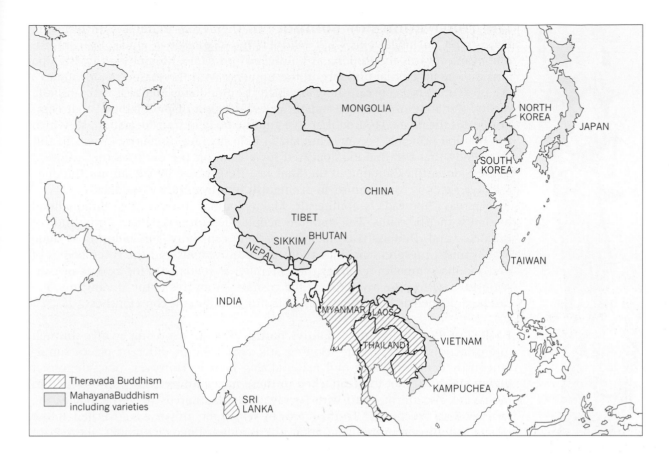

Map showing the approximate distribution of Theravada and Mahayana Buddhism in the world today.

The motivation to achieve Buddhahood in order to save all sentient beings is really a marvelous determination. That person becomes very courageous, warm-hearted, and useful in society.[20]

You are not just here for yourself alone, but for the sake of all sentient beings. Keep your mind pure, and warm.

Soen Nakagawa-roshi[21]

Bodhisattvahood is not just an ideal for earthly conduct; numerous heavenly Bodhisattvas are available to hear the pleas of those who are suffering. The heavenly Bodhisattvas are seen as aspects of the eternal Buddha. Each has a specific attribute, such as wisdom or compassion, and worshippers can pray to them for help.

The most popular Bodhisattva in East Asia is Kuan-yin (Japanese: *Kannon*), who symbolizes compassion and refuses help to no one. Although this being is depicted as a male (Avalokitesvara) in Indian images, the Lotus Sutra says that Kuan-yin will take any form that is needed to help others, and it lists thirty-three examples. In East Asia, Kuan-yin is typically represented as female, often as the giver or protector of babies. An image with a baby has become especially popular in East Asia as a refuge for aborted fetuses and their mothers.

Kuan-yin, "hearer of cries," Bodhisattva of mercy.

THE THREE BODIES OF BUDDHA In Theravada, Buddha is an historical figure who no longer exists but who left his *dharma* as a guide. By contrast, Mahayana regards the Buddha as a universal principle. Metaphysically, Buddha is said to be an eternal presence in the universe with three aspects, or "bodies": the pure universal consciousness in which the Buddha is identical with absolute reality; the body of bliss, that radiant celestial aspect of Buddhahood that communicates the *dharma* to Bodhisattvas; and the body of transformation, by which the Buddha principle becomes human to help liberate humanity. It was in this third body that the Buddha appeared for a time on the earth as the historical figure Siddhartha Gautama of the Shakyas. He is called "Shakyamuni Buddha" (Shakya sage) by Mahayanists to distinguish him from other Buddhas.

Whereas Theravada is nontheistic, Mahayana has thus elevated Buddhahood to almost theistic status. The common people therefore recognize a multitude of Buddhas and Bodhisattvas to whom they can pray for help. But some Mahayanists interpret teachings about the Bodhisattvas and the three bodies of the Buddha symbolically rather than literally, as metaphors for aspects of consciousness within the mysteries of the cosmos. From this point of view, nirvana can be described as the state of pure, blissful, and radiant consciousness.

EMPTINESS Mahayana scriptures portray Buddhas moving swiftly through intergalactic space and time, cloning and appearing at different places simultaneously, dematerializing and materializing at will. However, practitioners at higher stages are not to be attached to these appearances. Many schools within Mahayana also affirm, along with Theravadins, that there is an eternal reality, the transcendent "Suchness," Truth, or Law by which the universe is governed. In the Udana scripture from the Pali Canon, the Buddha stated, "O monks, there is an unborn, undying, unchanging, uncreated. If it were not so, there would be no point to life, or to training." However, as contemporary teacher Roshi Jiyu Kennett explains, "Buddhism states what the Eternal is not. ... It does not state what it is because if it did, then we would be stuck with a concept."[22]

Some of the most complex and paradoxical of Mahayana teachings concern the concept of **sunyata**, meaning voidness or emptiness. They were elaborated by the Indian philosopher Nagarjuna around the second and third century CE on the basis of the earlier Perfection of Wisdom scriptures. According to Nagarjuna, all earthly things arise and pass away, as a process of events dependent on other events, and having no independent origin and no eternal reality. The world of phenomena—*samsara*—is therefore empty of inherent existence. Nirvana is also empty in the sense that it is a thought construct, even though it is not dependent on conditions. Nirvana is not an eternal reality that can be acquired. In the paradoxical analyses of voidness, even ultimate reality is called *sunyata* because it transcends all thought constructs. In the Perfection of Wisdom scriptures, the student to whom the lengthy teachings on *sunyata* are given is at last asked if he has understood them. He declares, "In truth, nothing has been taught."

The Perfection of Wisdom scriptures that celebrate the liberating experience of emptiness are foundational texts for most of Mahayana. What is distinctive and startling about Mahayana is the application of the idea of emptiness to all things, even including the teachings of the Buddha. In the popular Heart Sutra that is used liturgically throughout East Asia, the core doctrines of traditional Buddhism are systematically shattered: Bodhisattva Kuan-yin sees that the five aggregates of a person (form, sensation, perception, reaction, and consciousness) are each empty of absolute self-nature; they exist only relative to other aggregates. With this realization, the Bodhisattva becomes free of all suffering. Next, birth and death, purity and defilement, increase and decrease are seen as empty; the six sense objects, the six sense organs, and the six sense awarenesses are seen to be empty; the Wheel of Life is seen as empty; the Four Noble Truths and Eightfold Path are seen as empty. Even knowledge and attainment are proclaimed to be empty. With this "perfection of wisdom," there are no obstacles, and therefore no fear, and going beyond delusions one attains nirvana, having emptied Buddhism of its central objects. The Heart Sutra replaces the doctrines with a mantra that it proclaims as supreme: *Gate, Gate, paragate, parasamgate, bodhi, svaha!* ("Gone, gone, gone beyond, gone to the other shore. O enlightenment, all hail!"). As Professor David Chappell observes,

> The systematic emptying of the central doctrines of the tradition is unparalleled in religious history. (Imagine a Christian saying that the Ten Commandments and Lord's Prayer and Apostles' Creed are empty!) And yet, insight into the impermanence of all things, and their connectedness, gives Mahayana a self-critical profundity and an inclusive acceptance of diversity, which provides balance in the midst of movement, and peace in the midst of compassion.[23]

Vajrayana: indestructible way to unity

Of the many branches of Mahayana Buddhism, perhaps the most prolific in creating elaborations is **Vajrayana**. It developed in the Tibetan area, but has also historically been practiced in Nepal, Bhutan, Sikkim, and Mongolia, and its practice is increasingly centered in the Tibetan diaspora and the United States.

Prior to the introduction of Buddhism from India, the mountainous Tibetan region may have been home to a shamanistic religion called Bon (pronounced "pern"). In the seventh century CE a particularly powerful king of Tibet, Songtsan, became interested in the religion that surrounded his isolated kingdom. He sent a group of students to study Buddhism in India, but they all died in the searing heat of the plains. Only one member of a second group survived the arduous trip across the Himalayas, returning with many Sanskrit texts. After some of these works were translated into Tibetan, Songtsan declared Buddhism the national religion and encouraged Buddhist virtues in his subjects.

The Bon shamans are said to have kept trying to sabotage this threat to their power until a tantric adept, Padmasambhava, was invited to the country

Tibetan Buddhist monks and nuns have set up a community in exile in the mountains of north India, Dharamsala, with the fourteenth Dalai Lama, but always remember their homeland in Tibet.

from Kashmir in the eighth century CE. Along the way, it is said, he subdued and converted the local Bon deities. He—and perhaps his consort, Yeshe Tsogyel—developed Tibetan Buddhism by combining elements of the Bon ways and esoteric tantric practices with Mahayana Buddhism. Many of the Bon gods and goddesses were adopted as lower grade tantric guardian deities, but animal sacrifice was replaced with symbolic forms of worship and black magic gave way to inner purification practices. When people interpreted tantric teachings literally, indulging freely in alcohol and perhaps sex in the name of spirituality, another teacher, Atisha, from the great center of Buddhist learning at Nalanda, India, was called in to set things right.

Under Atisha, Tibetan Buddhism became a complex path with three stages, said to have been prescribed by the Lord Buddha. While the Buddha did not develop them to their current state, he is said to have supported the idea of different levels of teachings for the less and more evolved. The first of these is called Hinayana by the Tibetans: quieting of the mind and relinquishing of attachments through meditation practices. The second is Mahayana: training in compassion and loving-kindness. The third is the advanced esoteric path called Vajrayana ("the diamond vehicle") or Tantrayana, said to be the speeded-up path that allows enlightenment within a single lifetime. It includes extremely rigorous practices derived from the tantric yoga of India. Adepts in this path attempt to construct an indestructible "diamond-body" for themselves that will allow them physically to sustain entries into the intense energies of higher levels of consciousness.

The "Hinayana" part of this process is similar to *vipassana* meditation. Meditators are advised to watch their emotions rising and falling, without attachment to them, without judgment. But whereas Theravadins doing this practice tend to emphasize revulsion over the emptiness of *samsara*, Tibetans use the center of emotions as a source of energy. Lama Tarthang Tulku explains:

> *With an attitude of acceptance, even our negative emotions have the potential to increase our energy and strength. Concentrate on the feeling, not on thoughts about it. Concentrate on the center of the feeling; penetrate into that space. There is a density of energy in that center that is clear and distinct. This energy has great power, and can transmit great clarity. Our consciousness can go into the emotion, contacting this pure energy so that our tension breaks. . . . The more we loosen our concepts and tightness, the more this energy flows.*[24]

After then developing tranquillity, freedom, and loving-kindness, as encouraged in Mahayana Buddhism, dedicated Vajrayana aspirants are guided through a series of tantric practices by gurus. The highest of these are **lamas**, who are revered as teachers. Some are considered as incarnate Bodhisattvas and carefully trained from a young age for their role as those who have realized the Supreme Truth and can help others advance toward it. The lamas' advice is often eminently practical, considering that we are living in Kali Yuga, the "dark age," as also identified by Hindu teachers. According to Buddhist teachings, Kali Yuga is characterized by five difficult conditions: (1) our life-force is weak; (2) delusions and emotional sickness prevail; (3) violence is rampant; (4) humans now living are of low character; and (5) false thoughts and attitudes are presumed to be true. Given this situation, the worst thing we could do is to follow social norms, for society is mistakenly veering away from truth. Therefore, in the eleventh century, Lama Drom Tonpa gave this practical advice:

> The masses have their heads on backwards. If you want to get things right, first look at how they think and behave, and consider going the opposite way. [25]

Vajrayana initiates are given practices in **deity yoga**: meditating on one of the many deities who embody various manifestations of energy in the universe. These radiant forms are themselves illusory, like the moon's image on water. But meditating on them is considered a way of reflecting on and thus bringing forth one's own true nature. Some of the deities are wrathful, such as Mahakala, defender of *dharma*. Buddhists understand that wrathful acts without hatred are sometimes socially necessary to protect truth and justice.

The highest form of Vajrayana is the use of the subtle vital energies of the body to transform the mind. A very high state of consciousness is produced after lengthy practice in which the "gross mind" is neutralized and the "subtle mind" manifests powerfully, "riding" on what Tibetans call "the clear light of bliss." This innermost subtle mind of clear light is considered the only aspect of existence that is eternal. Once it is uncovered, one is said to be capable of attaining Buddhahood in a single lifetime. The beloved seventh Dalai Lama of Tibet (1708–1757) gave this encouraging perspective:

> Even the most seemingly evil person has the primordial clear light mind at the heart of his or her existence. Eventually the clouds of distortion and delusion will be cleared away as the being grows in wisdom, and the evil behavior that emanates from these negative mindsets will naturally evaporate. That being will realize the essential nature of his or her own mind, and achieve spiritual liberation and enlightenment. [26]

The practices used to transform the mind also have as side-effects such abilities as levitation, clairvoyance, meditating continuously without sleep, and warming the body from within while sitting naked in the snow. Milarepa, the famous Tibetan poet-saint, whose enlightenment was won through great austerities, once sang this song:

> Blissful within, I don't entertain
> The notion "I'm suffering,"
> When incessant rain is pouring outside.
>
> Even on peaks of white snow mountains
> Amidst swirling snow and sleet
> Driven by new year's wintry winds
> This cotton robe burns like fire. [27]

Tibetans have suffered persecution by the communist Chinese, who overran the country in 1951, destroying ancient monasteries and scriptures and killing an estimated one-sixth of the people over decades of occupation. Since 1951, hundreds of thousands of Tibetans have escaped into exile. Among them is the highest of the lamas—the beloved fourteenth Dalai Lama, spiritual and political leader of the people. His speaking appearances around the world have been a major factor in the contemporary revival of interest in Buddhism. He has established his

Right *The Chinese communists dismantled the system whereby one quarter of the men in Tibet were monks, supported by the laity and holding considerable secular power. But spirituality persists among the people, who include full-length prostrations in their prayers.*

Far right *One of the most beloved of Tibetan Buddhist deities is Tara. She is savior and mother of the world; she protects us and helps us to achieve our spiritual longings. (Detail of Tibetan thang-ka, 18th/19th century, tempera on cotton.)*

headquarters, Dharamsala, in the mountains of northern India. A repository of traditional Tibetan culture, it has become a magnet for spiritual seekers.

Despite persecution, religious fervor and ceremony still pervade every aspect of Tibetan life, from house-raising to ardent pilgrimages. Monks and laypeople alike meditate on **thang-kas** and **mandalas**, visual aids to concentration and illumination, which portray a Buddha or Bodhisattva surrounded by deities in a diagram symbolically representing the universe. Both also chant mantras. A favorite one is the phrase associated with the beloved Tibetan Bodhisattva of mercy, Avalokitesvara: *Om mani padme hum.* It evokes awareness of the "jewel in the lotus of the heart," that beautiful treasure lying hidden within each of us. Because some emphasis is placed on the number of repetitions, mantras are written out thousands of times and spun in prayer wheels or placed on prayer flags which continue the repetition of the mantra as they blow in the wind.

Zen: the great way of enlightenment

Buddhism was transmitted from India to China around 50 CE and thence to Korea, Japan, and Vietnam, absorbing elements of Taoism along the way. Then, according to tradition, in the fifth century, Bodhidharma, a successor to the Buddha, traveled from southern China to a monastery in northern China. There he reportedly spent nine years in silent meditation, "facing the wall." On this

His Holiness the Dalai Lama

Surely one of the best-known and most-loved spiritual leaders in the world, His Holiness the fourteenth Dalai Lama is a striking example of Buddhist peace and compassion. Wherever he goes, he greets everyone with evident delight. Even when addressing audience of thousands, he looks around the hall with a broad, childlike grin, which seems directed to each person individually. His example is all the more powerful because he is the leader in exile of Tibet, a small nation that knew extreme oppression and suffering during the twentieth century.

The simplicity of His Holiness's words and bearing give no evidence of his intellectual power. His Holiness was only a peasant child of two in 1937 when he was located and carefully identified as the reincarnation of the thirteenth Dalai Lama. He was formally installed as the fourteenth Dalai Lama when he was only four and a half years old, thus becoming the spiritual and temporal ruler of Tibet. He was raised and rigorously educated in Lhasa in the Potala. One of the world's largest buildings, it then contained huge ceremonial halls, thirty-five chapels, meditation cells, the government storehouses, national treasures, all records of Tibetan history and culture in 7,000 huge volumes, plus 2,000 illuminated volumes of the Buddhist scriptures. He was educated according to the traditional system of Tibet, which stressed broadening and developing the mind to acquire many kinds of knowledge and also to study and practice advanced Buddhist teachings.

Such a rigorous grounding in religion, maintains the Dalai Lama, brings steadiness of mind in the face of any misfortunes. He says,

Humanitarianism and true love for all beings can only stem from an awareness of the content of religion. By whatever name religion may be known, its understanding and practice are the essence of a peaceful mind and therefore of a peaceful world. If there is no peace in one's mind, there can be no peace in one's approach to others, and thus no peaceful relations between individuals or between nations.[28]

The Dalai Lama's equanimity of mind must have been sorely challenged by the Chinese invasion and oppression of his small country. In 1959, when he escaped from Tibet to lessen the potential for bloodshed during a widespread popular revolt against the Chinese, Tibet was home to more than 6,000 monasteries. Only twelve of them were still intact by 1980. It is said that at least one million Tibetans have died as a direct result of the Chinese occupation, and the violence against the religion, the culture, and the people of Tibet continues today as Chinese settlers fill the country.

In the face of the overwhelming military power of the Chinese, and in any case armed with Buddhist precepts, the Dalai Lama has persistently tried to steer his people away from violent response to violence. Asserting that "Nonviolence is the only way. . . . It's a slower process sometimes, but a very effective one," he explains:

Practically speaking, through violence we may achieve something, but at the expense of someone else's welfare. That way, although we may solve one problem, we simultaneously seed a new problem. The best way to solve problems is through human understanding, mutual respect. On one side make some concessions; on the other side take serious consideration about the problem. There may not be complete satisfaction, but something happens. At least future danger is avoided. Non-violence is very safe.[29]

While slowly, patiently trying to influence world opinion so that the "weak" voice of Tibet will not be extinguished by Chinese might, the Dalai Lama has established an entire government in exile in Dharamsala, India, in the Himalayas. There he and Tibetan refugees have built schools, orphanages, hospitals, craft cooperatives, farming communities, monasteries, and groups preserving traditional music and drama. From this base, he travels tirelessly, and with a punishing schedule. In his effort to keep the voice of Tibet alive, he has also emerged as a great moral leader in the world. His quintessentially Buddhist message to people of all religions is that only through kindness and compassion toward each other and the cultivation of inner peace shall we all survive as a species.

experiential foundation, he became the first patriarch of the radical path that came to be called Ch'an Buddhism, from the Sanskrit *dhyana*, the yogic stage of meditation. Although this traditional account of its origins and founder is not fully accepted by scholars as absolute fact, it is known that this way was transmitted to Japan, where its name became **Zen**.

Zen claims to preserve the essence of the Buddha's teachings through direct experience, triggered by mind-to-mind transmission of the *dharma*. It dismissed scriptures, Buddhas, and Bodhisattvas in favor of training for direct intuition of cosmic unity, known as the **Buddha-nature** or the Void.

A central way of directly experiencing the underlying unity is *zazen* (sitting meditation). "To sit," said the Sixth Zen Patriarch, "means to obtain absolute freedom and not to allow any thought to be caused by external objects. To meditate means to realize the imperturbability of one's original nature."[30]

The Great Way is not difficult
for those who have no preferences.
When love and hate are both absent
everything becomes clear and undisguised.
Make the smallest distinction, however,
and heaven and earth are set infinitely apart.

Sengtsan[31]

Prescriptions for the manner of sitting are quite rigorous: one must take a specific upright posture and then not move during the meditation period, to avoid distracting the mind. Skillful means are then applied to make the mind one-pointed and clear. One beginning practice is simply to watch and count each inhalation and exhalation from one to ten, starting over from one if anything other than awareness of the breath enters the mind. Although this explanation sounds simple, the mind is so restless that many people must work for months before finally getting to ten without having to start over. Getting to ten is not really the goal; the goal is the process itself, the process of recognizing what comes up in the mind and gently letting it go without attachment or preferences.

As one sits in *zazen*, undisturbed by phenomena, as soon as one becomes inwardly calm, the natural mind is revealed in its original purity. This "original mind" is spacious and free, like an open sky. Thoughts and sensations may float through it like clouds, but they arise and then disappear, leaving no trace. What remains is reality, "True Thusness." In some Zen schools, this perception of thusness comes in a sudden burst of enlightenment, or **kensho**.

When the mind is calmed, action becomes spontaneous and natural. Zen practitioners are taught to have great confidence in their natural functioning, for it arises from our essential Buddha-nature. It is said that two Zen monks, on becoming enlightened, ran naked through the woods scribbling on rocks.

On the other hand, the Zen tradition links spontancity with intense, disciplined concentration. In the art of calligraphy, the perfect spontaneous brushstroke—executed with the whole body, in a single breath—is the outcome of years of attentive practice. Giving ourselves fully to the moment, to be aware only of pouring tea when pouring tea, is a simplicity of beingness that most of us have to learn. Then whatever we give ourself to fully, be it painting, or serving

Zen Oxherding Pictures

The ten Zen Oxherding Pictures metaphorically illustrate the stages along the spiritual path, with the meaning of each picture to be found through meditation. We are the herdsman (worldly self) who is searching for the elusive ox (our true nature) in the wilderness. In the second picture, the herdsman notices the footprints of the ox. In the third, he catches sight of the ox. In the fourth, he struggles mightily to grasp the ox. In the fifth, he tames the ox with tether and whip, until "well tended and domesticated, the ox grows pure and gentle."

In the sixth stage (illustrated upper right), the seeker has found and tamed the ox and leisurely returns home riding high upon it, playing tunes "full of infinite meaning." In the seventh, he reaches his home but the ox disappears.

In the eighth stage (below left), both ox and herdsman have disappeared—"Whip, tether, person, ox: ALL IS EMPTY! Blue sky, all and all around." In the ninth stage, Returning to the Source, "Inside his hut, he does not see any object outside." The final, tenth stage (below right), the enlightened one returns to the marketplace with helping hands and a wide grin on his face.[32]

Brush and ink drawings by Gyokusei Jikihara

Ceremonial tea in Japan, a ritual way of inculcating direct awareness, simplicity, and self-restraint.

tea, or simply breathing, reveals the "thusness of life," its unconditioned reality.

Another tool used in one Zen tradition is the **koan**. Here the attention is focused ardently on a question that boggles the mind, such as "What is the sound of one hand clapping?" or "What is your face before your parents' birth?" As Roshi (venerable teacher) Philip Kapleau observes, "*Koans* deliberately throw sand into the eyes of the intellect to force us to open our Mind's eye and see the world and everything in it undistorted by our concepts and judgments." To concentrate on a *koan*, one must look closely at it without thinking about it, experiencing it directly. Beyond abstractions, Roshi Kapleau explains, "The import of every *koan* is the same: that the world is one interdependent Whole and that each separate one of us is that Whole."[33]

The aim of Zen practice is enlightenment, or **satori**. One directly experiences the unity of all existence, often in a sudden recognition that nothing is separate from oneself. As one Zen master put it:

> *The moon's the same old moon,*
> *The flowers exactly as they were,*
> *Yet I've become the thingness*
> *Of all the things I see![34]*

All aspects of life become at the same time utterly precious, and utterly empty, "nothing special." This paradox can be sensed only with the mystically expanded consciousness; it cannot be grasped intellectually.

Pure Land: calling on Amida Buddha

Zen is essentially an inner awareness in which great attention is given to every action; it has little appeal for the laity. Other forms developed in India and the Far East have much greater popular appeal. One of the major trends is known as

Pure Land Buddhism. At times of great social upheaval (for instance, when the old Japanese feudal aristocracy was falling apart), it was widely thought that people had become so degenerate that it was nearly impossible for them to attain enlightenment through their own efforts. Instead, many turned to **Amida** Buddha, the Buddha of Boundless Light, to save them. Amida (first worshipped in India under the Sanskrit name Amitabha) was believed to have been an ancient prince who vowed to attain enlightenment. When he did, he used his virtue to prepare a special place of bliss, the Pure Land, for all those who called on his name.

Japan had an ancient tradition of worshipping mountains as the realm to which the dead ascend and from which deities descend to earth. The originally

Amida Buddha descends to welcome the faithful to the Western Paradise. Welcoming Descent of Amida Buddha, *Anon., 18th century.*

abstract Indian Buddhists' concept of the "Pure Land" far to the west to which devotees return after death was transformed in Japan into concrete images. They depicted Amida Buddha riding on clouds billowing over the mountains, coming to welcome his dying devotees.

Many people contributed to the growth of Pure Land Buddhism into a mass movement. In the tenth century, for example, a Japanese monk named Kuya encouraged others to join him as he danced through the streets with a bell about his neck, singing songs of devotion and chanting the name of Amida Buddha, "*Namu-amida-butsu.*" The influential thirteenth-century religious leader Shinran broke with monastic tradition by marrying, bringing greater emphasis on the principle that salvation comes only by repeating the name of Amida Buddha with sincere trust, not by any kind of good acts or separation from the life of society. "Self-power" is ineffectual; one must be empowered by the compassionate "other power." The Shin Buddhist path developed by Shinran's followers has become one of the major Buddhist movements throughout the world.

The results of loving trust in Amida Buddha were described very vividly by the monk Genshin. After graphic depictions of the eight hells, such as the burning vat in which people are cooked like beans, he describes the ineffable pleasures of being reborn into the Pure Land upon death:

> *Rings, bracelets, a crown of jewels, and other ornaments in countless profusion adorn his body. And when he looks upon the light radiating from the Buddha, he obtains pure vision, and because of his experiences in former lives, he hears the sounds of all things. And no matter what color he may see or what sound he may hear, it is a thing of marvel.*[35]

Many believers interpret these passages literally, anticipating that if they are sufficiently faithful they will enjoy a beautiful life after death. But some understand the Pure Land as a state that can be achieved in this life; a metaphor for the mystical experience of enlightenment, in which one's former identity "dies" and one is reborn into an expanded state of consciousness. According to this view, the lotus symbolizes the blooming of the pure lotus from the mire of ignorance and suffering, which the Buddha identified as the human condition.

In pragmatic China, Ch'an Buddhism—with its emphasis on personal effort and meditation—has often been combined with Pure Land Buddhism—with its devotional emphasis on salvation by Amida Buddha. Although reliance on "self-power" and reliance on "other power" seem contradictory, the combination of meditation and devotion is considered a practical way to single-minded concentration on the Buddha and thus to the Pure Land of enlightenment.

Nichiren: salvation through the Lotus Sutra

While some Pure Land Buddhists despair of purifying themselves by their own efforts and therefore humbly submit to the grace of Amida Buddha, a thirteenth-century Japanese fisherman's son, who named himself Nichiren, stressed the importance of striving to reform not only ourselves but also society. He blamed the political struggles of the time on false Buddhist paths, including the Pure Land focus on the next life rather than this one. For Nichiren, the highest truths of Buddhism were embodied in the Lotus Sutra, a large compilation of parables, verses, and descriptions of innumerable forms of beings who support the teachings of the World-Honored One, the Buddha. Nichiren gave particular attention to two of these beings: the Bodhisattva of Superb Action, who staunchly devotes himself to spreading the Perfect Truth, even in evil times, and the Bodhisattva Ever-Abused, who is persecuted because of his insistence on revering everyone with unshaken conviction that each person is potentially a Buddha. Nichiren himself was repeatedly abused by authorities but persisted in his efforts to reform Buddhism in Japan and then spread its purified essence, the Bodhisattva ideal, to the world.

The phrase chanted by Nichiren and his followers, *"Namu myoho rengekyo,"* refers to faith in the entire Lotus Sutra. Today it is chanted by Nichiren monks and nuns by the hour, slowly revealing its depths as it works inwardly, beyond thought. In our time, some in the Nichiren tradition undertake long peace walks, such as one sponsored by Nipponzan Myohoji in 1995. People walked from Auschwitz in Poland to Hiroshima and Nagasaki in Japan, to commemorate the fiftieth anniversary of the end of World War II with a plea for nonviolence and respect for all of life. They beat small hand drums while chanting *"Namu myoho rengekyo,"* and hope to contribute to world peace by truly bowing to the Buddha in each person, even if they encounter abuse. As the Most Venerable Nichidatsu Fujii, who passed away in 1985 at the age of one hundred and who influenced Gandhi's doctrine of nonviolence, has explained:

> *We do not believe that people are good because we see that they are good, but by believing that people are good we eliminate our own fear and thus we can intimately associate with them. To believe in the compassionate power of the Supreme Being which we cannot see is a discipline in order to believe in the invisible good in others.*[36]

Civilization has nothing to do with having electric lights, airplanes, or manufacturing atomic bombs. It has nothing to do with killing human beings, destroying things or waging war. Civilization is to hold one another in mutual affection and respect.[37]

The chanting of *"Namu myoho rengekyo"* has also caused seventy Peace Pagodas to arise thus far in Japan, England, Austria, India, and the United States, in fulfillment of the prophecy in the Lotus Sutra that wherever this "Scripture of the Lotus Blossom of the Fine Dharma" is preached, a beautiful stupa will spontaneously emerge as a physical reminder of the Buddha's "supernatural penetrations." These pagodas are built with donated materials and labor by people of all faiths who support the belief expressed by Nichidatsu Fujii, in hopes of world peace and the global elimination of all weapons.

Another new offshoot of Nichiren's movement is Soka Gakkai, based in Japan but having millions of members around the world. Its twentieth-century founders called for a peaceful world revolution through transformation of individual consciousness. The central practice is the chanting of Nichiren's phrase (which they transliterate as *"Nam myoho renge kyo"*) combined with modern social activism in areas such as humanitarian relief, environmental awareness, human rights, literacy, and cultural and interfaith exchanges. Members are encouraged to develop their "unlimited potential" for hope, courage, and altruism.

Yet another new branch of Buddhism inspired by the Lotus Sutra is Rissho

Kosei-kai, founded in the 1930s by Rev. Nikkyo Niwano and Myoko Naganuma to bring the message of the Lotus Sutra to the world in practical ways in order to encourage happiness and peace. Members meet to discuss ways of applying the Buddha's teachings to specific problems in their own lives. The organization, which is active in international inter-religious activities, asserts that "The Eternal Buddha, invisible but present everywhere, is the great life-force of the universe, which sustains each of us."[38]

> *The Bodhisattva loves all living beings as if each were his only child.*
> *Vimalakirtinirdesha Sutra 5*

Buddhism in the West

Images of the Buddha are now enshrined around the world, for what began in India has gradually spread to the West as well as the East. Much of this transmission occurred in the twentieth century, when the United States became a vibrant center of Buddhism. Scholars are studying Buddhist traditions at many universities, and many people are trying to learn Buddhist meditation practices.

A number of the highest Tibetan lamas, forced out of Tibet, have established spiritual communities in the United States, complete with altars full of sacred Tibetan artifacts. The majority of the five million Buddhists in the United States follow Tibetan Buddhism. Some have traveled to the Dalai Lama's community in exile in India to be personally given the complex *kalachakra* initiation by the Dalai Lama. Many Americans who have adopted Tibetan Buddhism have become its voice in the West, helping with translation work and establishing flourishing publishing houses. Hence in the last two decades, many books have appeared in English on Tibetan Buddhist traditions.

Intensive *vipassana* retreats of up to three months are carried out in centers such as the Insight Meditation Society in rural Barre, Massachusetts. Theravadin teachers from Southeast Asia and Europe make frequent appearances to conduct retreats, and American teachers undertake rigorous training in Southeast Asia under traditional meditation masters. In addition to numerous Zen centers, where Westerners who have undergone training in the East serve as teachers to lay practitioners of meditation, there are a number of Zen monasteries giving solid training in *zazen* and offering a monastic lifestyle as a permanent or temporary alternative to life in the world.

Many Buddhist centers in the United States are led by women, in contrast to the cultural suppression of females in the East. Leading women in American Buddhism have deeply imbibed traditional Buddhist teachings and are explaining them to Westerners in fresh, contemporary ways.

The American monk Venerable Sumedho, classically trained in Theravada Buddhism in Thailand, has established monastic forest communities and meditation centers in England, Switzerland, Italy, and the United States.

The Vietnamese monk Venerable Master Thich Nhat Hanh now lives in exile in France, where he conducts retreats for both women and men in his Plum

Village community. When he travels internationally, large audiences gather to be inspired by his teachings. He speaks simply, using homely examples, and emphasizes bringing the awareness fostered by meditation into everyday life, rather than making spirituality a separate compartment of one's life. He says:

> When we walk in the meditation hall, we make careful steps, very slowly. But when we go to the airport, we are quite another person. We walk very differently, less mindfully. How can we practice at the airport and in the market? That is engaged Buddhism.[39]

Buddhism has often been embraced by Westerners because of their longing for the peace of meditation. In the midst of a chaotic materialistic life, there is a desire to discover emptiness, to let the identity with self fall away, or to become familiar with the mind's tricks in the still simplicity of a *zendo*, a Zen meditation hall. Many psychotherapists are studying Buddhism for its insights into the mind and human suffering. Richard Clarke, who is both a Zen teacher and a psychotherapist, feels that a discipline such as Zen should be part of the training of therapists:

> Emptiness is . . . the source of infinite compassion in working with people: to really feel a person without any agenda, to be spacious to that person, to will that they be the way they are. When a person experiences that in someone's presence, then they can drop away those things that they've invented to present themselves with. Those faces, those armors, those forms of the self become unnecessary.[40]

A meditation teacher at the Buddhist Dharma School in Brighton, England, with her young students.

RELIGION IN PRACTICE

Life in a Western Zen Monastery

Side-by-side in still rows, with birdsong and sunlight streaming in through the tall windows, sit the monks and laypeople of Zen Mountain Monastery. For thirty-five minute blocks, separated by periods of attentive walking, they support each other by practicing *zazen* together in silence. With this group structure, many find it easier to carry on the rigorous discipline of serious Zen training than they would by themselves.

This particular monastery, located in the Catskill Mountains near Mount Tremper, New York, reflects the changing face of religion in the United States. A hundred years ago the main building was handcrafted of stone as a Benedictine monastery; later it became a Lutheran summer camp. Now

back-to-back with the Christ on the cross on the outside of the building is a statue of Buddha on the altar in the *zendo*. The monastery houses eleven fully ordained monastics (six of them women) who have taken lifetime vows of service, several novices and postulants in training (an aspect adopted from Western monasticism), lay residents who stay for up to a year, and groups of people who come for special retreats and classes. Increasingly these are professionals and family people from the mainstream culture, rather than the hippies who embraced Buddhism in the 1960s and 1970s. They do not come for a comfortable vacation, for *zazen* is hard work and the teachers are dedicated to creating snags that help people discover the places where they are not free. They are expected to practice intensely and then leave, carrying what they have learned back into the world. As the monk Shugen observes, "If Zen doesn't work in the world, it's not working."

In addition to long sessions of silent sitting and walking, *dharma* talks by the resident Zen master John Daido Loori Sensei (an American ordained in both authentic Zen lineages), and private coaching by the monks, monastery residents participate in structured nontheistic liturgical services designed to foster attentiveness and appreciation. They chant in Japanese and English, with frequent bowing to each other, to their meditation cushions, and to the Buddha on the altar in identification

John Daido Loori Sensei, abbot of Zen Mountain Monastery.

The stillness of the zendo *at Zen Mountain Monastery.*

Oriyoki, *a ceremonial meal, at Zen Mountain Monastery.*

with all beings and gratitude for the teachings. Zen master Daido notes that liturgy reflects the innards of a religion: "In Catholicism, cathedrals are awe-inspiring, the chants expansive; in Zen the form is simple and the chanting is grounded, not other-worldly."

The rest of the day is devoted to caretaking of the buildings and 200-acre (81-hectare) nature sanctuary, mindful practice done in silence, and work practice. Those with office jobs combine ancient and modern arts: they sit cross-legged on low cushions before their computers and use calligraphic skills to hand-letter signs. Meals are simple and include coarse breads donated by a nearby whole-grain bakery. Every action—even brushing one's teeth—is treated as liturgy, in the sense of bringing total attentiveness to the sacredness of even the most "mundane" activity as a teaching that enlightenment takes place in one's everyday experience.

Following the lead of their teacher Daido, who is at once highly disciplined in the pure mind-to-mind *dharma* transmission and very down-to-earth, approachable, compassionate, and married, monastery residents are human, playful, and loving. The women monks shave their heads when ordained and keep it very short thereafter, but for them near-baldness feels like freedom rather than self-sacrificing asceticism. The monk Myotai observes:

I could feel every breeze, and being bald definitely altered the way I saw the habit patterns I brought to my interactions with other people, clarifying how much "extra" was still there, to a degree that surprised me. There is a several-year entry period before ordination, to get clear on what it means, but one aspect of actually having no hair was that it really opened up the male–female dynamic. I no longer felt myself relating to men as a woman. That was very freeing. It was also wonderful to have this daily reminder of what I was doing with my life.

Despite the values of Buddhist principles and practices, are Westerners able to achieve enlightenment by taking Buddhist workshops here and there? Particularly in the case of Tibetan Buddhist practices, Westerners often want to be initiated into the highly advanced teachings without years of patiently practicing and being inwardly transformed by the step-by-step foundational teachings. A further question is whether teachings developed within a specific cultural context can be directly transplanted into the soil of an entirely different culture. Most Westerners who are adopting Buddhist practices are living in highly materialistic rather than monastic settings. And in their impatience to get results, many keep shopping around from one teacher to the next rather than persisting over a long time in one path. As Alan Wallace remarks,

> *In Tibetan society, fickleness is considered to be one of the worst of vices, while reliability, integrity, trustworthiness, and perseverance are held in high regard. So a few of the finest lamas are now refusing even to come to the West. Some are feeling—given the brevity and preciousness of human life—that devoting time to people with such fickleness and so little faith is time not very well spent.[41]*

The growing interest in Buddhism in the West is helping to revitalize Buddhism in Asia. As Asia entered the modern world, many of its peoples lost interest in their traditional religions, which became superficial re-enactments of ceremonial practices. But as Westerners themselves are taking strong interest in Buddhism, those who have grown up as Buddhists are reassessing their religion and finding new depths in it. There are now many laypeople interested in studying meditation, and their teachers include women who conduct special meditation retreats.

Buddhist women from West and East have joined hands to hold international gatherings to enhance the role of women in Buddhism. The international Association of Buddhist Women, Sakyadhita or "Daughters of the Buddha," established in Bodh Gaya in 1987, continues to work to improve conditions for women's Buddhist practice and education, full ordination of women, and training of women as teachers of Buddhism.

Socially engaged Buddhism

An emerging focus in contemporary Buddhist practice is the relevance of Buddhism to social problems. Contrary to popular assumptions, the Buddha did not advise people to permanently leave society to seek their own enlightenment. Sri Lankan Buddhist monk Walpola Rahula explains:

> *It may perhaps be useful in some cases for a person to live in retirement for a time in order to improve his or her mind and character, as preliminary moral, spiritual, and intellectual training, to be strong enough to come out later and help others. But if someone lives an entire life in solitude, thinking only of their own happiness and salvation, without caring for their fellow beings, this surely is not in keeping with the Buddha's teaching which is based on love, compassion, and service to others.[42]*

The Buddha's teachings on retraining and purifying the mind are far better known than his social commentaries, but he did make many pronouncements about the ways in which social suffering is to be corrected. No holy wars have been conducted in his name, for he preached nonviolence:

> *Hatred is never appeased by hatred. It is appeased by love. This is an eternal law. Just as a mother would protect her only child, even at the risk of her own life, even so let one cultivate a boundless heart towards all beings. Let one's thoughts of boundless love pervade the whole world.*[43]

Buddhists have therefore often been nonviolent social activists, protesting and trying to correct injustice, oppression, famine, cruelty to animals, nuclear testing, warfare, and environmental devastation. E. F. Schumacher preached what he called "Buddhist economics," to restore willingness to live simply, generously, and humanely with each other. Ajahn Pongsak, a Thai Buddhist monk, was so troubled by the devastation of the northern Thai forests that he rallied 5,000 villagers to reforest an area by building a tree nursery, terracing the eroded hillsides, planting nearly 200,000 seedlings, digging reservoirs and canals, laying irrigation pipes, and fencing the area to protect the new trees. He taught them the importance of a respectful relationship with the forest as their own home, their own parent. He says:

> *A mind that feels no gratitude to the forest is a coarse mind indeed—without this basic* siladhamma, *how can a mind attain enlightenment? . . . The times are dark*

Nipponzan Myohoji monks in the Peace Park, Hiroshima, Japan.

and siladhamma *is asleep, so it is now the duty of monks to reawaken and bring back* siladhamma. *Only in this way can society be saved.* Siladhamma *does not simply mean "morality" as commonly supposed. You may obey all the* silas *(commandments) in the book, it still doesn't mean that you have* siladhamma, *which in truth means "harmony," the correct balance of nature. From this comes true morality, the natural result of natural harmony. . . . Sanctity and holiness have their basis in purity of spirit. This purity still exists in the great mass of the people, especially in rural areas and may be reawakened for this purpose.*[44]

Venerable Maha Ghosananda of Kampuchea has led numerous long marches to promote peace in his country. Even though the country is now beginning to heal after thirty years of war, the walks continue, carrying a message of the necessity of developing inward peace through meditation and "learning and listening with mind and heart." Monks, nuns, and laypeople walk through still-dangerous areas that are heavily landmined, facing issues such as domestic violence, AIDS, deforestation, and dire poverty. Maha Ghosananda explains,

We must find the courage to leave our temples and enter the temples of human experience, temples that are filled with suffering. If we listen to the Buddha, Christ, or Gandhi, we can do nothing else. The refugee camps, the prisons, the ghettos and the battlefields will then become our temples. We have so much work to do.[45]

Buddhism was returned to its native India after some one thousand years' absence by the bold action of a converted Buddhist activist, Dr. B. R. Ambedkar (1891–1956). Born an untouchable Hindu, he was the chief architect of India's new democratic constitution, and built into it many provisions designed to end the oppression of the traditional Hindu caste system. In his personal search for a religion offering freedom and dignity to all human beings, he chose Buddhism. And when he publicly converted shortly before his death, he carried with him almost half a million untouchables. Despite this mass conversion, he openly questioned and changed certain Buddhist teachings. Among them were the Second Noble Truth that suffering results from desires and ignorance. He felt that such a concept may prevent recognition that some people are victims of oppression rather than their own faults, and thus may prevent action to end social injustices. Another traditional Buddhist ideal he challenged was the emphasis on renunciation and meditation rather than active social engagement, helping the people. His slogan was "Educate, Agitate, and Organize."

In Sri Lanka, a Buddhist schoolteacher started the Sarvodaya Shramadana Sangamaya movement, which has now spread to 5,000 villages. It engages people in working together to eliminate social decadence and poverty, through developing schools, nutrition programs, roads, and irrigation canals, and propagating the Four Noble Truths and the Eightfold Path. Sri Lanka's seventy percent Buddhist majority is now engaged in ethnic war with its Hindu minority. Old ethnic tensions have become politicized, turning this former paradise into a battlefield. But in the midst of the violence, the Buddhist monks of the Sarvodaya movement continue to work with Hindus and Christians as well as Buddhists, attempting to promote harmony and rural development. The founder, Dr. A. T. Ariyaratne, encourages people to look at their own egotism, distrust, greed, and competitiveness and to recognize that these are the cause of their suffering and inability to work together for progress.

Sulak Sivaraksa, founder of the International Network of Engaged Buddhists, explains that socially engaged Buddhism does not mean promoting Buddhism per se:

> *The presence of Buddhism in society does not mean having a lot of schools, hospitals, cultural institutions, or political parties run by Buddhists. It means that the schools, hospitals, cultural institutions, and political parties are permeated with and administered with humanism, love, tolerance, and enlightenment, characteristics which Buddhism attributes to an opening up, development, and formation of human nature. This is the true spirit of nonviolence.[46]*

Not to respond to the suffering around us is a sign of an insane civilization. Buddhism is thus as relevant today, and its insights as necessary, as in the sixth century, when Siddhartha Gautama renounced the life of a prince to save all sentient beings from suffering.

Suggested reading

Batchelor, Martine, *Walking on Lotus Flowers: Buddhist Women Living, Loving, and Meditating,* San Francisco: Thorsons/Harper Collins, 1996. Interesting personal accounts by a great variety of women who are nuns or lay practitioners.

Batchelor, Martine and Kerry Brown, eds., *Buddhism and Ecology*, World Wide Fund for Nature, 1992. Buddhist teachings, stories, and activities from various countries, illustrating the sympathetic relationship between Buddhism and nature.

Conze, Edward, Horner, I. B., Snellgrove, David, and Waley, Arthur, ed. and trans., *Buddhist Texts through the Ages*, Oxford, England: Oneworld Publications, 1995. A fine collection of Buddhist scriptures translated from the Pali, Sanskrit, Chinese, Tibetan, and Japanese.

Dalai Lama, His Holiness the, *A Policy of Kindness*, Ithaca, New York: Snow Lion Publications, 1993. Intimate articles by and about the world's most famous Buddhist leader.

Dalai Lama, His Holiness the, *My Land and My People,* New York: McGraw-Hill, 1962. Fascinating and compassionate autobiography of His Holiness the Dalai Lama, from his early experiences and training as the chosen child in Tibet to his exile.

Dresser, Marianne, ed., *Buddhist Women on the Edge: Contemporary Perspectives from the Western Frontier,* Berkeley, California: North Atlantic Books, 1996. Voices of American women who teach or practice Buddhism in America, exploring the issues involved therein.

Eppsteiner, Fred, ed., *The Path of Compassion: Writings on Socially Engaged Buddhism*, Berkeley, California: Parallax Press, 1988. A highly readable and relevant collection of essays by leading contemporary Buddhist teachers about the ways in which Buddhism can be applied to social problems.

Fremantle, Francesca, and Trungpa, Chogyam, trans., *The Tibetan Book of the Dead*, Boston and London: Shambhala Publications, 1975. The classic Tibetan Buddhist scripture on the projections of the mind and the practices of deity yoga to attain enlightenment.

Friedman, Lenore, *Meetings with Remarkable Women: Buddhist Teachers in America*, Boston and London: Shambhala Publications, 1987. Wisdom from Buddhist traditions shared in very personal, perceptive interviews.

Gross, Rita M., *Buddhism after Patriarchy*, Albany, New York: State University of New York Press, 1993. A feminist reconstruction of Buddhist history, revealing its core of gender equality but later overlays of sexism, plus analysis of key Buddhist concepts from a feminist point of view.

Hanh, Thich Nhat, *Being Peace,* New Delhi: Full Circle Books, 1997. Simply expressed wisdom arising from Buddhist practice.

Hanh, Thich Nhat, *The Heart of the Buddha's Teaching: Transforming Suffering into Peace, Joy, and Liberation*, New York: Broadway Books, 1998. In simple, compassionate language, the famous Vietnamese monk explains the efficacy of Buddhist teachings for dealing with today's problems.

Lal, P., trans., *The Dhammapada*, New York: Farrar, Straus & Giroux, 1967. A basic book attributed to the Buddha that covers the essentials of *dharma* in memorable, pithy verses.

Levine, Stephen, *A Gradual Awakening*, Garden City, New York: Doubleday, 1979 and London: Rider & Company, 1980. Gentle, poetic presentation of *vipassana* techniques in their relevance to contemporary life.

Lopez, Donald S., Jr., ed., *Buddhism in Practice*, Princeton: Princeton University Press, 1995. Annotated translation of original sources dealing with Buddhist practice around the world, organized around the Triple Jewels of Buddha, *dharma*, and *sangha*.

Queen, Christopher S. and King, Sallie B., eds., *Engaged Buddhism: Buddhist Liberation Movements in Asia*, Albany: State University of New York Press, 1996. A thorough survey of contemporary Buddhist activism in Asian countries.

Rahula, Walpola Sri, *What the Buddha Taught*, New York: Grove Press, 1974. The classic introduction to Buddhist teachings—an accurate and clear guide through the complexities of Buddhist thought and practice, with representative texts.

Reynolds, Frank E. and Jason A. Carbine, eds., *The Life of Buddhism*, Berkeley: University of California Press, 2000. Attempts to analyze Buddhist ways in their cultural and historical contexts.

Sivaraksa, Sulak, *Seeds of Peace: A Buddhist Vision for Renewing Society*, Berkeley, California: Parallax Press, 1992. A renowned Thai social activist examines the "politics of greed" and issues involved in transformation of society, from the point of view of Buddhist ideals.

Suzuki, Shunryu, *Zen Mind, Beginner's Mind*, New York and Tokyo: Weatherhill, 1970. A beautiful book, leading one gracefully and seemingly simply through the paradoxes of Zen.

Tulku, Tarthang, *Openness Mind,* Berkeley, California: Dharma Publishing, 1978.
A Tibetan lama teaches skillful means of understanding and controlling the mind.

Willis, Janice D., *Feminine Ground: Essays on Women and Tibet,* second edition, Ithaca,
New York: Snow Lion Publications, 1995. Essays by Western women scholars exploring
issues of women and the feminine in Tibetan Buddhism.

Wu Yin, Venerable Bhikshuni, *Choosing Simplicity,* trans. Bhikshuni Jendy Shih, Ithaca,
New York: Snow Lion Publications, 2001. Practical explanation of precepts for monastic
life by a Taiwanese nun.

CHAPTER 5

SIKHISM

"By the Guru's grace shalt thou worship Him"

Another great teacher made his appearance in northern India in the fifteenth century CE: Guru Nanak. His followers were called Sikhs, meaning "disciples, students, seekers of truth." In time, he was succeeded by a further nine enlightened Gurus, ending with Guru Gobind Singh (1666–1708). Despite the power of these Gurus, the spiritual essence of Sikhism is little known outside India and its **diaspora** (dispersed communities), even though Sikhism is the fifth largest of all world religions. Many Sikhs understand their path not as another sectarian religion but as a statement of the universal truth within, and transcending, all religions. Their beliefs have been interpreted as a synthesis of the Hindu and Muslim traditions of northern India, but Sikhism has its own unique quality, independent revelation, and history. As awareness of Sikh spirituality spreads, Sikhism is becoming a global religion, although it does not actively seek converts. Instead, it emphasizes the universality of spirituality and the relevance of spirituality in everyday life.

The *sant* tradition

Before Guru Nanak, Hinduism and Islam had already begun to draw closer to one another in northern India. One of the foremost philosophers in this trend was the Hindu saint Ramananda, who held theological arguments with teachers from both religions. But a deeper marriage occurred in the hearts of **sants**, or "holy people," particularly Sufi mystics, such as Shaikh Farid, and Hindu *bhaktas*, such as Sri Caitanya. They shared a common cause in emphasizing devotion to the Beloved above all else.

The most famous of the bridges between Hindu and Muslim is the fifteenth-century weaver Kabir (1440–1518). He was the son of Muslim parents and the disciple of the Hindu guru Ramananda. Rather than taking the ascetic path, he remained at work at his loom, composing songs about union with the divine that are at once earthly and sublime. He could easily transcend theological differences between religions, for he was opposed to outward forms, preferring ecstatic personal intimacy with God. Speaking for the One, he wrote:

O servant, where dost thou seek Me?
Lo! I am beside thee.

I am neither in temple nor in mosque:
  I am neither in Kaaba nor in Kailash:
Neither am I in rites and ceremonies; nor in yoga and renunciation.
If thou art a true seeker, thou shalt at once see Me: thou shalt meet Me in a moment
  of time.
Kabir says, "O Sadhu! God is the breath of all breath."[1]

Guru Nanak

When Guru Nanak (1469–c. 1539) was born, the area of northern India called
the Punjab was half-Muslim, half-Hindu, and ruled by a weak Afghan dynasty.
For centuries, the Punjab had been the lane through which outer powers had
fought their way into India. In 1398, the Mongolian leader Tamerlane had
slaughtered and sacked Punjabis on his way both to and from Delhi. Toward the
end of Nanak's life, it was the Mogul emperor Babur who invaded and claimed
the Punjab. This casting of the Punjab as a perpetual battleground later became a
crucial aspect of Sikhism.

Nanak was reportedly little concerned with worldly things. As a child he was
of a contemplative nature, resisting the formalities of his Hindu religion. Even
after he was married, it is said that he roamed about in nature rather than working and gave away any money he had to the poor. At length he took a job as an
accountant, but his heart was not in material gain.

When Nanak was thirty, his life was transformed after immersion in a river,
from which it is said he did not emerge for three days. Some people now think
he was meditating on the opposite side, but at the time he could not be found
until he suddenly appeared in town, radiant. According to one account, he had
been taken into the presence of God, who gave him a bowl of milk to drink,
saying that it was actually nectar (*amrit*) which would give him "power of prayer,
love of worship, truth and contentment."[2] The Almighty charged him to go back
into the tainted world to redeem it from Kali Yuga (the darkest of ages). Later
Nanak sang:

Me, the worthless bard, the Lord has blest with Service.
Be it night or day, many a time He gives His call,
And calls me verily into His presence.
And there I praise Him and receive the robe,
And the Nectar-Name [of God] becomes my everlasting food.[3]

After his disappearance in the river in 1499, Nanak began traveling through
India, the Himalayas, Afghanistan, Sri Lanka, and Arabia, teaching in his own
surprising way. When people asked him whether he would follow the Hindu or
Muslim path, he replied, "There is neither Hindu nor Mussulman [Muslim], so
whose path shall I follow? I shall follow God's path. God is neither Hindu nor
Mussulman."[4] Nanak mocked the Hindu tradition of throwing sacred river water
east toward the rising sun in worship of their ancestors—he threw water to the
west. If Hindus could throw water far enough to reach their ancestors thousands
of miles away in heaven, he explained, he could certainly water his parched land
several hundred miles distant in Lahore by throwing water in its direction.

Another tradition has it that he set his feet toward the Ka'bah when sleeping as a pilgrim in Mecca. Questioned about this rude conduct, he is said to have remarked, "Then kindly turn my feet toward some direction where God is not."

Again and again, Guru Nanak emphasized three central teachings as the straight path to God: working hard in society to earn one's own honest living (rather than withdrawing into asceticism and begging); sharing from one's earnings with those who are needy; and remembering God at all times as the only Doer, the only Giver. To a society that stressed distinctions of caste, class, gender, and religions, Guru Nanak introduced and practiced the idea of a new social order

Guru Nanak holding spiritual dialogue with Hindu ascetics. (Illustration from Biography of Guru Nanak *by Kartar Singh.)*

based on equality, justice, and service to all, in devotion to the One God whom Guru Nanak perceived as formless, pervading everywhere.

Nanak's commitment to practical faith, as opposed to external adherence to religious formalities, won him followers from both Hinduism and Islam. Before he died, they argued over who would dispose of his body. He reportedly told Muslims to place flowers on one side of his body, Hindus on the other; the side whose flowers remained fresh the next day could bury him. The next day they raised the sheet that had covered his body and reportedly found nothing beneath it; all the flowers were still fresh, leaving only the fragrance of his being.

> *Oh my mind, love God as a fish loves water:*
> *The more the water, the happier is the fish,*
> *the more peaceful his mind and body.*
> *He cannot live without water even for a moment.*
> *God knows the inner pain of that being without water.*
>
> *Guru Nanak*[5]

The succession of Gurus

There were eventually a total of ten Sikh Gurus. Before Nanak's death, he appointed a spiritual successor, his devoted disciple Angad Dev (1504–1552). This Second Guru strengthened the new Sikh tradition and developed a script for setting down its memorized teachings, which had been given orally in the common language. He emphasized by his own example the central Sikh virtues of humility and service. The Third and Fourth Gurus, Amar Das and Ram Das, developed organizational structures for the growing Sikh **Panth** (community) while also setting personal examples of humility. Ram Das founded the holy city of Amritsar, within which the Fifth Guru, Guru Arjun Dev (1536–1606), built the religion's most sacred shrine, the Golden Temple. The Fifth Guru also compiled the sacred scriptures of the Sikhs, the Adi Granth (original holy book, now known as the **Guru Granth Sahib**), from devotional hymns composed by Guru Nanak, the other Gurus, and Hindu and Muslim saints, including Kabir and many spiritual figures from low social castes. Among the latter are figures like Bhakta Ravi Das, a low-caste Hindu shoemaker who nonetheless achieved the heights of spiritual realization. His powerful poetry incorporated into the Guru Granth Sahib includes this song:

> *When I was, You were not.*
> *When You are, I am not.*
> *As huge waves are raised in the wind in the vast ocean,*
> *But are only water in water,*
> *O Lord of Wealth, what should I say about this delusion?*
> *What we deem a thing to be,*
> *It is not, in reality.*
> *It is like a king falling asleep on his throne*
> *And dreaming that he is a beggar.*

His kingdom is intact,
But separating from it, he suffers. . . .
Says Ravi Das, the Lord is nearer to us than our hands and feet.[6]

When a copy of the Adi Granth was sent to Emperor Akbar on his demand, he was so pleased with its universalism that he offered a gift of gold to the book. But apparently because of suspicions that the Fifth Guru, Arjun Dev, supported a rival successor to Akbar's throne, the Guru was tortured and executed by Akbar's son and successor, Jehangir, in 1606. It is said that the Guru Arjun Dev remained calmly meditating on God as he was tortured by heat, with his love and faith undismayed. His devotional hymns include words such as these:

Merciful, merciful is the Lord.
Merciful is my master.
He blesses all beings with His bounties.
Why waverest thou, Oh mortal? The Creator Himself shall protect you.
He who has created you takes care of you. . . .
Oh mortal, meditate on the Lord as long as there is breath in your body.[7]

From that point on, Sikhism took measures to protect itself and to defend the weak of all religions against tyranny. The Sixth Guru, Hargobind (1595–1644), established a Sikh army, carried two swords (one symbolizing temporal power, the other, spiritual power), and taught the people to defend their religion. The tender-hearted Seventh Guru, Har Rai (1630–1661), a pacifist who never used his troops against the Moguls, taught his Sikhs not only to feed anyone who came to their door, but moreover to:

do service in such a way that the poor guest may not feel he is partaking of some charity but as if he had come to the Guru's house which belonged to all in equal measure. He who has more should consider it as God's trust and share it in the same spirit. Man is only an instrument of service: the giver of goods is God, the Guru of us all.[8]

The Eighth Guru, Har Krishan (1656–1664), became successor to Guru Nanak's seat when he was only five years old and died at the age of eight. When taunted by Hindu *pandits* (learned men) the "Child Guru" reportedly touched a lowly deaf and dumb Sikh watercarrier with his cane, whereupon the watercarrier expounded brilliantly on the subtleties of the Hindu scripture, *Bhagavad-Gita*.

The ninth master, Guru Teg Bahadur (c. 1621–1675), was martyred. According to Sikh tradition, he was approached by Hindu *pandits* who were facing forced conversion to Islam by the Mogul emperor, Aurangzeb. The emperor viewed Hinduism as a totally corrupt, idolatrous religion, which did not lead people to God; he had ordered the destruction of Hindu temples and the mass conversion of Hindus throughout the land, beginning in the north with Kashmir. Reportedly, one of the Kashmiri *pandits* dreamed that only the Ninth Guru, the savior in Kali Yuga, could save the Hindus. With the firm approval of his young son, Guru Teg Bahadur told the Hindu *pandits* to inform their oppressors that they would convert to Islam if the Sikh Guru could be persuaded to do so. Imprisoned and forced to witness the torture and murder of his aides, the Ninth Guru staunchly maintained the right of all people to religious freedom. Aurangzeb beheaded him

TEACHING STORY

Guru Arjun Dev's Devotion

Throughout his life, Guru Arjun Dev, the Fifth Sikh Guru, responded with calm faith in God to jealous plots against him. His martyrdom by torture was the ultimate demonstration of his devotion.

The Mogul emperor Jehangir claimed that the Adi Granth—the sacred scripture that Guru Arjun Dev had compiled—was negative toward Hindus and Muslims, even though both were becoming followers of the gentle Guru. Jehangir ordered that all references to Hinduism and Islam be deleted from the holy book and that the Guru be fined 200,000 rupees. The Guru reportedly replied that the hymns of the Sikh Gurus and Muslim and Hindu saints were inspired praises of God and that no one could change them. Furthermore, monies were not his own property but rather belonged to the Sikh community, to be used for the welfare of those in need. Even though his Sikhs started collecting money to pay the fine, the Guru stopped them, saying that he had not done anything wrong and that compromising with wrong is irreligious.

Ostensibly for his refusal to follow the emperor's orders—but more likely to end his popular influence—the Guru was subjected to torture by heat, during the already terrible heat of summer. He was made to sit on a hot iron sheet.

Hot sand was dumped onto his body and he was placed into boiling water.

As these tortures were being inflicted, Mian Mir, an established saint of Islam who reportedly laid the foundation stone of the Holy Temple at Amritsar, pleaded with the Guru to let him use his mystical power against the persecutors. Guru Arjun Dev refused, telling Mian Mir to patiently accept the reality that everything is under God's control; every leaf that moves does so by God's will.

The daughter-in-law of Chandu, the rich man of Lahore who had turned the emperor against the Guru, tried to offer sherbet to the Guru to ease his agony. But just as he had refused attempts to wed his son to Chandu's daughter, saying that a rich man's daughter would not be happy in the home of a dervish, he refused her food, saying that he would accept nothing. Nonetheless, he blessed her for her devotion.

Through five days of torture, Guru Arjun Dev persisted in calm faith in God. His torturers then forced him to bathe in the river alongside the Mogul fort. His followers wept to see the blisters covering his body. As he walked on blistered feet, he repeated again and again, "Your will is sweet, Oh God; I only seek the gift of Your Name." Calmly, he walked into the water and breathed his last.

before a crowd of thousands. But as his son later wrote, "He has given his head, but not his determination."[9]

The martyred Ninth Guru was succeeded by his young son, who became the tenth master, Guru Gobind Singh (1666–1708). It was he who turned the intimidated Sikhs into saint-warriors for truth.

In 1699 he reportedly told a specially convened assembly of Sikhs that the times were so dangerous that he had developed a new plan to give the community strength and unity. Total surrender to the master would be necessary, he said, asking for volunteers who would offer their heads for the cause of protecting religious ideals. One at a time, five stepped forward. Each was escorted into the Guru's tent, from which the Tenth Guru emerged alone with a bloody sword. After this scene was repeated five times, the Guru brought all the men out of the tent, alive. Some say the blood was that of a goat, in a test of the people's loyalty; others say that Guru Gobind Singh had actually killed the men and then resurrected them. At any rate, their willingness to serve and bravely to sacrifice themselves was dramatically proven, and the Five Beloved Ones became models for Sikhs. It is noteworthy that those who became the Five Beloved Ones all came from the lowest classes.

Guru Gobind Singh instituted a special initiation rite using **amrit**: water, which was stirred with a double-edged sword to turn his followers into heroes and mixed with sugar symbolizing that they would also be compassionate. After initiating the Five Beloved Ones, he established a unique Guru–Sikh relationship by asking that they initiate him—thus underscoring the principle of equality among all Sikhs. The initiated men were given the surname *Singh* ("lion"); the women were all given the name *Kaur* ("princess") and treated as equals. Together, they formed the **Khalsa** (Pure Ones), a community pledged to a special code of personal discipline. They were sworn to wear five distinctive symbols of their dedication: long unshorn hair bound under a turban or a veil, a comb to keep it tidy, a steel bracelet as a personal reminder that one is a servant of God, short underbreeches for modesty, and a sword for dignity and the willingness to fight for justice and protection of the weak.

Guru Gobind Singh writing Jaap Sahib, *a hymn praising the attributes of God, "without form, beyond religion." (Painting by Mehar Singh.)*

These "5 Ks" (so called because all the words begin with a "K" in Punjabi) clearly distinguished Sikhs from Muslims and Hindus, supporting the assertion that they constituted a third path with its own right to spiritual sovereignty. All of these innovations were designed to turn the meek into warriors capable of shaking off Mogul oppression and protecting freedom of religion; the distinctive dress made it impossible for the Khalsa to hide from their duty by blending with the general populace. In Sikh history, their bravery was proven again and again. For example, it is reported that the Tenth Guru's own teenage sons were killed as they single-handedly engaged several thousand Mogul soldiers in battle.

In addition to transforming the Sikh faithful into a courageous, unified community, Guru Gobind Singh ended the line of bodily succession to Guruship. As he was dying in 1708, he transferred his authority to the Adi Granth rather than to a human successor. Thenceforth, it was called the Guru Granth Sahib—the living presence of the Guru embodied in the sacred scripture, to be consulted by the congregation for spiritual guidance and decision-making.

As the Mogul Empire began to disintegrate and Afghans invaded India, the Sikhs fought for their own identity and sovereignty. At the end of the eighteenth century and beginning of the nineteenth century under Maharaja Ranjit Singh, they formed the Sikh Empire, a non-sectarian government noted for its generous tolerance toward Muslims, despite the earlier history of oppression by the Muslim rulers. Maharaja Ranjit Singh is said to have been unusually kind to his subjects and to have humbly accepted chastisement by the Sikh religious authorities for his rather immoral private life. The Sikh Empire attempted to create a pluralistic society, with social equality and full freedom of religion. It also blocked the Khyber Pass against invaders. The empire lasted only half a century, for the British subdued it in 1849.

Resistance to oppression became a hallmark of Sikhism, for the times were grim for India's people. Despite heavy losses, Guru Gobind Singh's outnumbered Sikhs began the protection of the country from foreign rule, a process that continued into the twentieth century. During the Indian struggle against British rule, despite their military abilities Sikhs set heroic examples of nonviolent resistance to oppression. One famous story concerns Guru ka Bagh, a garden and shrine that had been used by Sikhs for cutting wood for the community free kitchen. After tearing up that agreement, the British police began arresting and then beating and even killing Sikhs who went to the garden to collect firewood. Every day a new wave of one hundred Sikhs would come voluntarily to suffer fierce beatings and perhaps even be killed, without a murmur except for the Name of God on their lips, to resist injustice.

At one point, Sikh political prisoners arrested at Guru ka Bagh were being shifted by train. The Sikh community in Hasanavdal asked the stationmaster there to stop the train so they could offer food to the prisoners. He refused, saying that it was a special train and would not stop at Hasanavdal. Determined to care for the prisoners, three leading Sikhs told the **sangat** (congregation) to bring food and then courageously lay down on the tracks to force the train to stop. It ran over them, crushing their bodies, and then stopped. As the *sangat* tried to help the dying martyrs, one of them ordered, "Don't care for us. Feed the prisoners." Thus the **langar** (communal meal) was served to the prisoners on the train, and the Sikhs who had laid their bodies on the track died.

High praise for Guru Gobind Singh's military effect has been offered by Dr. S. Radhakrishnan, the respected second President of India:

> *For one thousand years, after the defeat of Raja Jaipal, India had lain prostrate. The raiders and invaders descended on India and took away the people, to be sold as slaves. . . . Guru Gobind Singh raised the Khalsa to defy religious intolerance, religious persecution and political inequality. It was a miracle that heroes appeared out of straws and common clay. Those who grovelled in the dust rose proud, defiant and invincible in the form of the Khalsa. They bore all sufferings and unnamable tortures cheerfully and unflinchingly. . . . India is at long last free. This freedom is the crown and climax and a logical corollary to the Sikh Guru's and Khalsa's terrific sacrifices and heroic exploits.[10]*

In addition to the bravery evident in Sikh history, stories of the Gurus are full of miracles that reportedly happened around them, such as the Eighth Guru's empowering a lowly watercarrier to give a profound explanation of the *Bhagavad-Gita*. Neither age, nor caste, nor gender is thought to have any relevance in Sikh spirituality. In contrast to the restricted position of women in Indian society, the Sikh Gurus accorded full respect and freedom of participation to women.

> *God is like sugar scattered in the sand. An elephant cannot pick it up. Says Kabir, the Guru has given me this sublime secret:*
>   *"Become thou an ant and partake of it."*
>
> *Kabir, Guru Granth Sahib 1377*

Although the Sikh Gurus gave their followers no mandate to convert others, their message was spread in a nonsectarian way by the **Udasis**, renunciates who do not withdraw from the world but rather practice strict discipline and meditation while at the same time trying to serve humanity. Their missionary work began under Baba Siri Chand, the ascetic elder son of Guru Nanak. He had a close relationship with the Sikh Gurus and was highly respected by people of all castes and creeds because of his spiritual power, wisdom, and principles. During the reign of the Mogul emperor Shah Jahan, a census showed that Baba Siri Chand had the largest following of any holy person in India. Nevertheless, he directed all attention and praise to his father, and never claimed to be a Guru himself. Udasi communities and educational institutions are still maintained in the subcontinent, and old Udasi inscriptions have been discovered in Baku, Azerbaijan.

Baba Siri Chand, elder son of Guru Nanak, combined the power of intense meditation with the power of hard work.

Central beliefs

Sikhism's major focus is loving devotion to one God, whom Sikhs recognize as the same One who is worshipped by many different names around the world. God is formless, beyond time and space, the only truth, the only reality. This boundless concept was initially set forth in Guru Nanak's Mul Mantra (basic sacred chant), which prefaces the Guru Granth Sahib, and **Jap Ji**, the first morning prayer of Sikhs:

> *There is One God*
> *Whose Name is Truth,*
> *The Creator,*
> *Without fear, without hate,*
> *Eternal Being,*
> *Beyond birth and death,*
> *Self-existent,*
> *Realized by the Guru's grace.*[11]

Following Guru Nanak's lead, Sikhs often refer to God as *Sat* ("truth") or as *Ik Onkar*, the One Supreme Being. God is pure being, without form.

Guru Gobind Singh, a great custodian of scholars who kept many poets in his court, offered a litany of praises of this boundless, formless One. His inspired composition, *Jaap Sahib*, includes 199 verses such as these:

> *Immortal*
> *Omnipotent*
> *Beyond Time*
> *And Space*
> *Invisible*
> *Beyond name, caste, or creed*
> *Beyond form or figure*
> *The ruthless destroyer*
> *Of all pride and evil*
> *The Salvation of all beings ...*
> *The Eternal Light*
> *The Sweetest Breeze*
> *The Wondrous Figure*
> *The Most Splendid.*[12]

The light of God shines fully through the Guru, the perfect master. The light of God is also present in the Guru Granth Sahib, **shabd**, the Holy Word of God, and in all of creation, in which **Nam**, the Holy Name of God dwells. God is not separate from this world. God pervades the cosmos and thus can be found within everything. As the Ninth Guru wrote:

> *Why do you go to the forest to find God? He lives in all and yet remains distinctly detached. He dwells in you as well, as fragrance resides in a flower or the reflection in a mirror. God abides in everything. See him, therefore, in your heart.*[13]

Sikhism does not claim to have the only path to God, nor does it try to convert others to its way. It has beliefs in common with Hinduism (such as *karma* and

Sikhs young or old may read from the Guru Granth Sahib, in which are enshrined the writings of Hindu and Muslim saints as well as Sikh Gurus.

reincarnation) and also with Islam (such as monotheism). It is said that the respected Muslim mystic, Mian Mir, was invited to lay the cornerstone of the Golden Temple in Amritsar. It was constructed with four doors, inviting people from all traditions to come in to worship. When Guru Gobind Singh created an army to resist tyranny, he admonished Sikhs not to feel enmity toward Islam or Hinduism, the religions of the oppressors. The enemy, he emphasized, was oppression and corruption.

Sikh soldier-saints are pledged to protect the freedom of all religions. Sikhism is, however, opposed to empty ritualism, and Guru Nanak and his successors sharply challenged hypocritical religious practices. "It is very difficult to be called a Muslim," sang Guru Nanak. "A Muslim's heart is as soft as wax, very compassionate, and he washes away the inner dirt of egotism."[14] By contrast, said Guru Nanak, "The Qazis [Muslim legal authorities] who sit in the courts to minister justice, rosary in hand and the name of *Khuda* (God) on their lips, commit injustice if their palm is not greased. And if someone challenges them, lo, they quote the scriptures!"[15]

According to the Sikh ideal, the purpose of life is to realize God within the world, through the everyday practices of work, worship, and charity, of sacrificing love. All people are to be treated equally, for God's light dwells in all and ego is a major hindrance to God-realization. From Guru Nanak's time on, Sikhism has refused to acknowledge the traditional Indian caste system. In their social services, such as hospitals, leprosariums, and free kitchens, Sikhs observe a tradition of serving everyone, regardless of caste or creed. A special group of Sikhs, known as Seva Panthis, place great emphasis on this aspect of Sikhism, refusing to accept any offerings to support their services to the needy. They are inspired by the example of Bhai Kanahia, who in the time of Guru Gobind Singh was found offering water to the fallen opponents as well as to Guru Gobind Singh's wounded soldiers. The Guru's people complained about his behavior to the Guru, who questioned Bhai Kanahia about what he was doing. Bhai Kanahia reportedly said that he was obeying the Sikh Gurus' teaching that one should look upon all with the same eye, whether friend or foe. Guru Gobind Singh praised him and gave him ointment, with the instruction not only to give water but also to soothe the wounds of soldiers from both armies.

In contrast to the low status of women in Indian society, the Gurus accorded considerable respect to women. Guru Nanak asked: "Why denounce her, who even gives birth to kings?"[16] Many women are respectfully remembered in Sikh history. Among them are Guru Nanak's sister Bibi Nanaki, who first recognized her brother's great spiritual power and became his first devotee. A group of Guru Gobind Singh's soldiers deserted him in the face of seemingly impossible odds when his citadel at Anandpur was being besieged, but their women refused to allow them to return to their homes. The women threatened to dress in the men's clothes and return to fight for the Guru, to expunge the shame of the men's cowardice. One woman—Mai Bhago—did so and helped to lead forty of the deserters back to battle on the Guru's side against Muslim attackers. The men all died on the battlefield, asking the Guru to forgive them, but Mai Bhago survived and

Surrounded by a sacred pool, the central structure in the Golden Temple at Amritsar houses the Guru Granth Sahib. It has a door on each of its four sides, symbolizing its openness to people of all faiths.

remained in the Guru's personal security guard, dressed as a man, with his permission. When *amrit* was first prepared for Khalsa initiation, it was Guru Gobind Singh's wife who added sugar crystals to make the initiates sweet-tempered as well as brave. In Brahmanic Hindu tradition, such an action by a woman would have been considered a defilement. During the fifteenth century, women were active as missionaries carrying Guru Gobind Singh's program. A preference for sons persisted, in part because of the heavy dowry burden traditionally expected of females in India. To counter this trend, Guru Gobind Singh reportedly forbade female infanticide, and in 2001, the chief Sikh authorities issued an order that anyone practicing female foeticide would be excommunicated from the faith.

In developing the military capabilities of his followers in order to protect religious freedom, Guru Gobind Singh set forth very strict standards for battle. He established five stringent conditions for "righteous war": (1) Military means are a last resort to be used only if all other methods have failed; (2) Battle should be undertaken without any enmity or feeling of revenge; (3) No territory should be taken or captured property retained; (4) Troops should be committed to the cause, not mercenaries fighting for pay, and soldiers should be strictly disciplined, forswearing smoking, drinking, and abuse of opponents' women; and (5) Minimal force should be used and hostilities should end when the objective is attained.

Like Hinduism, Sikhism conceives a series of lives, with *karma* (the effects of past actions on one's present life) governing transmigration of the soul into new bodies, be they human or animal. The ultimate goal of life is mystical union with the divine, reflected in one's way of living.

I was separated from God for many births, dry as a withered plant,
But by the grace of the Guru, I have become green.

Guru Arjun, the Fifth Guru[17]

Sacred practices

To be a true Sikh is to live a very disciplined life of surrender and devotion to God, with hours of daily prayer, continual inner repetition of the Name of God (Nam), and detachment from negative, worldly mind-states. Nam carries intense spiritual power, making a person fearless, steady, inwardly calm and strong in the face of any adversity, willing to serve without any reward, and extending love in all directions without any effort. Why is it so powerful? It comes from the guru as a transmission of spiritual blessing that automatically transforms people and links them with God. Some feel that Nam is the essence of creation, the sound and vibration of which the cosmos is a material manifestation. The mystics and gurus whose writings are included in the Guru Granth Sahib refer to many Names of God, such as *Sohang* (What You are, I am), *Narain* (the One present in water), *Allah*, and *Ram*. Some Sikhs recite *"Wahe Guru,"* (God wondrous beyond words), some say *"Ik Onkar Sat nam Siri Wahe Guru"* (God is One, the Truth Itself, Most Respectful, Wondrous beyond words), some recite the whole Mul Mantra.

In the Sikh path, at the same time that one's mind and heart are joined with God, one is to be working hard in the world, earning an honest living, and helping those in need. Of this path, the Third Sikh Guru observed:

The way of devotees is unique; they walk a difficult path.
They leave behind attachments, greed, ego, and desires, and do not speak much.
The path they walk is sharper than the edge of a sword and thinner than a hair.
Those who shed their false self by the grace of the Guru are filled with the fragrance
    of God.[18]

The standards set by Guru Gobind Singh for the Khalsa are so high that few people can really meet them. In addition to outer disciplines, such as abstaining from drugs, alcohol, and tobacco, the person who is Khalsa, said the Guru, will always recite the Name of God:

The Name of God is light, the Light which never extinguishes, day or night. Khalsa
recognizes none but the One. I live in Khalsa; it is my body, my treasure store.[19]

The one who is Khalsa renounces anger and does not criticize anybody. He fights on the front line against injustice and vanquishes the five evils (lust, anger, greed, attachment, and ego) in himself. He burns his *karmas* and thus becomes egoless. Not only does he not take another person's spouse, he doesn't even look at the things that belong to others. Perpetually reciting Nam is his joy, and he falls in love with the words of the Gurus. He faces difficulties squarely, always attacks evil, and always helps the poor. He joins other people with the Nam, but he is not bound within the forts of narrow-mindedness.[20]

The Sikh Gurus formed several institutions to help create a new social order with no caste distinctions. One is *langar*, the communal meal, which is freely offered to all who come, regardless of caste. This typically takes place at a **gurdwara**, the building where the Guru Granth Sahib is enshrined and public worship takes place. The congregation is called the *sangat*, in which all are equal; there is no priestly class nor servant class. During communal worship as well as langar, all strata of people sit together, though men and women may sit separately, as in the Indian custom. People of all ethnic origins, ideologies, and castes, including Untouchables, may bathe in the tank of water at Sikh holy places. Baptism into the Khalsa does away with one's former caste and makes a lowly person a chief. At least one-tenth of one's income is to be contributed toward the welfare of the community. In addition, the Sikh Gurus glorified the lowliest forms of manual labor, such as sweeping the floor and cleaning shoes and dirty pots, especially when these are done as voluntary service to God.

The morning and evening prayers take about two hours a day, starting in the very early morning hours. The first morning prayer is Guru Nanak's *Jap Ji. Jap*, meaning "recitation," refers to the use of sound, especially the Name of God (Nam), as the best way of approaching the divine. Like combing the hair, hearing and reciting the sacred word combs all negative thoughts out of the mind. Much of the *Jap Ji* is devoted to the blessings of Nam. For example,

The devotees are forever in bliss, for by hearing the Nam their suffering and
    sins are destroyed.
Hearkening to the Nam bestows Truth, divine wisdom, contentment.

His Holiness Baba Virsa Singh

For decades, His Holiness Baba Virsa Singh (born c. 1934) has been developing farms and communities in India in which people are trying to live by the teachings of the Sikh Gurus. Not only Sikhs but also Hindus, Muslims, and Christians, literate and illiterate, live and work side by side as brothers and sisters there. Baba Virsa Singh himself is illiterate, the son of a village farmer. From childhood he had an intense yearning for communion with God. He relates,

His Holiness Baba Virsa Singh

From childhood, I kept questioning God, "In order to love Jesus, must one become a Christian or just love?" He told me, "It is not necessary to become a Christian. It is necessary to love him."

I asked, "To believe in Moses, does one have to observe any special discipline, or just love?" The divine command came: "Only love." I asked, "Does one have to become a Muslim in order to please Muhammad, or only love?" He said, "One must love." "To believe in Buddha, must one become a monk or a Buddhist?" He replied, "No. To believe in Buddha is to love." God said, "I created human beings. Afterward, human beings created sectarian religions. But I created only human beings, not religions."[21]

Intense spirituality is the base of Baba Virsa Singh's communities, which are known collectively as Gobind Sadan ("The House of God"). Volunteers work hard to raise record crops on previously barren land. The harvests are shared communally and also provide the basis for Gobind Sadan's continual free kitchens (*langar*) for people of all classes, free medical services, and celebrations of the holy days of all religions. Devotions are carried on around the clock, with everyone from gardeners and pot washers to governors and professors helping to clean the holy areas and maintain perpetual reading of the Sikh scriptures. Everyone is empowered to do useful work, including small children, elderly men and women, mentally disturbed people, and people with physical handicaps. Thus under Baba Virsa Singh's guidance, there is a living example of the power of Guru Nanak's straightforward, nonsectarian spiritual program: Work hard to earn your own honest living, share with others, and wake early to meditate upon and remember God in your everyday life.

Another social effect of the work of Baba Virsa Singh is an easing of the tensions that have arisen between people of different religions in India. Even the most rigid proponents of their own religions come to Babaji and are gently convinced to open their eyes toward the validity of other faiths. He teaches Sikhs that their own scripture repeatedly praises and invokes the "Hindu" gods and goddesses. He teaches Hindu extremists that there is no one tradition that can be called "Hinduism" and that to take the name of Ram is to invoke the heights of moral character and selfless service to humanity. He likewise encourages Muslims to appreciate the spiritual depths of their religion.

Another area in which Baba Virsa Singh is influencing public life in India and other countries is his effect on government officials. He urges them to attend to the practical needs of the people and to uphold order and justice in society.

Speaking from his prodigious visionary powers, Baba Virsa Singh also gives people spiritual hope for a new world order. To editors of a Russian magazine, he explained,

Truth is always tested. Who tests it? Evil—evil attacks the truth. But truth never stops shining, and evil keeps falling back. Truth's journey is very powerful, with a very strong base. It never wavers. It is definitely a long journey, full of travails, but evil can never suppress the truth.[22]

He told the former ambassador to the United States and the ambassador from the Ukraine to India,

After the year 2000, many good people will arise in the world and the corrupt and criminal elements will fade away, because they will be disturbed by their own evils. When they taste what is emerging, all negativity will fall away, and a new light and joy will arise which will far exceed any earthly joy. As Guru Nanak says, "In the twinkling of an eye, God can change the whole Creation." The whole cosmos is like His puppet show, and if people so desire, perhaps the time is coming when He will change it all. From a worldly point of view, we wonder where the water will come from to quench such a massive fire. But behind all of this is the divine. The Master of the Mind can transform all minds instantly.[23]

By hearing the Nam, the blind find the path of Truth and realize the Unfathomable.[24]

Langar, *a free meal, is provided daily at some gurdwaras and all visitors are expected to partake. Rich and poor must sit side-by-side, with no distinction.*

"The Lord is stitched into my heart and never goes out of it even for a moment."
Fifth Guru, Jaitsri

The second morning prayer is Guru Gobind Singh's universal Jaap Sahib. It names no prophet, nor creates any religion. It is sheer homage to God. The Guru addresses God as having no form, no country, and no religion but yet as the seed of seeds, song of songs, sun of suns, the life force pervading everywhere, ever merciful, ever giving, indestructible. Complex in its poetry and profound in its content, *Jaap Sahib* asserts that God is the cause of conflict as well as of peace, of destruction as well as of creation; God pervades in darkness as well as in light. In verse after verse, devotees learn that there is nothing outside of God's presence, nothing outside of God's control.

In addition to recitation of prayers, passages from the Guru Granth Sahib are chanted or sung as melodies, often with musical accompaniment. This devotional tradition of **kirtan** was initiated by Guru Nanak. But great discipline is required to attend the pre-dawn songs and recitations every day, and in contrast to the self-respect developed by Guru Gobind Singh in the Khalsa, worshippers humble themselves before the sacred scriptures. The Granth is placed on a platform, with a devotee waving a whisk over the sacred book to denote the royalty of the scripture. Worshippers bow to it, bring offerings, and then sit reverently on the floor before it. Every morning and evening, the spirit of God reveals its guidance to the people as an officiant opens the scripture at random, intuitively guided, and reads a passage that is to be a special spiritual focus for the day. For many occasions, teams of people carry out Akhand Path, reading the entire Guru Granth Sahib from start to finish within forty-eight hours, taking turns of two hours each.

Some *gurdwaras*, including the Golden Temple in Amritsar, have previously allowed only men to read publicly from the Guru Granth Sahib, to preach, to officiate at ceremonies, or to sing sacred songs. This has been a cultural custom, however, for nothing in the Sikh scriptures or the Code of Conduct bars women from such privileges. Indeed, Guru Gobind Singh initiated women as well as men into the Khalsa and allowed women to fight on the battlefield. In 1996, the central body setting policies for Sikh gurdwaras ruled that women should be allowed to perform sacred services.

In addition to group chanting, singing, and listening to collective guidance from the Guru Granth Sahib, devout Sikhs are encouraged to begin the day with private meditations on the name of God. As one advances in this practice and abides in egoless love for God, one is said to receive guidance from the inner guru, the living word of God within each person.

Sikhism today

Sikhism is spreading around the world, largely by emigration from India, but the center of Sikhism remains the Punjab. The area of this territory, which is under Indian rule, was dramatically shrunk by the partition of India in 1947, for two-thirds of the Punjab was in the area thenceforth called Pakistan. The two million Sikhs living in that part were forced to migrate under conditions of extreme hardship. Some managed to migrate to other countries and parts of India other than the Punjab. Emigration continued, and there are now large Sikh communities in Britain, Canada, the United States, Malaysia, and Singapore. The global Sikh community reconverged in the Punjab in 1999, when a massive celebration of the 300th anniversary of the birth of the Khalsa was held in Anandpur Sahib. The event turned out to be the largest human gathering in history without any accident of any sort. Such an atmosphere of peace and joy prevailed that witnesses attributed the peacefulness to the blessings of Guru Gobind Singh himself.

In India, Sikhs and Hindus have lived side by side in mutual tolerance until recent years, when violent clashes occurred between Hindus and Sikhs. Sikh separatists want to establish an independent Sikh state, called Khalistan, with a commitment to strong religious observances. Another purpose of Khalistan would be to protect Sikhs from oppression and exploitation by the much larger Hindu community. In 1984, Prime Minister Indira Gandhi chose to attack the Golden Temple, Sikhism's holiest shrine, for Sikh separatists were thought to be using it as a shelter for their weapons. The attack seemed an outrageous desecration of the holy place, and counter-violence increased. The Prime Minister

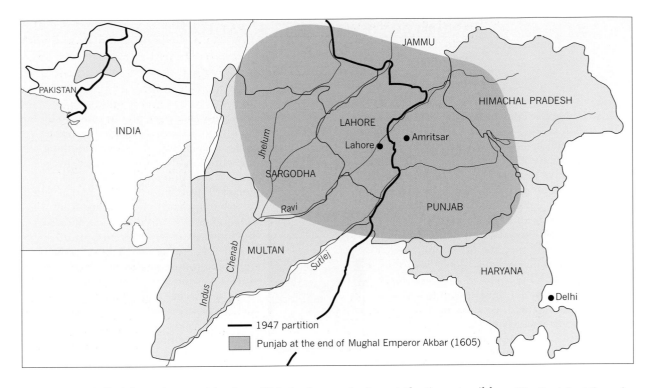

herself was killed later in 1984 by her Sikh bodyguards. In retribution, terrible killings of Sikhs followed. At least 8,000 Sikhs were murdered by mobs in Delhi alone.

Many Sikhs have "disappeared" in the Punjab, allegedly at the hands of both separatists and police terrorists. Sikhs in India generally are going on with their lives now that violence has abated, but tensions are kept alive by Sikhs living outside India who persist in demanding the formation of Khalistan. Many Internet websites have been set up devoted to this purpose and to promoting a militant, rigid version of the religion.

Historical tensions have also arisen within Sikhism, as it became institutionalized and used by some factions for their own ends, such as acquiring the landholdings of the *gurdwaras*. Leadership of *gurdwaras* is democratic, by elected committees, but this provision has not stopped fractiousness within the organizations. In 1998, factions of a Canadian *gurdwara* had to be separated by police in their fight over the issue of using chairs and tables in the *langar* rather than the tradition of sitting in rows on the ground.

There are also tensions between those Sikhs who favor a more spiritual and universal understanding of their religion and those who interpret it more rigidly and exclusively. During the years when Sikhs were asserting their distinct identity, lest they be subsumed under Hinduism, the ecumenical nature of Sikhism was not generally emphasized. There were no forcible attempts to convert anyone else to Sikhism, but Sikhs became proud of their heroic history and tended to turn inward.

In the diaspora, Sikhs attempted to resist assimilation to the surrounding cultures and to raise their children according to their Indian traditions. In the wake

The Punjab at the end of the reign of the Mogul (Mughal) emperor, Akbar. The 1947 partition of India left two-thirds of the Punjab, including many of its Sikh temples, inside Pakistan, a Muslim state.

AN INTERVIEW WITH G. S. JAUHAL

Living Sikhism

G. S. Jauhal is a Punjabi Sikh, a commandant in the Indian military service and a member of Gobind Sadan established by Baba Virsa Singh. His words illustrate the humility which characterizes those who truly live the teachings of the Sikh Gurus:

"I am not an authority. I'm just a student in the very beginning stage. I want to learn so much. I've been a Sikh since birth and I'm forty-seven now. But I think one needs many births and then the Guru's grace — then only can he learn Sikhism. It is so deep, so vast.

"We can only get something if first of all Guru's grace is there. Then we keep on endeavoring sincerely, from the core of our heart, and keep on learning. Again and again reading, reciting Guru Granth Sahib, trying to understand what it means. I myself feel that I am one of those who, without understanding ourselves, we try to teach others. This is a pity. Whatever the Guru has given in the Granth Sahib, we are supposed to practice so that everyone knows that what we say, we do. Otherwise people will not take us as true persons. This is the teaching of Guru Granth Sahib — whatever you do outwardly, the same thing should be in your heart. I do try to recite and follow Gurbani, but I am far, far away from the goal which is desired by the Guru.

"There are five things which we should not have — lust, anger, greed, attachment to worldly things, ego. These things take us toward the worldly side and away from the true path. The difficult path is chosen by the Gurus. Once man is trying from his inner being to follow that path, and he prays to his Gurus to help him to achieve that path, the Guru always helps this small being, and there is nothing difficult in the world. As the Guru described, to perfect ourself is a very thin path the Sikh is supposed to walk.

"When I was young, I learned from my mother. She was totally uneducated. She knew some hymns from Guru Granth Sahib which she learned verbally from her brother. She used to recite when I was just a small child; she used to put me on her lap and recite the Name. Still I remember today some of the words recited by my mother, so it has gone deep into my mind.

"I think Sikhism is a unique religion, and the latest. All the good things of all the religions have been combined in one. It is meant to be spread all over the world. We should understand other religions also; there are so many good things in other religions. But I find that the work toward spreading our religion in other parts of the world has not been done as much as it should have been. That could have been possible if the message of the Gurus had been printed in all the languages and then taken to the doorsteps of the other people. People will not come to you to learn your religion in your language. So it was our duty to make it convenient, to translate our Guru Granth Sahib and Guru's teachings into simple speaking language and take it to the people in their own languages. It is a world religion, and we should not have kept it in our closed doors."

of the terrorist attacks in New York and Washington in 2001, many Sikhs in the diaspora who had kept their traditional dress and long hair with beards and turbans found themselves the mistaken victims of hate crimes, since they were confused with Afghanis. They found it necessary to explain their religion publicly, and in doing so, inevitably stressed its universality, democratic nature, and the spirit of religious tolerance.

Without going so far as to deny the uniqueness or continuing tradition of Sikhism, many contemporary Sikh and non-Sikh scholars are appreciating the message of the Sikh Gurus as supporting the underlying unity of people of all religions. There is a growing consciousness of Sikhism as a world religion that can establish itself in any soil. His Holiness Baba Virsa Singh (see box, p. 426) expresses this point of view:

That which we call dharma, that which we call Sikhism, that which we call the religion of Guru Nanak, that which we call the command of Guru Gobind Singh is this: That we should not forget God even for one breath.

Guru Nanak prepared a lovely ship, in which all the seats were to be given to those who were doing both manual work and spiritual practice.

The religion of Guru Gobind Singh, of Guru Nanak was not given to those of one organization, one village, one country. Their enlightened vision was for the whole cosmos. Guru Granth Sahib is not for some handful of people. It is for everyone.[25]

In the words of Guru Gobind Singh:

Same are the temple and the mosque
And same are the forms of worship therein.
All human beings are one though apparently many,
Realize, therefore, the essential unity of mankind.[26]

The Guru Ganth Sahib arrived in state atop an elephant for the three hundredth anniversary of the Khalsa at Anandpur Sahib, which drew Sikhs from around the world.

Suggested reading

Cole, W. Owen, and Sambhi, Piara Singh, *The Sikhs: Their Religious Beliefs and Practices*, second edition, Sussex, England: Academic Press, 1995. A clearly written survey of the Sikh tradition.

Macauliffe, Max Arthur, *The Sikh Religion: Its Gurus, Sacred Writings, and Authors*, sixteen vols., Oxford: Oxford University Press, reprinted in Delhi: S. Chand and Company, 1963. The most respected general account of Sikhism in English, even though its author was not Sikh.

McLeod, W. H., trans. and ed., *Textual Sources for the Study of Sikhism*, Totowa, New Jersey: Barnes and Noble Books, 1984 and Manchester: Manchester University Press, 1984. Interesting compilation of Sikh literature, from selections from the Adi Granth to rules for the Khalsa initiation ceremony, all with explanatory comments.

Singh, Dharam, *Sikhism: Norm and Form*, New Delhi: Vision and Venture, 1997. Convincing discussion of Sikhism as a vision of a new social order: a classless and casteless brotherhood of enlightened humans.

Singh, Guru Gobind, *Jaap Sahib*, English translation by Surendra Nath, New Delhi: Gobind Sadan Publications, 1997. Powerful praises of the formless, ultimately unknowable God, without reference to any particular religion.

Singh, Dr. Gopal, *A History of the Sikh People 1469–1978*, New Delhi: World Sikh University Press, 1979. Thorough and scholarly history of the Sikhs to modern times.

Singh, Harbans, ed., *The Encyclopedia of Sikhism*, Patiala: Punjabi University, 1992–1999. Four volumes on all aspects of Sikhism prepared by leading scholars.

Singh, Khushwant, trans., *Hymns of Guru Nanak*, New Delhi: Orient Longmans Ltd., 1969. Stories about Guru Nanak's life and selections from his sacred songs.

Singh, Manmohan, trans., *Sri Guru Granth Sahib*, eight vols., Amritsar: Shromani Gurdwara Parbandhak Committee, 1962. A good English translation of the Sikh sacred scripture.

Singh, Nikky-Guninder Kaur, *The Name of My Beloved: Devotional Poetry from the Guru Granth and the Dasam Granth*, San Francisco: HarperSanFrancisco, 1995. Daily devotional hymns in contemporary English translation.

Singh, Trilochan, Singh, Jodh, Singh, Kapur, Singh, Bawa Harkishen, and Singh, Khushwant, trans., *The Sacred Writings of the Sikhs*, New York: Samuel Weiser, 1973. Selections from the Adi Granth and hymns by Guru Gobind Singh in English translation.

CHAPTER 6
TAOISM AND CONFUCIANISM

The unity of opposites

While India was giving birth to Hinduism, Jainism, and Buddhism, three other major religions were developing in East Asia. Taoism and Confucianism grew largely in China, and later spread to Japan and Korea; Shinto was distinctively Japanese. These religions have remained associated primarily with their home-lands. In this chapter we will explore the two that developed in China from simi-lar roots but with different emphases: Taoism and Confucianism. Shinto will be the subject of Chapter 7. Buddhism also spread to East Asia, and its practice has often been mixed with the native traditions.

In East Asia, religions that will be treated as separate entities in this chapter and the next are, in fact, more subtly blended and practiced. Taoism and Confucianism, though they may seem quite opposite to each other, co-exist as complementary value systems in East Asian societies, and a person's thought and actions may encompass both streams. Contemporary political shifts in China, however, have made it difficult to pin-point or predict the continued existence of religious ways there.

Ancient traditions

Chinese civilization is very old and continuous. By 2000 BCE, people were living in settled agrarian villages in the Yellow River Valley, with a written language, musical instruments, and skillful work in bronze, silk, ceramics, and ivory. The spiritual ways of this early civilization permeate all later religious developments in China, Korea, and Japan. One major feature is the veneration of ancestors. The spirits of deceased ancestors remain very closely bonded to their living descen-dants for some time. Respect must be paid to them—especially the family's found-ing ancestor and those recently deceased—through funerals, mourning rites, and then continuing sacrifices. The sacred rituals are called *li*. They are essential because the ancestors will help their descendants, if treated with proper respect, or cause trouble if ignored.

Kings, even those of the earliest Chinese dynasty, sought their ancestors' help through the medium of oracle bones. These were shells or bones onto which the divining specialist scratched questions the king wanted the ancestors to answer. Touching the bones with a hot poker made them crack, forming patterns, which

TAOISM AND CONFUCIANISM

	BCE	
	Legendary Yellow Emperor	
Ancient Traditions **TAOISM**	Shang Dynasty (c.1751–1123)	Ancient Traditions **CONFUCIANISM**
between c.600–300 Life of Lao-tzu c.365–290 Life of Chuang-tzu	Chou Dynasty (c.1122–221)	c.551–479 Life of Confucius c.390–305 Life of Mencius c.340–245 Life of Hsun Tzu
Immortality movements Queen Mother of the West cult	Chin Dynasty (221–206)	Confucian scholars suppressed, books burned
Early religious Taoist sects Heavenly Master tradition begins	Han Dynasty (206 BCE– 220 CE)	Confucian Classics used as basis of civil service exams
	—— CE ——	
Mutual influences between Taoism and Buddhism. 748 Taoist Canon first compiled	T'ang Dynasty (618–907)	Buddhism reaches peak, then is persecuted. Confucianism makes comeback
Tai-chi chuan appears Northen Taoist sects flourish	Sung Dynasty (960–1280)	Neo-Confucianism 1130–1200 Life of Chu Hsi
1911 Imperial dynasty overthrown	1900	1911 Last imperial dynasty overthrown. Confucianism de-established as state religion
National Association of Taoism (White Clouds Temple, Beijing)	1950	1949 onward Chairman Mao's red book replaces Confucian Classics
Temples and books destroyed	Cultural Revolution (1966–1976)	Temples and books destroyed
	1980	1989 Scholars' requests refused at Tiananmen Square
Taoist sects, temples re-established. First Taoist Grand Ritual. Popular faith and practices	1990–2000	Confucian Classics reintroduced in schools. Confucius's birthday celebrated. International Association of Confucians established

the diviner interpreted as useful answers from the ancestors. Later, demons and ghosts who had been ignored or ill-treated during their lifetime, were seen as causing so much mischief that many efforts were made to thwart them, including evil-deflecting charms, gongs, and firecrackers, appeals through mediums, spirit-walls to keep them from entering doorways, exorcisms, prayers, incense, and fasts. These activities continue today.

To the early Chinese and in continuing popular belief, the world is full of invisible spirits. In addition to ancestors, there are charismatic humans who have died but are still available to help the people.

As is understood in indigenous religions everywhere, the world is also full of nature spirits. Plants, animals, rivers, stones, mountains, stars—all parts of the natural world are vitalized by cosmic energy and often personified and honored as deities. From early times, Chinese people made offerings to these beings and sought their aid with personal problems, sometimes through the mediumship of a shaman who can communicate with the spirit world.

According to Chinese belief, which can be traced back at least to the earliest historical dynasty, the Shang (c. 1751–1123 BCE), there also exists a great spiritual being referred to as **Shang Ti**, the Lord-on-High, ruler of the universe, the supreme ancestor of the Chinese. Deities governing aspects of the cosmos and the local environment are subordinate to him. This deity is conceived of as being masculine and closely involved in human affairs, though not as a Creator God.

During the Chou dynasty (c. 1122–221 BCE), which overthrew the Shang, the focus shifted to Heaven as an impersonal power controlling the universe. Rulers then developed the idea of the "Mandate of Heaven" to justify their rule. The Mandate is the self-existing moral law of virtue, the supreme reality. According to the Chou rulers, human destiny is determined by virtuous deeds. Rulers have a moral duty to maintain the welfare of the people and a spiritual duty to conduct respectful ceremonies for the highest heavenly beings.

In addition to ancestors, spirits, and Heaven, there has long existed in China a belief that the cosmos is a manifestation of an impersonal self-generating energy called *ch'i*. This force has two aspects whose interplay causes the ever-changing phenomena of the universe. **Yin** is the dark, receptive, "female" aspect; **yang** is the bright, assertive, "male" aspect. Wisdom lies in recognizing their ever-shifting, but regular and balanced, patterns and moving with them. This creative rhythm of the universe is called the **Tao**, or "way." As traditionally diagrammed, yin and yang interpenetrate each other (represented by the small circles). As soon as one aspect reaches its fullest point, it begins to diminish, while its polar opposite increases.

To harmonize with the ancestors and gods, and yin and yang, the ancients devised many forms of divination. One system developed during the Chou dynasty was eventually written down as the *I Ching*, or *Book of Changes*. It is a common source for both Taoism and Confucianism and is regarded as a classic text in both traditions. The *I Ching* was highly elaborated with commentaries by scholars beginning in the Han dynasty (206 BCE–220 CE). To use this subtle system, one respectfully purifies the divining objects—such as yarrow stalks or coins, which symbolize yin and yang—asks a question, casts the objects six times, and then consults the *I Ching* for symbolic interpretation of the yin–yang combinations.

The pattern of throws is diagrammed in the *I Ching* as a hexagram, with yin represented as a broken line and yang by a straight line. For example,

In ancient Chinese tradition, the universe arises from the interplay of yin and yang. They are modes of energy commonly represented as interlocking shapes, with dominance continually shifting between the dark, receptive yin mode and the bright, assertive yang mode.

hexagram number 46, called Sheng or "Pushing Upward," has been likened by some commentators to a tree emerging from the earth, growing slowly and invisibly:

> *Thus the superior person of devoted character*
> *Heaps up small things*
> *In order to achieve something high and great.*[1]

Another set of commentaries is based on the two trigrams within the hexagram. In the case of hexagram 46, the upper pattern of three yin lines can be interpreted as devotion and yielding, and the lower pattern of two yang lines above one yin line suggests gentleness. According to the commentaries, these non-aggressive qualities will ultimately lead to supreme success.

By studying and systematizing the ways of humans and of nature, the ancient Chinese tried to order their actions so that they might steer a coherent course within the changing cosmos. They recognized that any extreme action will produce its opposite as a balancing reaction and thus they strived for a middle way of subtle discretion and moderation. From these ancient roots gradually developed two contrasting ways of harmonizing with the cosmos—the more mystically religious ways, which are collectively called Taoism, and the more political and moral ways, which are known as Confucianism. Like yin and yang, they interpenetrate and complement each other, and are themselves evolving dynamically.

Taoism—the way of nature and immortality

Taoism is as full of paradoxes as the Buddhist tradition it influenced: Ch'an or Zen Buddhism. It has been adored by Westerners who seek a carefree, natural way of life as an escape from the industrial rat race. Yet beneath its words of the simple life in harmony with nature is a tradition of great mental and physical discipline. As it has developed over time, Taoism includes efforts to align oneself with the unnamable original force (the Tao), ceremonial worship of deities from the Jade Emperor to the kitchen god, and cultivation of physical and spiritual strength. Some Taoist scriptures counsel indifference about birth and death; others teach ways of attaining physical immortality. These variations developed within an ancient tradition that had no name until it had to distinguish itself from Confucianism. "Taoism" is actually a label invented by scholars and awkwardly stretched to cover a philosophical or "literati" tradition, a multitude of so-called longevity techniques, and an assortment of religious sects whose relationship to the literati tradition is complex, but which probably developed at least in part from the early philosophical texts and practices. Religious Taoism itself is often an amalgam, with the Taoist way of natural life and meditation as its base, plus Confucian virtues, health disciplines, Buddhist-like rituals, and immortality as its final goal.

Teachings of Taoist sages

Aside from its general basis in ancient Chinese ways, the specific origin of Taoist philosophy and practices is unclear. In China, tradition attributes the publicizing of these ways to the Yellow Emperor, who supposedly ruled from 2697 to 2597 BCE. He was said to have studied with an ancient sage and to have developed meditation, health, and military practices based on what he learned. After ruling for one hundred years, he ascended to heaven on a dragon's back and became one of the Immortals.

The hexagram Sheng is a visual symbol of the various meanings attached to "Pushing Upward."

The philosophical or literati form of Taoism has been pursued by intellectuals and artists over the millennia. Its foundation is expounded in the famous scripture, the *Tao-te Ching* ("The Classic of the Way and the Power"). It is second only to the Bible in the number of Western translations, for its ideas are not only fascinating but also elusive for translators working from the terse ancient Chinese characters and confronting variations in existing copies of the Chinese text.

Even the supposed author of the *Tao-te Ching* is obscure. According to tradition, the book was dictated by Lao-tzu (or Lao-tse), a curator of the royal library of the Chou dynasty, to a border guard as he left society for the mountains at the reported age of 160. The guard recognized Lao-tzu as a sage and begged him to leave behind a record of his wisdom. Lao-tzu reportedly complied by inscribing the 5,000 characters now known as the *Tao-te Ching*. This is traditionally said to have happened during the sixth century BCE, with Lao-tzu purportedly fifty-three years older than Confucius. But recent archaeological finds date the existent version of the *Tao-te Ching* to 350 BCE and suggest it was an alternative to Confucianism. Some think the *Tao-te Ching* was an oral tradition, derived from the teachings of several sages, and question whether Lao-tzu ever existed.

The book's central philosophy, which shines through widely varying translations, is a practical concern with improving harmony in life. It says that one can best harmonize with the natural flow of life by being receptive and quiet. These teachings were elaborated more emphatically and humorously by a sage named Chuang-tzu (c. 365–290 BCE). He, too, was a minor government official for a while but left political involvement for a hermit's life of freedom and solitude. Unlike Lao-tzu, whose philosophy was addressed to those in leadership positions, Chuang-tzu asserted that the best way to live in a chaotic, absurd civilization is to become detached from it.

FLOWING WITH TAO   At the heart of Taoist teachings is the idea of Tao, the "unnamable," the "eternally real."[2] Contemporary Master Da Liu asserts that Tao is so ingrained in Chinese understanding that it is a basic concept that cannot be defined, like "goodness." Moreover, Tao is a mystical reality that cannot be grasped by the mind. The *Tao-te Ching* says:

The Tao that can be told of
  Is not the Absolute Tao,
The Names that can be given
  Are not Absolute Names.
The Nameless is the origin of Heaven and Earth;
The Named is the Mother of All Things . . .

Lao-tzu, one of the major conveyers of the Taoist tradition, is often depicted as a humorous old man riding off into the mountains after reportedly drawing the 5,000 characters of the Tao-te Ching.

These two (the Secret and its manifestations)
 Are (in their nature) the same; . . .
They may both be called the Cosmic Mystery:
Reaching from the Mystery into the Deeper Mystery
Is the Gate to the Secret of All Life.[3]

Chapter 25 of the *Tao-te Ching* is more explicit about the mysterious Unnamable:

There is a thing confusedly formed,
Born before heaven and earth.
Silent and void
It stands alone and does not change,
Goes round and does not weary.
It is capable of being the mother of the world.
I know not its name
So I style it "the way."
I give it the makeshift name of "the great."[4]

Although we cannot describe the Tao, we can live in harmony with it. Ideally, says Lao-tzu:

Humans model themselves on earth,
Earth on heaven,
Heaven on the way,
And the way on that which is naturally so.[5]

TEACHING STORY

Three in the Morning

Whether you point to a little stalk or a great pillar, a leper or the beautiful Hsi-shih, things ribald and shady or things grotesque and strange, the Way makes them all into one. . . . Only the man of far-reaching vision knows how to make them into one. So he has no use [for categories], but relegates all to the constant. The constant is the useful; the useful is the passable; the passable is the successful; and with success, all is accomplished. He relies upon this alone, relies upon it and does not know he is doing so. This is called the Way.

But to wear out your brain trying to make things into one without realizing that they are all the same—this is called "three in the morning." What do I mean by "three in the morning"? When the monkey trainer was handing out acorns, he said, "You get three in the morning and four at night." This made all the monkeys furious. "Well, then," he said, "you get four in the morning and three at night." The monkeys were all delighted. There was no change in the reality behind the words, yet the monkeys responded with joy and anger. Let them, if they want to. So the sage harmonizes with both right and wrong and rests in Heaven the Equalizer.

Chuang-tzu[6]

There are several basic principles for the life in harmony with Tao. One is to experience the transcendent unity of all things, rather than separation. Professor Chang Chung-yuan observes that "the value of Tao lies in its power to reconcile opposites on a higher level of consciousness."[7] This higher level can only be attained when one ceases to feel any personal preferences. Everything has its own nature and function, says Chuang-tzu. But disfigured or beautiful, small or large, they are all one in Tao. Taoism is concerned with direct experience of the universe, accepting and cooperating with things as they are, not with setting standards of morality, not with labeling things as "good" or "bad." Chuang-tzu asserts that herein lies true spirituality:

Such a man can ride the clouds and mist, mount the sun and moon, and wander beyond the four seas. Life and death do not affect him. How much less will he be concerned with good and evil![8]

In addition to experiencing oneness, the Taoist sage takes a low profile in the world. He or she is like a valley, allowing everything needed to flow into his or her life, or like a stream. Flowing water is a Taoist model for being. It bypasses and gently wears away obstacles rather than fruitlessly attacking them, effortlessly nourishes the "ten thousand things" of material life, works without struggling, leaves all accomplishments behind without possessing them. Lao-tzu observes:

Water is the softest thing on earth,
Yet its silken gentleness
Will easily wear away the hardest stone.

Everyone knows this;
Few use it in their daily lives.
Those of Tao yield and overcome.[9]

This is the uniquely Taoist paradox of **wu-wei**—"non-action," or taking no intentional or invasive action contrary to the natural flow of things. *Wu-wei* is spontaneous, creative activity proceeding from the Tao, action without ego-assertion, letting the Tao take its course. Chuang-tzu uses the analogy of a butcher whose knife always stays sharp because he lets his hand be guided by the makeup of the carcass, finding the spaces between the bones where a slight movement of the blade will glide through without resistance. Even when difficulties arise, the sage does not panic and take unnecessary action.

Sites for Taoist and Buddhist temples in China were traditionally chosen according to the ancient art of feng-shui, *or geomancy, the awareness of the presence and movement of natural energies. The energies of waterfalls and mountains were considered conducive to spiritual practices. (*Buddhist Temple Amid Clearing Mountain Peaks, *Northern Sung, c.940–67 CE.)*

> *Sweet music and highly seasoned food*
> *Entertain for a while,*
> *But the clear, tasteless water from the well*
> *Gives life and energy without exhaustion.*   *Lao-tzu*[10]

The result of *wu-wei* is non-interference. Much of Lao-tzu's teaching is directed at rulers, that they might guide society without interfering with its natural course. Nothing is evil, but things may be out of balance. The world is naturally in harmony; Tao is our original nature. But according to tradition, the Golden Age of Tao declined as humans departed from the "Way." "Civilization," with its intellectual attempts to improve on things and its rigid views of morality, actually leads to world chaos, the Taoists warn. How much better, Lao-tzu advises, to accept not-knowing, moving freely in the moment with the changing universe.

Then again, Taoism places great value on withdrawal from the madding crowd to a contemplative life and love of nature. The latter is greatly aided by **feng-shui** (geomancy), an increasingly popular practice in China and other countries today. By observing the contours of the land and the flows of wind and water, specialists in *feng-shui* could reportedly determine the best places for the harmonious placement of a temple, dwelling place, or grave. By examining the flow of *ch'i* within a dwelling, they decide on the optimal placement of furniture and wall decorations.

Whether in a peaceful or chaotic environment, the literati Taoist seeks to find the still center, save energy for those times when action is needed, and take a humble, quiet approach to life. As asserted in a fourth-century BCE essay on inner training:

> *The vitality of all people inevitably comes from their peace of mind.*
> *When anxious, one loses this guiding thread; when angry, one loses this basic point.*
> *When one is anxious or sad, pleased or angry, the Way has no place to settle. . . .*
> *That mysterious vital energy within the mind, one moment it arrives, the next it*
>   *departs.*
> *So fine nothing can be contained within it, so vast nothing can be outside it.*
> *The reason we lose it is because of the harm caused by agitation.*[11]

Organized Taoism

Beginning in the second century CE, Taoist-organized groups or sects developed, employing practices such as alchemy, faith-healing, sorcery, and the use of power objects, which seem to have existed from ancient times in China, converting them into institutionalized and distinctive social movements with detailed rituals, clergy, and revealed texts. This institutionalization of ancient practices developed as the Han dynasty (206 BCE–220 CE) was declining amidst famine and war. An array of revelations and prophecies predicted the end of the age and finally led to the rise of religious/political organizations. For example, Kan Ji received a visionary revelation that yin and yang were no longer in balance in heaven or on earth, for the rulers had forgotten to follow the ways of nature, and that in 184 CE the blue heaven of the Han would be replaced by the yellow heaven. In that year, inspired by this vision of Great Peace, hundreds of thousands of followers of a leader who was known as a faith healer and advocate of egalitarian ideas rebelled in eight of China's twelve provinces; their rebellion took several years to suppress and presaged the fall of the Han dynasty. Simultaneously, in western China, Chang Tao-ling had a vision of Lao-tzu as the heavenly Lord Lao in which he was appointed representative of the Tao on earth and given the title Celestial Master. He advocated similar practices of healing by faith and developed a quasi-military organization of religious officials, attracting numerous followers. The older Han religion had involved demons and exorcism, belief in an afterlife, and a god of destinies, who granted fortune or misfortune based on heavenly records of good and bad deeds. These roles were now ascribed to a pantheon of celestial deities, who in turn were controlled by the new Celestial Master priesthood led by Chang's family. This hereditary clergy performed imperial investitures as well as village festivals, with both men and women serving as libationers in local dioceses.

After the sack of the northern capitals early in the fourth century, the Celestial Masters and other aristocrats fled south and established themselves on Dragon-Tiger Mountain in southeast China. Today the sixty-fourth patriarch in the lineage lives in Taiwan, although practices are being revived on Dragon-Tiger Mountain in mainland China.

In approximately 365 CE another aristocratic family in exile in southern China began receiving revelations from a deceased member, Lady Wei. These revelations of the names and powers of newly discovered deities, meditation methods, alchemy, and rituals were recorded in exquisite calligraphy and transmitted to a few advanced disciples. This elite group of celibates, who resided on Mount Mao, called their practices "Highest Purity Taoism." They looked down on the Celestial Master tradition and its sexual rituals as crude, and they avoided village rituals and commoners. Instead, they focused on personal immortality through meditations for purifying the body with divine energies so as "to rise up to heaven in broad daylight." Although the Highest Purity Taoism did not reach the mass of the people, its texts and influence continue to be revered today as the elite tradition of Taoism.

In the late fourth century, another group arose in the wake of Highest Purity: the Numinous Treasure school. It assimilated many elements of Buddhism, creating a medley of new meditation practices, divine beings, rituals, scriptures, heavens, rebirth, and hells. This tradition was in turn succeeded in the twelfth century by Complete Perfection, which has been the dominant monastic school ever since. It unites Taoist inner alchemy with Ch'an Buddhist meditation and Confucian social morality, harmonizing the three religions. Actively monastic, it focuses on meditation and non-attachment to the world. Today its major center is the White Cloud Monastery in Beijing, the headquarters of the government-approved Chinese Taoism Association. Complete Perfection is also the foundation for most Hong Kong Taoist temples and martial arts groups.

The many revealed scriptures of Taoist movements were occasionally compiled and canonized by the court. The present Taoist canon was compiled in 1445 CE. Containing about 1,500 sophisticated scriptures, it has only recently begun to be studied by non-Taoist scholars. It includes a wealth of firsthand accounts by mystical practitioners—poems of their visionary shamanistic journeys, encounters with deities, advanced meditation practices, descriptions of the perfected human being, methods and elixirs for ascending to heavenly realms and achieving immortality, and descriptions of the Immortals and the heavenly bureaucracies. The rituals and inner cultivation practices of the canon are in use today, typically in one of two modes: rites of cosmic renewal for the living, and rituals to be employed after death. At death either Taoist or Buddhist priests may be hired by private families to perform rituals to help the deceased appear before the Ten Hell Judges, as well as to join in communal rituals of grave-cleaning in April and of universal liberation and feeding of hungry ghosts in August. Every temple has a side shrine to T'u-ti Kung, Lord of the Earth, who can transport offerings to deceased loved ones.

LONGEVITY TAOISM   Flowing with Tao is easy and natural, while controlling the spirits is ritually formalized. But both require masterful spiritual discipline, which forms the third major aspect of Taoism. Lao-tzu describes what mastery entailed:

> *The ancient Masters were profound and subtle.*
> *Their wisdom was unfathomable. . . .*
> *They were careful*
> *as someone crossing an iced-over stream.*
> *Alert as a warrior in enemy territory.*
> *Courteous as a guest.*
> *Fluid as melting ice.*
> *Shapable as a block of wood.*
> *Receptive as a valley.*
> *Clear as a glass of water.*[12]

The mastery to which Taoist writers refer may be the result of powerful unknown ascetic practices traditionally passed down secretly from teacher to pupil. These teachers lived in the mountains; great Taoist teachers are said to be still hidden in the remote mountains of China and Korea.

The aim of the longevity practices is to use the energy available to the body in order to become strong and healthy and intuitively perceive the order of the universe. Within our body is the spiritual micro-universe of the "three treasures" necessary for the preservation of life: generative force (*ching*), vital life-force (*ch'i*), and spirit (*shen*). These three are activated with the help of various methods: breathing techniques, vocalizations, diets, gymnastics, absorption of solar and lunar energies, sexual control, visualizations, and meditations. Combined in various ways, these methods are today known as ***ch'i-kung***, or energy training, and applied both for medical and spiritual purposes. Some people today claim they are helpful in thwarting the ravages of AIDS, for instance. Traditionally they were employed as the foundation of inner alchemy.

Inner alchemy began with the practitioner's building a reservoir of *ching* energy in the "cauldron" several inches below the navel, whence it rises up the spine as a vapor, transmuted into *ch'i* energy. *Ch'i* is in turn transmuted into *shen* in an upper cauldron in the head (an area similar to the Third Eye of Indian yogic practice), drops down to illuminate the heart center, and then descends to an

One of the goals of esoteric Taoist practice is to separate the spirit from the body so that the former can operate independently, both before and after death.

inner area of the lower cauldron. There it forms what is called the Immortal Fetus, which adepts can reportedly raise through the Heavenly Gate at the top of the head and thus leave their physical body for various purposes, including preparation for life after death. In addition, the adept learns to draw the *ch'i* of the macro-universe of heaven and earth into the micro-universe of the body, unifying and harmonizing inner and outer, heaven and earth.

> *The secret of the magic of life consists in using action in order to attain non-action.*
> *The Secret of the Golden Flower*[13]

THE LURE OF IMMORTALITY   Taoist texts on immortality specify a twofold process: physically regaining and expanding health and vitality, and spiritually merging into the greater oneness of the Tao through total harmony. Immortality is both a refinement of the body and an overcoming of the limits of worldly existence. Already Chuang-tzu counseled indifference to birth and death: "The Master came because it was time. He left because he followed the natural flow. Be content with the moment, and be willing to follow the flow."[14] Lao-tzu referred enigmatically to immortality or long life realized through spiritual death of the individual self, the body and mind transmuted into selfless vehicles for the eternal. Still, for many the first step is good enough. As Professor Huai-Chin Han puts it, people who are interested in Taoist practices:

> usually forget the highest principles, or the basis of philosophical theory behind the cultivation of Tao and the opening of the ch'i routes for longevity. . . . Longevity consists of maintaining one's health, slowing down the ageing process, living without illness and pain, and dying peacefully without bothering other people. Immortality does not mean indefinite physical longevity; it indicates the eternal spiritual life.[15]

A quiet contemplative life in natural surroundings, with sexual abstinence, peaceful mind, health-maintaining herbs, practices to strengthen the inner organs and open the meridians (subtle energy pathways known to Chinese doctors), and meditations to transmute vital into spiritual energy bring a marked tendency to longevity. Chinese literature and folk knowledge contain many references to venerable sages thought to be centuries old. They live hidden in the mountains, away from society, and are said to be somewhat translucent. Their age is difficult to verify. The Chinese sage Li Ch'ing Yuen claimed that he was 250 years old, shortly before he died early in the twentieth century, apparently from the effects of being exposed to "civilization." The most famous of the legendary long-lived are the Eight Immortals, humans who were said to have gained immortality, each with his or her own special magical power.

For instance, since ancient times, one of the most revered celestial beings has been the Queen Mother of the West. She guards the elixir of life and is the most wondrous incarnation of yin energy. The Taoist canon also includes the writings of some female Taoist sages who undertook the great rigors of Taoist meditation practices and reportedly mastered its processes of inner transformation. In her mystical poetry, the twelfth-century female sage Sun Bu-er describes the ultimate realization:

All things finished.
You sit still in a little niche.
The light body rides on violet energy,
The tranquil nature washes in a pure pond.
Original energy is unified, yin and yang are one;
The spirit is the same as the universe.[16]

Another form of energy practice is **T'ai-chi ch'uan**. Developed in the eighteenth century as a training for martial arts, it is still practiced today by many Chinese at dawn and dusk for their health. It looks like slow swimming in the air, with continual circular movement through a series of dance-like postures. They are ideally manifestations of the unobstructed flow of *ch'i* through the body. According to the *T'ai-chi Ch'uan Classics*, "In any action the entire body should be light and agile and all of its parts connected like pearls on a thread."[17] *Ch'i* is cultivated internally but not expressed externally as power. In combat, the practitioner of T'ai-chi is advised to "yield at your opponent's slightest pressure and adhere to him at his slightest retreat,"[18] using mental alertness to subtle changes rather than muscular strength in order to gain the advantage.

T'ai-chi is also a physical way of becoming one with the eternal interlocking of yin and yang, and of movement and stillness. T'ai-chi master Al Chung-liang Huang says:

Think of the contrasting energies moving together and in union, in harmony,
interlocking, like a white fish and a black fish mating. If you identify with only one
side of the duality, then you become unbalanced. . . . Movement and stillness
become one. One is not a static point. One is a moving one, one is a changing one,
one is everything. One is also that stillness suspended, flowing, settling, in motion.[19]

Al Huang embodies the fluidity of T'ai-chi ch'uan, practiced both for physical health and for teaching the mind to flow with change so that action is effortless.

Taoism today

All forms of Taoist practice are still actively undertaken today, both in communist mainland China and Chinese communities elsewhere, and also increasingly in the West. They tend to merge with popular religion, New Age philosophies, and health culture. In China, they form part of domestic and family religion. To the present day, there are numerous rituals in the home, such as the farewell party to the stove god on the lunar New Year's eve (late January or February). In hopes that the god of the kitchen, who sits in the corner watching what the family does, will speak well of them in his annual report to the Jade Emperor, god of the present, families offer sweets, incense, and paper horses, with the prayer: "When you go to heaven you should report only good things, and when you come down from heaven you should protect us and bring peace and safety to us."[20]

Also, both Taoist and Buddhist groups continue to be recipients of new revelations and scriptures. These texts, which are known as "precious scrolls," emanate from deities such as the Golden Mother of the Celestial Pool. It is believed that in the past the Divine Mother sent Buddha and Lao-tzu as her messengers but that now the crisis of the present world requires her direct intervention.

Contemporary religion also follows the ancient practice of worshipping certain people as divine, appointed to heavenly office after they died. There are many examples, such as the valiant and loyal late Han dynasty general Kuan-kung, who is honored everywhere in China as the righter of wrongs and supporter of justice. A virtuous daughter of the Lin family saved members of her own family and others in distress during the Sung dynasty, and now she is worshipped as Tien-hou, the Holy Mother in Heaven, especially in coastal regions. Recently in mainland China, worship has revived for the Great Emperor Who Protects Life, who is traced back to an inspired eleventh-century doctor. The reverence that is still shown to the twentieth-century liberator of China, Mao Zedong (1893–1976), likewise reflects the Chinese pattern of recognizing certain humans as possessing divine power to help and save the people.

Historically, whenever the central Chinese government has been strong, it has tended to demand total allegiance to itself as a divine authority and to challenge or suppress competing religious groups. The emperors of ancient China either claimed divine origin or referred to themselves as the Sons of Heaven appointed from on high. Confucian scholars were suppressed and their books were burned by the Ch'in dynasty (221–206 BCE), shamans were forbidden during the Han dynasty, Buddhists were persecuted during the T'ang dynasty, the T'ai-p'ing rebellion of the nineteenth century attempted to purge China of Taoism and Buddhism, and during the Cultural Revolution of 1966 to 1976, zealous young Red Guards destroyed Taoist, Buddhist, and Confucian temples and books. However, during the economic liberalization of the late twentieth century in mainland China, in spite of an atheistic communist ideology, temples were maintained as historic sites, pilgrimages to temples in natural sites and religious tourism were encouraged, and an explosion of temple building occurred.

Interest in Taoist practices and philosophy has boomed in the West from the middle of the twentieth century, and by now there are many masters and centers in the United States. They typically fall into the same three categories that have

Taoist religion is still practiced in non-communist Chinese areas. At the Matsu Yen Tao Temple in Anping, Taiwan, Taoist elements are incorporated into worship of the goddess Matsu.

long characterized Taoism in the East: organized religious institutions, societies for self-cultivation, and practitioners of techniques for spiritual development and longevity.

Nonetheless, a new wave of repression began in 1999 with severe persecution of followers of Falun Gong or Falun Dafa. This is a hybrid of Buddhist virtues and Taoist energy practices initiated by Li Hongzhi in 1992. It involves five daily exercises for developing the *ch'i*, plus attempts to develop three cardinal virtues: honesty, benevolence toward all beings, and forbearance, such that one does not react against others' wrongdoings. Li, who now lives in the United States, claims that practitioners of Falun Gong develop excellent health, supernatural power, and cosmic enlightenment. The practices are taught for free, by volunteers. "Master Li" now has hundreds of thousands—perhaps millions—of followers around the world. But those in China are being imprisoned and tortured because the movement is regarded as a political threat. In 1999, the Chinese government labeled it an "evil religion," "spiritual opium," and an "heretical cult suspected of illegal management crimes." Legislation has been passed that may be used to suppress any mystical Chinese group, in addition to any religious group that has not been sanctioned by the Communist Party. But interest in Falun Gong and Taoism in general is running high in other countries, complete with numerous websites and international Taoist organizations and scholarly conferences, and is likely to continue growing rather than receding.

Confucianism—the practice of virtue

To trace a different strand of Eastern religion, we return to the sixth century BCE, which was a period of great spiritual and intellectual flourishing in many cultures. It roughly coincided with the life of the Buddha and perhaps of Lao-tzu, the Persian Empire, the Golden Age of Athens, the great Hebrew prophets, and in China with the life of another outstanding figure. Westerners call him Confucius and his teaching Confucianism. His family name was K'ung; the Chinese honored him as K'ung Fu-tzu (Master K'ung) and called his teaching **Juchiao** (the teaching of the scholars). It did not begin with Confucius. Rather, it is based on the ancient Chinese beliefs in the Lord on High, the Mandate of Heaven, ancestor worship, spirits, and the efficacy of rituals. Confucius developed from these roots a school of thought that emphasizes the cultivation of moral virtues and the interaction between human rulers and Heaven, with political involvement as the way to transforming the world.

This philosophy became highly influential in China and still permeates the society, despite great political changes. It exists not only as a school of thought but also as the practice of religious ethics, as a political ideology, and as the link between the state and the Mandate of Heaven.

For two thousand years, Taoism, Buddhism, and Confucianism have co-existed in China, contributing mutually to the culture. Both Taoism and Buddhism emphasize the ever-changing nature of things in the cosmos, whereas Confucianism focuses on ways of developing a just and orderly society.

Individuals often harmonize the apparently opposite characteristics of Taoism and Confucianism in their own lives. For example, elderly Taoist Master An speaks on one hand of the fact that he and his fellows sweep the temple when they feel like it—"We're not caught up in routines"—and on the other of the ways that his father's teaching of Confucian maxims shaped his life:

> My father was very cultured and adamant about teaching us the true Tao. He mastered the classics, and would write out quotations all the time. Over on the wall there is a quotation by Confucius he wrote:
>
> If I'm not generous with those below me,
> If I'm disrespectful toward the proprieties,
> Or if I do not properly mourn at a funeral,
> How can I have self-esteem?
>
> He'd paste these quotations on our wall above the bed. I'd turn my head and there it was, sinking in my brain. . . . Confucius also said, "One who seeks the Tao cannot be deficient in manners."[21]

Professor Yu Yingshi explains that Taoism and Confucianism can co-exist because in Chinese tradition there are no major divisions between mind and matter, utopian ideals and everyday life:

> For Chinese, the transcendental world, the world of the spirit, interpenetrates with the everyday world though it is not considered identical to it. If we use the tao to represent the transcendental world and the Confucian ideal of human relationships to represent the human world, we can see how they interface. The tao creates the

character of these human relations. For these relations to exist as such, they must follow the tao, they cannot depart from the tao for a moment. These two worlds operate on the cusp of interpenetration, neither dependent on or independent of the other. So mundane human relationships are, from the very beginning, endowed with a transcendental character.[22]

Master K'ung's life

Young K'ung Ch'iu was born in approximately 551 BCE, during the Chou dynasty, into a family whose ancestors had been prominent in the previous dynasty. They had lost their position through political struggles, and Ch'iu's father, a soldier, died when the boy was only three years old. Although young Ch'iu was determined to be a scholar, the family's financial straits necessitated his taking such humble work as overseeing granaries and livestock. He married at the age of nineteen and had at least two children.

Ch'iu's mother died when he was twenty-three, sending him into three years of mourning. During this period he lived ascetically and studied ancient ceremonial rites (*li*) and imperial institutions. When he returned to social interaction, he gained some renown as a teacher of *li* and of the arts of governing.

It was a period of political chaos, with the stability of the early Chou dynasty having given way to disorder. As central power weakened, feudal lords held more power than kings of the central court, ministers assassinated their rulers, and sons killed their fathers. Confucius felt that a return to classical rites and standards of virtue was the only way out of the chaos, and he earnestly but unsuccessfully sought rulers who would adopt his ideas.

Confucius turned to a different approach: training young men to be wise and altruistic public servants. He proposed that the most effective strategy was for the rulers to perform classical rites and music properly so that they would remain of visibly high moral character and thus inspire the common people to be virtuous. He thus revived and instructed his students in the "Six Classics" of China's cultural heritage: the *I Ching*, poetry, history, rituals, music and dance, and the Spring and Autumn Annals of events in his state, Lu. According to tradition, it was Confucius who edited older documents pertaining to these six areas and who put them into the form now known as the Confucian Classics. There are now only five; the treatises on music were either destroyed or never existed. Of his role, Confucius claimed only: "I am a transmitter and not a creator. I believe in and have a passion for the ancients."[23]

Confucius's work and teachings were considered relatively insignificant during his lifetime. After his death in 479 BCE, interstate warfare increased, ancient family loyalties were replaced by large and impersonal armies, and personal virtues were replaced by laws and state control. After the brutal reunification of China by the Ch'in and Han dynasties, however, rulership required a more cultured class of bureaucrats who could embody the virtues advocated by Confucius. In the second century BCE the Confucian Classics thus became the basis of the civil service examinations for the scholar-officials who were to serve in the government. The life of the gentleman-scholar devoted to proper government became the highest professed ideal. Eventually temples were devoted to the worship of Confucius himself as the model for unselfish public service, human kindness, and

Confucianism idealized gentlemen-scholars, who became the highest class in China until the 20th-century revolution.

scholarship. However, the official state use of the Confucian Classics can be seen as a political device to give the government a veneer of civility.

The Confucian virtues

Foremost among the virtues that Confucius felt could save society was **jen**. Translations of this central term include innate goodness, love, benevolence, perfect virtue, humaneness, and human-heartedness. In Chapter IV of *The Analects*, Confucius describes the rare person who is utterly devoted to *jen* as one who is not motivated by personal profit but by what is moral, is concerned with self-improvement rather than public recognition, is ever mindful of parents, speaks cautiously but acts quickly, and regards human nature as basically good.

The prime example of *jen* should be the ruler. Rulers were required to rule not by physical force but by the example of personal virtue:

> *Confucius said: If a ruler himself is upright, all will go well without orders. But if he himself is not upright, even though he gives orders they will not be obeyed. . . . One who governs by virtue is comparable to the polar star, which remains in its place while all the stars turn towards it."*[24]

Asked to define the essentials of strong government, Confucius listed adequate troops, adequate food, and the people's trust. But of these, the only true necessity is that the people have faith in their rulers. To earn this faith, the ruling class should "cultivate themselves," leading lives of virtue and decorum. They should continually adhere to *jen*, always reaching upward, cherishing what is right, rather than reaching downward for material gain.

The Chinese character for *jen* is a combination of "two" and "person," conveying the idea of relationship. Those relationships emphasized by Confucius are the interactions between father and son, older and younger siblings, husband and wife, older and younger friend, ruler and subject. In these relationships, the first is considered superior to the second. Each relationship is nonetheless based on distinct but mutual obligations and responsibilities. This web of human relationships supports the individual like a series of concentric circles.

At the top, the ruler models himself on Heaven, serving as a parent to the people and linking them to the larger cosmic order through ritual ceremonies. Confucius says that this was the source of the greatness of Yao—a sage king of c. 2357 BCE: "It is Heaven that is great and Yao who modelled himself upon it."[25]

In Confucius's ideal world, there is a reciprocal hierarchy in which each knows his place and respects those above him. As the *Great Learning* states it, peace begins with the moral cultivation of the individual and order in the family. This peace extends outward to society, government, and the universe itself like circular ripples in a pond.

The heart of moral rectification is filial piety to one's parents. According to Confucian doctrine, there are three grades of filial piety: the lowest is to support one's parents, the second is not to bring humiliation to one's parents and ancestors, and the highest is to glorify them. In the ancient *Book of Rites*, as revived by Confucius, deference to one's parents is scrupulously defined. For instance, a husband and wife should go to visit their parents and parents-in-law, whereupon:

> *On getting to where they are, with bated breath and gentle voice, they should ask if their clothes are (too) warm or (too) cold, whether they are ill or pained, or uncomfortable in any part; and if they be so, they should proceed reverently to stroke and scratch the place. They should in the same way, going before or following after, help and support their parents in quitting or entering (the apartment). In bringing in the basin for them to wash, the younger will carry the stand and the elder the water; they will beg to be allowed to pour out the water, and when the washing is concluded, they will hand the towel. They will ask whether they want anything, and then respectfully bring it. All this they will do with an appearance of pleasure to make their parents feel at ease.*[26]

Confucius also supported the ancient Chinese custom of ancestor veneration, as an extension of filial piety—indeed, as the highest achievement of filial piety.

Confucius said relatively little about the supernatural, preferring to focus on the here-and-now: "While you are not able to serve men, how can you serve the ghosts and spirits?"[27] He made a virtue of *li* (the rites honoring ancestors and deities), but with the cryptic suggestion that one make the sacrifices "as if" the spirits were present. According to some interpreters, he encouraged the rites as a way of establishing earthly harmony through reverent, ethical behavior. The rites should not be empty gestures; he recommended that they be outwardly simple and inwardly grounded in *jen*.

Although Confucius did not speak much about an unseen Reality, he asserted that *li* are the earthly expressions of the natural cosmic order. *Li* involves right conduct in terms of the five basic relationships essential for a stable society: kindness in the father and filial piety in the son; gentility in the older brother and respect in the younger; righteous behavior in the husband and obedience in the wife; humane consideration in the older friend and deference in the younger friend; and benevolence in rulers and loyalty in subjects.

Everything should be done with a sense of propriety. Continually eulogizing the typical gentleman of China's ancient high civilization as the model, Confucius used examples such as the way of passing someone in mourning. Even if the mourner were a close friend, the gentleman would assume a solemn expression and "lean forward with his hands on the crossbar of his carriage to show respect; he would act in a similar manner towards a person carrying official documents."[28] Even in humble surroundings, the proprieties should be observed: "Even when a meal consisted only of coarse rice and vegetable broth, [the gentleman] invariably made an offering from them and invariably did so solemnly."[29]

Divergent followers of Confucius

The Confucian tradition has been added to by many later commentators. Two of the most significant were Mencius and Hsun Tzu, who differed in their approach.

A little over a hundred years after Confucius died, the "Second Sage" Meng Tzu (commonly latinized as Mencius) was born. During his lifetime (c. 390–305 BCE) Chinese society became even more chaotic. Like his predecessor, the Second Sage tried to share his wisdom with embattled rulers, but to no avail. He, too, took up teaching, based on stabilizing aspects of the earlier feudal system.

Mencius's major additions to the Confucian tradition were his belief in the goodness of human nature and his focus on the virtue of **yi**, or righteous conduct. Mencius emphasized the moral duty of rulers to govern by the principle of humanity and the good of the people. If rulers are guided by profit motives, this self-centered motivation will be reflected in all subordinates and social chaos will ensue. On the other hand, "When a commiserating government is conducted from a commiserating heart, one can rule the whole empire as if one were turning it in one's palm."[30] This is a natural way, says Mencius, for people are naturally good: "The tendency of human nature to do good is like that of water to flow downward."[31] Heaven could be counted on to empower the righteous.

Another follower quite disagreed with this assessment. This was Hsun Tzu, who seems to have been born when Mencius was an old man. Hsun Tzu argued that human nature is naturally evil and that Heaven is impersonal, operating according to natural laws rather than intervening on the side of good government or responding to human wishes ("Heaven does not suspend the winter because men dislike cold"[32]). Humans must hold up their own end. Their natural tendency, however, is to envy, to hate, and to desire personal gain and sensual pleasure. The only way to constrain these tendencies is to teach and legally enforce the rules of *li* and *yi*. Though naturally flawed, humans can gradually attain sagehood by persistent study, patience, and good works and thereby form a cooperative triad with Heaven and earth.

Hsun Tzu's careful reasoning provided a basis for the new legalistic structure of government. The idealism of Mencius was revived much later as a Chinese response to Buddhism and became required for the civil service examinations from the thirteenth to the twentieth centuries. However, their points of agreement are basic to Confucianism: the appropriate practice of virtue is of great value; humans can attain this through self-cultivation; and study and emulation of the ancient sages are the path to harmony in the individual, family, state, and world.

The state cult

Since ancient times, as we have seen, rulers have been regarded as the link between earth and Heaven. This understanding persisted in Chinese society, but Confucius and his followers had elaborated the idea that the ruler must be virtuous for this relationship to work. During the Han dynasty, Confucius's teachings were at last honored by the state. The Han scholar Tung Chung-shu (c. 179– c. 104 BCE) set up an educational system based on the Confucian Classics that lasted until the twentieth century. He used Confucian ideals to unite the people behind the ruler, who himself was required to be subject to Heaven.

It was during this period that civil service examinations based on the Confucian classics were first established as a means of attaining government positions. The Confucian Classics were established as the Five Classics and the Four Books as the standard textbooks for education during the Sung dynasty by the Neo-Confucian scholar, Chu Hsi (1130–1200 CE). *His Reflections on Things at Hand* gave a metaphysical basis for Confucianism: the individual is intimately linked with all of the cosmos, "forming one body with all things." According to Chang Tsai's *Western Inscription*:

> *Heaven is my father and earth is my mother and even such a small creature as I finds an intimate place in their midst. Therefore, that which extends throughout the universe I regard as my body and that which directs the universe I regard as my nature. All people are my brothers and sisters and all things are my companions. The great ruler [the emperor] is the eldest son of my parents [Heaven and Earth], and the great ministers are his stewards. . . . To rejoice in Heaven and to have no anxiety—this is filial piety at its purest.[33]*

By becoming more humane one can help to transform not only oneself but also society and even the cosmos. The Neo-Confucianists thus stressed the importance of meditation and dedication to becoming a "noble person."

The Temple of Heaven in Beijing. Since ancient times in China, there has been an open-air altar used by the emperor himself once or twice a year to make sacrifices to Heaven, the main governing and guiding force of the Confucian universe.

Women were encouraged to offer themselves in total sacrifice to others. Confucian women had previously been expected to take a subordinate role in the family and in society, but at the same time to be strong, disciplined, wise, and capable in their relationships with their husbands and sons. In Neo-Confucianism, such virtues were subsumed under an extreme ideal of self-sacrifice.

Although Confucius had counseled restrained use of *li*, Neo-Confucianism also included an increased emphasis on sacrifice, as practiced since ancient times and set forth in the traditional *Book of Rites* and *Etiquette and Ritual*, which had been reconstructed during the Han dynasty. These rites were thought to preserve harmony between humans, Heaven, and earth. At the family level, offerings were made to propitiate the family ancestors. Government officials were responsible for ritual sacrifices to beings such as the gods of fire, literature, cities, mountains, waters, the polar star, sun, moon, and former rulers, as well as spirits of the earth and sky.

The most important ceremonies were performed by the emperor, to give thanks and ask blessings from Heaven, earth, gods of the land and agriculture, and the dynastic ancestors. Traditionally these were performed at the tops of five holy mountains in the four cardinal directions and the center of the kingdom, each associated with a particular season and symbolic meaning, such as rites for spring and new growth that were held in the east. Of these, the highest ritual was the elaborate annual sacrifice to Shang Ti at the white marble Altar of Heaven by the emperor. He was considered Son of Heaven, the "high priest of the world." Both he and his large retinue prepared themselves by three days of fasting and keeping vigil. In a highly reverent atmosphere, he then sacrificed a bull, offered precious jade, and sang prayers of gratitude to the Supreme, such as this one:

> With reverence we spread out these precious stones and silk, and, as swallows rejoicing in the spring, praise Thy abundant love. . . . Men and creatures are emparadised, O Ti, in Thy love. All living things are indebted to Thy goodness, but who knows whence his blessings come to him? It is Thou alone, O Lord, who art the true parent of all things.[34]

Confucianism under communism

The performance of rituals was a time-consuming and major part of government jobs, carried out on behalf of the people. But as China gradually opened to the West in recent centuries, a reaction set in against these older ways, and the last of the imperial dynasties was overthrown in 1911. Although worship of Confucius continued, in the 1920s Republic, science and social progress were glorified by radical intellectuals of the New Culture movement who were opposed to all the old systems. Under the communist regime established in 1949, communism took the place of religion, attempting to transform the society by secular means. Party Chairman Mao Zedong was venerated almost as a god, with the "Little Red Book" of quotations from Chairman Mao replacing the Confucian Classics.

During the Cultural Revolution (1966–76), Confucianism was attacked as one of the "Four Olds"—old ideas, culture, customs, and habits. The Cultural Revolution attempted to destroy the hierarchical structure that Confucianism had idealized and to prevent the intellectual elite from ruling over the masses. Contrary to the Confucian virtue of filial piety, young people even denounced their parents at public trials, and scholars were made objects of derision. An estimated one million people were attacked. Some were killed, some committed suicide, and millions suffered.

Mao said that he had hated Confucianism from his childhood. What he so disliked was the intellectual emphasis on the study of the Classics, the "superstitious" rituals, and the oppression of the lowest members of hierarchical Chinese society—women and peasants. He had urged peasants to overthrow all authoritarian traditions, including religion:

> A man in China is usually subjected to the domination of three systems of authority: (1) the state system (political authority) . . . ; (2) the clan system (clan authority), ranging from the central ancestral temple and its branch temples down to the head of the household; and (3) the supernatural system (religious authority), ranging from the King of Hell down to the town and village gods belonging to the nether world, and from the Emperor of Heaven down to all the various gods and spirits belonging to the celestial world. As for women, in addition to being

During the years of Mao Zedong's ascendency, the Chairman was treated as a larger-than-life hero of a grand drama that replaced but also resembled religion.

dominated by these three systems of authority, they are also dominated by the men (the authority of the husband). These four authorities—political, clan, religious and masculine—are the embodiment of the whole feudal-patriarchal system and ideology, and are the four thick ropes binding the Chinese people, particularly the peasants.[35]

Nevertheless, in some respects, Confucian morality continued to form the basis of Chinese ethics. Mao particularly emphasized the (Confucian) virtues of selfless service to the people and of self-improvement for the public good:

All our cadres, whatever their rank, are servants of the people, and whatever we do is to serve the people. How then can we be reluctant to discard any of our bad traits?[36]

For decades, communist China prided itself on being the most law-abiding country in the world. The streets were safe, and tourists found that if they could not understand the currency, they could trust taxi drivers to take the exact amount, and no more, from their open wallets. But recently there has been a rise in crime and official corruption. The society has changed abruptly since China opened its doors to the West in 1978, undermining traditional Confucian virtues. The government blames the influx of materialistic values, resulting from the indiscriminating embrace of the underside of Western culture and the rapid shift toward a free market economy. In 1989, Chao Tzu-yang, then Communist Party leader, urged officials to maintain Confucian discipline (without naming it that) in the midst of the changes: "The Party can by no means allow its members to barter away their principles for money and power."[37] But when the people picked up this cry, aging leaders chose brutally to suppress popular calls for greater democracy and an end to official corruption; they did so in the name of another Confucian value: order in society.

For their part, the intellectuals of the democracy movement had tried to do things in the proper way but were caught on the horns of the poignant Chinese dilemma. Under Confucian ethics, it has been the continuing responsibility of scholars to morally cultivate themselves and properly remonstrate with their rulers, to play the role of upright censors. On the other hand, scholars had to remain loyal to the ruler, for they were subjects and observing one's subservient position as a subject preserved the security of the state. The leaders of the democracy movement tried to deal with this potential conflict by ritualized, respectful action: they formally walked up the steps of the Great Hall of the People in Tiananmen Square to present their written requests to those in power. But they were ignored and brutally suppressed.

Again, in 1995, forty-five of China's most distinguished scholars and scientists delivered a petition to the government urging freedom of thought and accountability of the government to the public, in order to end socially corrosive corruption. Some observers speculate that slow transformations will bring a new form of Confucian tradition. Already, interest in Confucian thought is increasing among intellectuals. Conferences have recently been held on the mainland in China and also in Taiwan and Singapore to discuss Confucianism. Today it is being analyzed not as an historical artifact but as a tradition that is relevant to modern life. Even though it may not be practiced in the same ways as before, it

Students demonstrating for democracy in Tiananmen Square, May 1989, after breaking through police blockades. Leaders of this movement presented their requests formally at the Great Hall of the People, but the movement was forcefully suppressed.

may nonetheless contribute significantly to cultural identity, economic progress, social harmony, and a personal sense of the meaning of human life.

Confucianism may inform capitalistic behavior as well as Marxist communism. There is now talk of "Capitalist Confucianism"—business conducted according to Confucian ethics such as humanity, trustworthiness, sincerity, and altruism. The Confucian value system has significant potential for informing capitalist freedom of choice. As Professor Xinzhong Yao explains,

> *Free choice is the foundation of modern society, and the pre-condition of market economy. However, freedom without responsibility would result in the collapse of the social network and in the conflict between individuals and between individuals and society, and would lead to the sacrifice of the future in order to satisfy short-term needs. This has become a serious challenge to human wisdom and to human integrity. In this respect, Confucianism can make a contribution to a new moral sense, a new ecological view and a new code for the global village.*[38]

Confucian values are also being reappraised as a significant addition to holistic education. In them is imbedded the motivation to improve oneself and become a responsible and ethical member of one's family and society. Self-perception, according to Confucian ideals, is a lifelong process. Thus the Neo-Confucians studied education methods and developed multi-stage learning programs that extend beyond the years of formal schooling. Confucianism has always promoted education as the only means to social reform, and further encourages a sense of voluntary service to the community.

In the moral and spiritual vacuum left after the demise of fervent Maoism, Confucianism may also help restore a sense of holy purpose to people's lives. The traditional feeling was that the Mandate of Heaven gives transcendent meaning to human life. Professor Tu Wei-ming, a modern Neo-Confucian, explains:

> *We are the guardians of the good earth, the trustees of the Mandate of Heaven that enjoins us to make our bodies healthy, our hearts sensitive, our minds alert, our souls refined, and our spirits brilliant. . . . We serve Heaven with common sense, the lack of which nowadays has brought us to the brink of self-destruction. Since we help Heaven to realize itself though our self-discovery and self-understanding in day-to-day living, the ultimate meaning of life is found in our ordinary, human existence.*[39]

Revived interest in Confucianism is occurring not only among intellectuals. Chinese authorities have recently reintroduced the teaching of Confucius in elementary schools throughout the country as a vehicle for encouraging social morality. After a gap of more than half a century, the Confucian-based civil service examinations are being partially reintroduced in the selection of public servants. Earlier castigated as "feudal institutions," Confucian academies are being described as fine centers for learning. Chinese authorities are also reviving aspects of the religious cult, such as observance of the birthday of Confucius, perhaps mostly for the sake of tourism. But believers such as members of the Confucian Academy in Hong Kong take such observances seriously. In rural areas, observance of Confucian virtues has remained rather steady through time.

Living Confucianism

Ann-ping Chin grew up in Taiwan, the daughter of parents from the northern part of mainland China. She teaches Confucianism and Taoism at Wesleyan University and has visited China five times to do research on the continuing changes in that society. Of the contemporary situation there with regard to traditional values she says:

"Lots of things are changing in China. First of all, the economic boom is changing women's perceptions of themselves and of their family. For instance, if a woman is determined to have a profession of her own, in this huge marketplace of China this implies that she would become involved in a private enterprise or begin one herself. If she does that, this means that she would have to consider child-rearing as secondary. Usually these women depend on their parents or in-laws to bring up their children, in their own homes.

"Divorce is very common. Family units are breaking up and children have less security—there are all the problems that we associate with divorce in the West. The woman simply says, 'Look—I'm going to leave or you leave.'

"Making money is now the most important thing for the Chinese. It's finally a free market. Even though it's economic freedom, it's some kind of freedom. 'So,' they feel, 'why not make the most of that sort of freedom? Political freedom can wait. Let's make the most of this that we have, and not ask too much.'

"From an initial impression, perhaps you can say that the fundamental Confucian values are disappearing. Through more than two thousand years of Chinese history, both in traditional Confucian teachings and in Taoist teachings as well, you find a tremendous deprecation of the idea of making money—of taking advantage or making a profit, be it in money or in human relationships. Now unless you have the determination to make money, you are not considered a true man in Chinese society.

"On the other hand, if you really delve into their private lives, and try to understand what is really important to the Chinese, I would say that the very basic relationships of parents and children, and of friends to friends are still very strong. The Chinese have given up their relationship with the ruler; that's really a joke. The relationship between husband and wife is much more complicated. Men love the idea of having a very devoted wife. They know that is perhaps impossible, but they still yearn for it. And they still value the traditional qualities that you find in the biographies of virtuous women. If they can find that in their mothers, they still appreciate those values.

"Other values have been abandoned. I'm very disturbed and saddened, pained, by what is happening to the Chinese scholars. They cannot go out and do private enterprise, for they are scholars. They get paid a very pathetic amount of money each month, not enough to make ends meet. Scholars have always been really respected even though people didn't understand them. But now there isn't even that respect since the society is placing so much emphasis on making money.

"My parents both came from very scholarly backgrounds. They passed down to us the traditions without the formalities, without the rigidities, so we were extremely fortunate. I think my father passed down to us his love of students, his love of teaching, and of the very special relationship between teachers and disciples. That relationship is a very special one in Chinese tradition. If you are lucky, you can still see that between an elderly teacher and his disciples. It's not obedience—rather, it's a concern that the disciple expresses toward the teacher.

"In looking at what I've absorbed from my parents, there's also the matter of character. My father's character had a profound effect on me. I just intuitively know that he always tried to do the right thing. And to do the right thing sometimes can be so difficult. This was the only way that he could live—to always try to do the right thing, whether it was for a friend, or for us, for my mom, for his own parents, or for strangers. He would never compromise that."

Confucianism in East Asia

Countries near China, which have historically been influenced by China politically and culturally, also show signs of having been influenced by Confucian values. The city-state of Singapore has since 1978 sponsored an annual courtesy campaign to inspire virtuous behavior in the midst of fast-paced modern life. In 1997, the focus of the campaign was courteous use of mobile phones and pagers. It was politely suggested that one should turn them off in theaters, places of worship, and public functions to avoid disturbing others.

In Korea, where few people now consider themselves adherents of Confucianism as a religion, lectures and special events are being sponsored by hundreds of local Confucian institutes to promote Confucian teachings. In some cases, Confucianism is associated with particular clans in East Asia, and thus with political favoritism. Some of the Korean institutes are politically conservative, opposing women's efforts to revise family laws. The Korean Overseas Information Service advocates a flexible, liberal version of the tradition, open to other cultures and to all religions but still providing a firm foundation for social order:

> *Confucianism can present contemporary Koreans with a set of practical standards of conduct in the form of rituals and etiquette. Extensive introduction of Western modes of behavior led to the confusion and adulteration of Korea's native behavior pattern. Civility and propriety in speech and deportment enhance the dignity of man. Rites and conduct befitting to a civilized people should be refined and adjusted to the conditions of the time. ... Korea should, through its Confucian heritage, sustain the tradition of propriety and modesty and defend the intrinsically moral nature of man from submergence in economic and materialistic considerations.[40]*

Various Confucian organizations have developed in Hong Kong, Taiwan, and other parts of East Asia which are attempting to restore religious versions of Confucianism, such as the worship of Confucius himself or study of the Confucian Classics in Sunday schools.

Confucian thought has also played a significant role in Japan. It entered Japan during the seventh century when Chinese political thought and religious ideas first began to have significant influence there. It left its mark on the first constitution of Japan, on the arrangement of government bureaucracy, and in the educational system. From the twelfth to the sixteenth century, Confucianism was studied in Zen Buddhist monasteries. Then from the seventeenth to nineteenth century, Confucianism began to spread more widely among the people of Japan because of its adoption as an educational philosophy in public and private schools. Confucian moral teachings became the basis for establishing proper human relationships in the family and in Japanese society.

Both Confucianism and Shinto were manipulated by the military during the pre-war period to inculcate a nationalist expansionist ideology. More in keeping with the original motives of Confucianism, some scholars have observed that Japan's notably effective modernization in the last one hundred years is partly due to values derived from Confucianism. These values include a high regard for diligence, consensus, education, moral self-cultivation, frugality, and loyalty.

Suggested reading

Chang, Wing-Tsit, *A Sourcebook in Chinese Philosophy*, Princeton: Princeton University Press, 1963. A large and helpful anthology of Confucian, Taoist, and Buddhist texts.

de Bary, William Theodore, *East Civilizations: A Dialogue in Five Stages*, Cambridge: Harvard University Press, 1988. A masterful overview of 3,000 years of East Asian civilization, including the classical legacy, the Buddhist age, the Neo-Confucian stage, and East Asia's modern transformation.

de Bary, William Theodore, Chan, Wing-tsit, and Watson, Burton, eds., *Sources of Chinese Tradition*, New York: Columbia University Press, 1960. Useful commentaries and extensive texts from Confucian and Taoist schools.

The I Ching, translated into German by Richard Wilhelm and thence into English by Cary Baynes, third edition, Princeton, New Jersey: Princeton University Press, 1967. Insights into the multiple possibilities of the interplay of yin and yang in our lives.

Kohn, Livia, *The Taoist Experience*, Albany, New York: State University of New York Press, 1993. Interesting translations of ancient and more recent texts covering the various aspects of Taoism.

Kohn, Livia, *Daoism and Chinese Culture*, Cambridge, Massachusetts: Three Pines Press, 2001. Concise survey of different forms of Taoism in chronological order, considering comparative aspects and providing additional bibliography.

Lopez, Donald S., ed., *Religions of China in Practice*, Princeton, New Jersey: Princeton University Press, 1996. Excellent articles illustrating the overlap between Confucianism, Taoism, and Buddhism in traditional and contemporary practice, with translations of original texts.

Mencius, trans. by D. C. Lau, New York: Viking Penguin, 1970.

Robinet, Isabelle, *Taoist Meditation: The Mao-shan Tradition of Great Purity*, trans. Julian Pas and Norman Girardot, Albany, New York: State University of New York Press, 1993. A careful analysis of the central scriptures and practices used by elite Taoists to become Immortals.

Schipper, Kristofer M., *The Taoist Body*, trans. Karen Duvall, Berkeley: University of California Press, 1992. Explores integration of religious and philosophical Taoism within the Celestial Masters movement, from the Han dynasty to contemporary Taiwan.

Sommer, Deborah, ed., *Chinese Religions: An Anthology of Sources*, New York/Oxford: Oxford University Press, 1995. Interesting primary source material from Taoist, Confucian, Buddhist, and communist writings about religious topics.

Tao-te Ching, attributed to Lao-tzu, available in numerous translations, including the English translation by D. C. Lau, London: Penguin Books, 1963.

Taylor, Rodney, *The Religious Dimensions of Confucianism*, Albany: State University of New York Press, 1990. A collection of essays dealing with the central question of whether Confucianism is a religion.

Tu Wei-ming, *Confucian Thought: Selfhood as Creative Transformation*, Albany: State University of New York Press, 1985. A collection of Tu's seminal essays on his concern that Confucian humanity be understood as a living tradition with something distinctive to contribute to contemporary discussions in philosophy and comparative religions.

Watson, Burton, *Chuang Tzu: Basic Writings*, New York: Columbia University Press, 1964. An engaging translation of major writings by Chuang Tzu, with an introduction that is particularly helpful in dealing with this paradoxical material.

CHAPTER 7

SHINTO

The way of the kami

Japan has embraced and adapted many religions that originated in other countries, but it also developed its own unique path, closely tied to nature and the unseen world: Shinto. According to current scholarship, Shinto is not a single self-conscious religious tradition but rather an overarching label applied to ways of honoring the spirits in nature that have evolved since ancient times in Japan. These ways have at times been combined with imperial myths supporting the worldly rulers.

Of those modern Japanese who are religious, many combine practices from several religions, for each offers something different. Confucianism informs organizations and ethics, Buddhism and Christianity offer ways of understanding suffering and the afterlife, traditional veneration of ancestors links the living to their family history, and the way called "Shinto" harmonizes people with the natural world.

The essence of Shinto

The spiritual heart of Shinto has no founder, no orthodox canon of sacred literature, and no explicit code of ethical requirements. It is so deep-seated and ancient that the symbolic meanings of many of its elaborate rituals have been forgotten by those who practice them. It seems to have begun as the local religion of agricultural communities and had no name until Buddhism was imported in the sixth century CE. To distinguish the indigenous Japanese way from the foreign one, the former was labeled *shin* (divine being) *do* (way). During one period it was used by the central government to inspire nationalism, but since the forced separation of church and state after World War II Shinto has quietly returned to its roots. They can be described through three central aspects of the path: affinity with natural beauty, harmony with the spirits, and purification rituals.

Kinship with nature

Before industrial pollution and urbanization, Japan was a country of exquisite natural beauty, and to a certain extent, it still is. The islands marry mountains to sea, and the interiors are laced with streams, waterfalls, and lush forests. Even the agriculture is beautiful, with flowering fruit trees and terraced fields. The people lived so harmoniously with this environment that they had no separate word for

The Japanese people have traditionally honored the natural beauty of their land and have considered Mount Fuji to be its most sacred peak. Pilgrims have long made the arduous climb up Fuji seeking purification and good fortune.

"nature" until they began importing modern Western ideas late in the nineteenth century.

Living close to nature, the people experienced life as a continual process of change and renewal. They organized their lives around the turn of the seasons, honoring the roles of the sun, moon, and lightning in their rice farming. Mount Fuji, greatest of the volcanic peaks that formed the islands, was honored as the sacred embodiment of the divine creativity that had thrust the land up from the sea. It has never been called Mount Fuji by the Japanese, but rather Fuji-san, indicating a friendship and intimacy with the mountain. The sparkling ocean and rising sun, so visible along the extensive coastlines, were loved as earthly expressions of the sacred purity, brightness, and awesome power at the heart of life.

> *To be fully alive is to have an aesthetic perception of life because a major part of the world's goodness lies in its often unspeakable beauty.*
>
> *Rev. Yukitaka Yamamoto, Shinto priest* [1]

Although industrialization and urbanization have blighted some of the natural landscape, the sensitivity to natural beauty survives in small-scale arts. In traditional rock gardening, flower arranging, the tea ceremony, and poetry, Japanese artists continue to honor the simple and natural. If a rock is placed "just right" in a garden, it seems alive, radiating its natural essence. In a tea ceremony, great attention is paid to each natural sensual delight, from the purity of water poured from a wooden ladle to the genuineness of the clay vessels. These arts are often linked with Zen Buddhism, but the sensitivities seem to derive from the ancient Japanese ways.

Honoring the kami

Surrounded by nature's beauty and power, the Japanese people found the divine all around them. In Shinto, the sacred is both immanent and transcendent. In Japanese mythology, the divine originated as one essence:

> *In primeval ages, before the earth was formed, amorphous matter floated freely about like oil upon water. In time there arose in its midst a thing like a sprouting reedshoot, and from this a deity came forth of its own.[2]*

This deity gave birth to many **kami**, or spirits, two of which—the Amatsu *Kami*—were told to organize the material world. Standing on the Floating Bridge of Heaven, they stirred the ocean with a jeweled spear. When they pulled it out of the water, it dripped brine back into the ocean, where it coagulated into eight islands, with mountains, rivers, plants, and trees (these may be interpreted either as Japan or the whole world). To rule this earthly kingdom they created the Kami Amaterasu, Goddess of the Sun. Through their union, the Amatsu Kami also gave birth to the ancestors of the people of Japan. All of the natural world—land, trees, mountains, waters, animals, people—is thus joined in kinship as the spiritual creation of the *kami*.

Although the word *kami* (a way of pronouncing the character *shin*) is usually translated as "god" or "spirit," these translations are not exact. *Kami* can be either singular or plural, for the word refers to a single essence manifesting in many places. Rather than evoking an image, like the Hindu or Mahayana Buddhist

Shinto shrines are set apart by a torii, *an ever-open sacred gateway at the entrance to all shrine precincts. This floating* torii *is the symbolic gate to Itsukushima Jjinja shrine, Miyajima.*

deities, *kami* refers to a quality. It means that which evokes wonder and awe in us. The *kami* harmonize heaven and earth and also guide the solar system and the cosmos. It/they tend to reside in beautiful or powerful places, such as mountains, certain trees, unusual rocks, waterfalls, whirlpools, and animals. In addition, it/they manifest as wind, rain, thunder, or lightning. *Kami* also appear in abstract forms, such as the creativity of growth and reproduction. Since the seventh century CE, using the imported Chinese idea of the Mandate of Heaven, the emperor himself came to be revered as a *kami*—a living god, the divinely descended ruler upon whom the well-being of the country depends. In general, explains Sakamiki Shunzo, *kami* include:

> *all things whatsoever which deserve to be dreaded and revered for the extraordinary and preeminent powers which they possess. . . . [Kami] need not be eminent for surpassing nobleness, goodness, or serviceableness alone. Malignant and uncanny beings are also called* kami, *if only they are the objects of general dread.*[3]

Shrines

Recognizing the presence of *kami*, humans have built shrines to honor it/them. There are even now more than 100,000 Shinto shrines in Japan. Shrines may be as small as bee-hives or elaborate temple complexes covering thousands of acres. Some honor *kami* protecting the area; some honor *kami* with special responsibilities, such as healing or protecting crops from insects. The shrines are situated on sites thought to have been chosen by the *kami* for their sacred atmosphere. At one time, every community had its own guardian *kami*.

It is thought that the earliest Shinto places of worship were sacred trees or groves, perhaps with some enclosure to demarcate the sacred area. Shrine complexes that developed later also have some way of indicating where sacred space begins: tall gate-frames, known as *torii*, walls, or streams with bridges, which must be crossed to enter the holy precinct of the *kami*. Water is a purifying influence, and basins of water are also provided for washing one's mouth and hands before passing through the *torii*. Statues of guardian lions further protect the *kami* from evil intrusions, as do ropes with pendants hanging down.

In temple compounds, one first comes to a public hall of worship, behind which is an offering hall where priests conduct rites. Beyond that is the sacred sanctuary of the *kami*, which is entered only by the high priest. Here the spirit of the *kami* is invited to come down to dwell within a special natural object or perhaps a mirror, which reflects the revered light of brightness and purity, considered the natural order of the universe. If there is a spiritually powerful site already present—a waterfall, a crevice in a rock, a hot spring, a sacred tree—the spirit of the *kami* may dwell there. Some shrines are completely empty at the center. In any case, the eyes of the worshippers do not fall on the holy of holies; their worship is imageless. As Kishimoto Hideo explains,

> *A faithful believer would come to the simple hall of a Shinto sanctuary, which is located in a grove with a quiet and holy atmosphere. He may stand quite a while in front of the sanctuary, clap his hands, bow deeply, and try to feel the deity in his heart. . . . Shinto being a polytheistic religion, each sanctuary has its own particular deity. But seldom do the believers know the individual name of the deity whom they*

Modern Japanese visit Shinto shrines for many purposes, asking the blessing of kami *on the patterns of their lives. Most Shinto shrines are built with an appreciation for simple natural materials, and the larger ones are periodically rebuilt with great ceremony.*

are worshipping. They do not care about that. . . . The more important point for them is whether or not they feel the existence of the deity directly in their hearts.[4]

The *kami* of a place may be experienced as energies. They are not necessarily pictured as forms, and at times Shintoism has been strongly iconoclastic (opposed to images of the divine). In the eighteenth century, for instance, a famous Shinto scholar wrote:

Never make an image in order to represent the Deity. To worship a deity is directly to establish a felt relation of our heart to the living Divinity through sincerity or truthfulness on our part. If we, however, try to establish a relation between Deity and man indirectly by means of an image, the image will itself stand in the way and prevent us from realizing our religious purpose to accomplish direct communion with the Deity. So an image made by mortal hands is of no use in Shinto worship.[5]

Ceremonies

To properly encourage the spirit of the *kami* to dwell in the holy sanctuary, long and complex ceremonies are needed. In some temples, it takes ten years for the priests to learn them. The priesthood was traditionally hereditary. One temple has drawn its priests from the same four families for over a hundred generations. Not uncommonly, the clergy are women priestesses. Neither priests nor priestesses live as ascetics; it is common for them to be married, and they are not traditionally expected to meditate. Rather, they are specialists in the arts of maintaining the connection between the *kami* and the people.

Everything has symbolic importance, even when people do not remember quite what it is, so rites are conducted with great care. The correct kind of wood, cloth, and clay in temple furnishings, the nine articles held by priests during ceremonies (such as branch, gourd, sword, and bow), the bowing, the sharp clapping of hands, beating of drums, the waving of a stick with paper strips—everything is established by tradition and performed with precision. Traditionally, there are no personal prayers to the *kami* for specific kinds of help, but rather a reverent recognition of the close relationship between the *kami*, the ancestors, the people, and nature. When people have made a pilgrimage to a special shrine, they often take back spiritual mementos of their communion with the *kami*, such as a paper symbol of the temple encased within a brocade bag.

Followers of the way of the *kami* may also make daily offerings to the *kami* in their home. Their place of worship usually consists of a high shelf on which rests a miniature shrine, with only a mirror inside. The daily home ritual may begin with greeting the sun in the east with clapping and a prayer for protection for the household. Then offerings are placed before the shrine: rice for health, water for cleansing and preservation of life, and salt for the harmonious seasoning of life. When a new house is to be built, the blessings of the *kami* are ceremonially requested.

To acknowledge and follow the *kami* is to bring our life into harmony with nature, Shintoists feel. The word used for this concept is **kannagara**, which is the same word used for the movements of the sun, moon, stars, and planets. Yukitaka Yamamoto, ninety-sixth Chief Priest of the Tsubaki Grand Shrine, says *kannagara* could be translated as "Natural Religion":

> *Natural Religion is the spontaneous awareness of the Divine that can be found in any culture. . . . The Spirit of Great Nature may be a flower, may be the beauty of the mountains, the pure snow, the soft rains or the gentle breeze. Kannagara means being in communion with these forms of beauty and so with the highest level of experiences of life. When people respond to the silent and provocative beauty of the natural order, they are aware of* kannagara. *When they respond in life in a similar way, by following ways "according to the* kami,*" they are expressing* kannagara *in their lives. They are living according to the natural flow of the universe and will benefit and develop by so doing.*[6]

Purification

In the ancient traditions now referred to as Shinto, there is no concept of sin. The world is beautiful and full of helpful spirits. Sexuality *per se* is not sinful; the world was created by mating deities, and people have traditionally bathed together communally in Japan. However, there is a great problem of ritual impurity that may offend the *kami* and bring about calamities, such as drought, famine, or war.

RELIGION IN PRACTICE

Purification by Waterfall

The cleansing power of waters, plentiful in natural Japan, is often used. One may take a ritual bath in the ocean, source of life. Or, in a lengthy ritual called **misogi**, a believer may stand beneath a waterfall, letting its force hit the shoulders and carry impurities and tensions away. Before even entering the waterfall, those seeking purification must undergo preliminary purification practices because the waterfall itself is *kami*. The women put on white kimonos and headbands, the men white loincloths and headbands.

The *misogi* ritual proceeds with shaking the soul by bouncing the hands up and down in front of the stomach, to help the person become aware of the soul's presence. Next comes a form of warm-up calisthenics called Bird Rowing. Following a leader, the participants then shout invocations that activate the soul, affirm the potential for realizing the infinite in one's own soul, and unify the people with the *kami* of earth, guidance, water, life, and the *ki* energy (which the Chinese know as *ch'i*).

Before entering the waterfall, the participants raise their metabolism and absorb as much *ki* as possible by practicing a form of deep breathing. They are sprinkled with purifying salt and are given *sake* to spray into the stream in three mouthfuls. The leader counts from one to nine, to symbolize the impurity of the mundane world and then cuts the air and shouts "Yei!" to dispel this impurity. With ritual claps and shouts the participants then enter the waterfall, continually chanting "*Harae-tamae-Kiyome-tamae-ro-kon-sho-jo!*" This phrase requests the kami to wash away all **tsumi** from the six elements that form the human being, from the senses, and from the mind. This part of the ritual has been scientifically proven to lower the blood pressure.

After this powerful practice, participants dry off, spend time in meditation to calm the soul, and share a ceremonial drink to unify themselves with the *kami* and with each other. The whole *misogi* ceremony is designed to restore one's natural purity and sense of mission in life. As Yukitaka Yamamoto explains:

> *As imperfect beings, we often fail to recognize our mission. These failures come about because we have lost something of our natural purity. This is why purification, or* misogi, *is so central to Shinto. It enables man to cultivate spirituality and to restore his or her natural greatness.*[7]

Misogi, *or ritual purification by standing beneath a waterfall.*

The quality of impurity or misfortune is called *tsumi*. It can arise through defilement by corpses or menstruation, by unkind interaction between humans, between humans and the environment, or through natural catastrophes. In contrast to repentance required by religions that emphasize sin, *tsumi* requires purification. Followers of the way of the *kami* have various means of removing *tsumi*. One is paying attention to problems as they arise:

> *To live free of obstructing mists, problems of the morning should be solved in the morning and those of the evening should be solved by evening. Wisdom and knowledge should be applied like the sharpness of an axe to the blinding effect of the mists of obstruction. Then may the* kami *purify the world and free it of* tsumi.[8]

The *kami* of the high mountain rapids will carry the *tsumi* to the sea, where the whirlpool *kami* will swallow it and the wind *kami* will blow it to the netherworld, where *kami* of that place absorb and remove it.

> *After this has been completed, the heavenly* kami, *the earthly* kami *and the myriad of* kami *can recognise man as purified and everything can return to its original brightness, beauty and purity as before since all* tsumi *has wholly vanished from the world.*[9]

People may also be purified spontaneously by a kind of grace that washes over them, often in nature, bringing them into awareness of unity with the universe. Hitoshi Iwasaki, a young Shinto priest, says that he likes to look at the stars at night in the mountains where the air is clear:

> *When I am watching the thoroughly clear light of the stars, I get a pure feeling, like my mind being washed. I rejoice to think this is a spiritual* misogi *[purification ritual]. . . . Master Mirihei Ueshiba, the founder of Aikido, is said to have looked upon the stars one night, suddenly realized he was united with the universe, and burst into tears, covering his face with his hands. We human beings, not only human beings but everything existing in this world, are one of the cells which form this great universe.*[10]

In addition to these personal ways of cleansing, there are ritual forms of purification. One is **oharai**, a ceremony commonly performed by Shinto priests, which includes the waving of a piece of wood from a sacred tree, to which are attached white streamers (the Japanese version of the shaman's medicine fan of feathers or the Hindu yak-tail whisk, all used to sweep through the air and thus purify an area). This ceremony is today performed on cars and new buildings. A version used to soothe a *kami* that is upset by an impurity was called for in 1978 when there was a rash of suicides in a Tokyo housing complex by residents jumping off roofs.

Before people enter a Shinto shrine, they will splash water on their hands and face and rinse their mouth to purify themselves in order to approach the *kami*. Water is also used for purification in powerful ascetic practices, such as *misogi*, which involves standing under a waterfall (see box, opposite). Sprinkling salt on the ground or on ritual participants is also regarded as purifying.

Such ritual practices all have inner meaningfulness. At Tsubaki Grand Shrine in Japan, priests purify more than two hundred new cars every weekend, and the same practice is being adopted at Tsubaki Shrine in California. There, Tetsuji

Ancient and modern ways are juxtaposed in Stockton, California, where a traditional Shinto priest purifies and blesses new cars.

Ochiai explains to new car owners whose cars are being ritually purified that they themselves must also practice mental purification for the sake of traffic safety. Just as they attended the ceremony for their car with a calm mind, they should be calm as they drive. Thus, even though the ceremony is not guaranteed to protect them from accidents, it will help them to concentrate their energy on safe driving.

Festivals

In addition to elaborate regular ceremonies, Shintoism is associated with numerous special festivals throughout the year and throughout a person's life. They begin four months before the birth of a baby, when the soul is thought to enter the fetus. Then, thirty-two or thirty-three days after the infant's birth, its parents take it to the family's temple for initiation by the deity. In a traditional family, many milestones—such as coming of age at thirteen, or first arranging one's hair as a woman at age sixteen, marriage, turning sixty-one, seventy-seven, or eighty-eight—are also celebrated with a certain spiritual awareness and ritualism.

The seasonal festivals are reminders to the people that they are descendants of the *kami*. This means remembering to live in gratitude for all that they have received. Festivals became exuberant affairs in which the people and the *kami* join in celebrating life. Many have an agricultural basis, ensuring good crops and then giving thanks for them. Often the local *kami* is carried about the streets in a portable shrine.

Among the many local and national Japanese festivals with Shinto roots, one of the biggest is New Year's. It begins in December with ceremonial housecleaning, the placing of bamboo and pine "trees" at doorways of everything from homes to offices and bars to welcome the *kami*, and dressing in traditional kimonos. On December 31, there is a national day of purification. On New Year's day, people may go out to see the first sunrise of the year and will try to visit a shrine as well as friends and relatives.

Many ceremonies honor those reaching a certain age. For instance, on January 15, those who are twenty years old are recognized as full-fledged adults, and on November 15, children who are three, five, or seven years old (considered delicate ages) are taken to a shrine to ask for the protection of the *kami*. On February 3, the end of winter, people throw beans to toss out bad fortune and invite good, and at shrines the priests shoot arrows to break the power of misfortune. A month-long spring festival is held from March to April, with purification rites and prayers for a successful planting season. The month of June is devoted to rites to protect crops from insects, blights, and bad weather. Fall brings thanksgiving rites for the harvest, with the first fruits offered to the *kami* and then great celebrating in the streets.

Buddhist and Confucian influences

Over time, the ways of the *kami* that have been labeled "Shinto" have blended with other religions imported into Japan. The two religions with which Shinto has been most blended are Buddhism, first introduced into Japan in the sixth century CE, and Confucianism, which has been an intimate part of Japanese culture since its earliest contact with Chinese influences.

Buddhism is still practiced side-by-side with Shinto. The fact that their theologies differ so significantly has been accepted by the people as covering different kinds of situations. The Japanese often go to Shinto shrines for life-affirming events, such as conception, birth, and marriage, and to Buddhist temples for death rites. Shingon Buddhist monks tried long ago to convince the Japanese that the Shinto *kami* were actually Buddhist deities. The two religions were therefore closely interwoven in some people's minds until the Meiji government extricated its version of Shinto from Buddhism in the nineteenth century. But the parallel worship of the two paths continues, with some villages having stone monuments to the *kami* and statues of Nichiren placed next to each other.

As for Confucianism, seventeenth-century Japanese Confucian scholars attempted to free themselves from Buddhism and to tie the Chinese beliefs they were importing to the ancient Japanese ways. One, for instance, likened li to the way of the *kami* as a means of social cohesion. Another stressed reverence as the common ground of the two paths and was himself revered as a living *kami*. The Neo-Confucianists' alliance with Shinto to throw off the yoke of Buddhism actually revived Shinto itself and made the ancient, somewhat formless tradition more self-conscious. Scholars began to study and interpret its teachings. The combination of Confucian emphasis on hierarchy and devotion to the *kami* helped pave the way for the establishment in 1868 of the powerful Meiji monarchy.

State Shinto

The Meiji regime distinguished Shinto from Buddhism and took steps to promote Shinto as the spiritual basis for the government. The state cult, amplifying the Japanese traditions of ancestor veneration, had taught since the seventh century

*On the nearest Sunday to November 15, boys of five and girls of three or seven years are dressed in traditional clothes and taken to a Shinto shrine by their parents to pray for health and good fortune. This father and daughter are celebrating this Seven-Five-Three (*Shichi-go-san*) festival in Narita, Japan.*

that the emperor was the offspring of Amaterasu, the Sun Goddess. *Naobi no Mitma* ("Divine Spirit of Rectification"), written in the eighteenth century, expressed this ideal:

> *This great imperial land, Japan, is the august country where the divine ancestral goddess Amaterasu Omikami was born, a superb country. . . . Amaterasu deigned to entrust the country with the words, "So long as time endures, for ten thousand autumns, this land shall be ruled by my descendants."*
>
> *According to her divine pleasure, this land was decreed to be the country of the imperial descendants . . . so that even now, without deviation from the divine age, the land might continue in tranquility and in accord with the will of the* kami, *a country ruled in peace.*[11]

It had been customary for the imperial family to visit the shrine to the Sun Goddess at Ise to consult the supreme *kami* on matters of importance. But Emperor Meiji carried this tradition much farther. He decreed that the way of the *kami* should govern the nation. The way, as it was then interpreted, was labeled State Shinto. It was administered by government officials rather than bona fide Shinto priests, whose objections were silenced, and many of the ancient spiritual rituals were suppressed. State Shinto became the tool of militaristic nationalists as a way to enlist popular support for guarding the throne and expanding the empire.

An illustration of the profound changes in Shinto ushered in by the Meiji "Restoration" occurs in pre- and post-Meiji versions of the Oracles of the Three Shrines. These are scrolls with sayings attributed to the *kami* of three major shrines. The versions popular before the Meiji Restoration emphasize virtues such as honesty, compassion, and purity. For instance:

If you plot and connive to deceive men, you may fool them for a while, and profit thereby, but you will without fail be visited by divine punishment. To be utterly honest may have the appearance of inflexibility and self-righteousness, but in the end, such a person will receive the blessings of sun and moon. Follow honesty without fail.[12]

A version prepared in the Meiji period is taken from the eighth-century imperial cult, with passages such as this one asserting a direct link between the *kami* and the emperor:

Amaterasu Sumeomikami commanded her August Grandchild, saying: "This Reed-plain-1500-autumns-fair-rice-ear Land is the region which my descendants shall be lords of. Do thou, my August Grandchild, proceed thither and govern it. Go! and may prosperity attend thy dynasty, and may it, like Heaven and Earth endure for ever.[13]

By the time that Japan was defeated in World War II, Emperor Hirohito, Meiji's grandson, may have been little more than a ceremonial figurehead. But he had been held up as a god, not to be seen or touched by ordinary people. At the end of the war he officially declared himself human.

During the social changes of the nineteenth and twentieth centuries, many new religious sects appeared that had their roots in Shinto beliefs and practices of communicating with the *kami*. These new sects were also labeled "Sect Shinto" by the Meiji regime. One of these new sects, Tenrikyo, will be considered separately in Chapter 8. Another, called Oomoto, developed from revelations given to Madame Nao Deguchi when she was reportedly possessed by the previously little-known *kami* Ushitora no Konjin in 1892. The revelations criticized the "beastly" state of humanity, with:

the stronger preying on the weaker. . . . If allowed to go on in this way, society will soon lose the last vestiges of harmony and order. Therefore, by a manifestation of Divine Power, the Greater World shall undergo reconstruction, and change into an entirely new creation. . . . The Greater World shall burst into bloom as plum blossoms at winter's end.[14]

As developed by Madame Deguchi's relatives and successors, the Oomoto movement survived persecution by the Meiji regime. It has denied that it is a Shinto sect and now has a universalist approach, recognizing founders of other religions as *kami*. Its leaders travel around the world encouraging self-examination, environmental restoration, and global religious cooperation.

Shinto today

In general, the ways of Shintoism are indigenous to Japan, and they remain so. Outside Japan, Shinto beliefs and practices are common only in Hawaii and Brazil, because many Japanese have settled there. Shintoism has not been a proselytizing religion (that is, it does not seek to convert others). Most Japanese people who visit shrines and pray to the *kami* during festivals do not even think of themselves as "Shintoist." This label is applied mostly by the priestly establishment.

Within Japan, reaction to the horrors of World War II, the elimination of the imperial mythology of State Shinto, and a desire for modernization threatened to leave Shinto in the shadows of the past. After the war, the Japanese Teachers Association began teaching rejection of patriotism, of the imperial family, of Japanese history, and also of the beliefs and practices associated with Shintoism. The Japanese national flag—a red circle on a white background—became a symbol of the past, although its symbolism transcends history. The red circle signifies the rising sun and the white background purity, righteousness, and national loyalty. As Hitoshi Iwasaki notes (see box, opposite), for a time it was difficult for young people to learn about Shintoism. But the shrines remain and are visited by more than 80 million Japanese at New Year. People often visit more as tourists than as believers, but many say they experience a sense of spiritual renewal when they visit a shrine. Long-established households still have their *kami* shelf, often next to the Buddhist family altar, which combines tablets memorializing the dead with scrolls or statues dedicated to a manifestation of the Buddha. In Japan, Shinto also survives as the basis for the seasonal holidays.

Despite the fact that Japan is now one of the most technologically advanced countries in the world, with business its primary focus, there still seems to be a place for ritual—and in some cases, heartfelt—communion with the intangible *kami* that, in Shinto belief, permeate all of life. Before Japanese scientists launched their first satellite in 1970, the most senior scientists of the Space Development Agency went to the Chichibu Shinto shrine near Tokyo to request the shrine deity—the North Star—that their mission should be successful. When it was, they returned to the shrine to express their gratitude.

Modern life, instead of distancing Japanese from their ancient traditions, has ultimately encouraged renewed interest in Shinto beliefs. Rapid and extreme urbanization and industrialization in twentieth-century Japan brought extremes of pollution and disease. Minamata disease, for example, inflicted paralysis and painful suffering in an area of southern Japan where a chemical factory had been dumping mercury into the bay, contaminating the fish eaten by the residents. In another area of southern Japan, iron and steel factories had so polluted the air that children developed severe respiratory diseases and the sky was never blue. However, citizens' groups—many of them led by concerned mothers—are intervening to protest the despoliation of the environment and of human health and to urge a new appreciation of the natural beauty of the islands. Such actions can perhaps be seen as practical applications of Shinto sentiments.

Some Shintoists now explain their path as a universal natural religion, rather than an exclusively Japanese phenomenon, and try to explain the way of harmony with the *kami* to interested non-Japanese, without striving for conversions. A Shinto shrine has been built in California, offering ritual ways of experiencing one's connection with nature and learning to see the divine in the midst of life.

Within Japan, there are new attempts to teach children the thousands-of-years-old rice cultivation ceremony, and with it, Shinto values such as co-existence and "co-prosperity" with the natural environment and with each other. The Association of Shinto Shrines feels that it can play a role in helping people to remember the natural world. The Association recently stated:

AN INTERVIEW WITH HITOSHI IWASAKI

Living Shinto

Hitoshi Iwasaki is a young Shinto priest struggling to educate himself in the suppressed ancient ways of his people. He has officiated at the Shinto shrine in Stockton, California, and at its parent shrine in Japan, Tsubaki Grand Shrine in the Mie Prefecture, where a fine waterfall is used for *misogi*.

"We Japanese are very fortunate. We are grateful for every natural phenomenon and we worship the mountain, we worship the river, we worship the sea, we worship the big rocks, waterholes, winds.

"Unfortunately, after World War II, we were prohibited from teaching the Shinto religion in schools. We never learned about Shinto at school. Many young Japanese know the story of Jesus Christ, but nothing about Shinto. The government is not against Shinto. [The silence comes from] newspapers, the media, and the teachers' union, because they were established just after World War II. They have a very left-wing attitude [and associate Shinto with State Shinto]. Ordinary Japanese people don't link Shinto with politics nowadays, but the teachers' union and newspapers never give credence to religion, Shinto, or Japanese old customs.

"Against this kind of atmosphere, we learned in the school that everything in Japan was bad. Shinto and Japanese customs were bad. Many young people are losing Japanese customs. But I went to Ise Shrine University, where I learned that Shinto is not just State Shinto. Some young people like me study Japanese things and they become super-patriots. That's the problem. There is no middle, just super-left or super-right.

"I learned Shinto partly by learning aikido. The founder was a very spiritual person who studied in one of the Shinto churches. In Shinto we don't have services, we don't preach, we don't do anything for people who want to be saved. But I want to introduce the idea of Shinto to the people of the United States and young Japanese and I can do it through aikido. I think I learned the way of nature through aikido practice. We are born as a child of *kami*, which means we are part of the universe, like a tree. People practice aikido not to fight but to be a friend, to unite.

"In Japan some people are going to Shinto. They were all doing Zen before, but Zen is very difficult. In waterfall purification there is no choice, just standing under the waterfall.

"My friend, a Shinto priest, went to the Middle East, in complete desert. He says it was difficult to explain Shinto there. For them, nature is the enemy. They have to fight nature.

"In Japan we have water everywhere. Now the big rivers and streams are polluted. But people come to the shrines. People gather because this is a sacred place from ancient times where people have come to pray. And other people want to go where people are gathered, so some of the shrines become vacation places, surrounded by souvenir shops. Many come to Shinto shrines and pray Buddhist prayers. Why not? Buddha is one of the *kami*. Everything has *kami*."

[Traditionally] the Japanese viewed nature not as an adversary to be subdued, but rather as a sacred space overflowing with the blessings of the kami, *and toward which they were to act with restraint. . . . While the Japanese have loathed environmental destruction, the advance of civilization centered on science and technology, and the rush toward economic prosperity has created a tidal wave of modernization that has frequently resulted in the loss of that traditional attitude*

handed down from ancestors. . . . By reconsidering the role of the sacred groves possessed by the some eighty thousand shrines in Japan, we hope to heighten Japanese consciousness, and expand the circle of active involvement in environmental preservation.[15]

Suggested reading

Bocking, Brian, *A Popular Dictionary of Shinto*, Richmond, Surrey: Curzon Press, 1996. Thorough discussions of ancient and contemporary facets of Shinto, including shrines, festivals, *kami*, new religious movements, historical events, and key figures.

Breen, John and Mark Teeuwen, eds., *Shinto in History: Ways of the Kami*, Honolulu: University of Hawaii Press, 2000. Scholarly essays distinguishing between unnamed shrine cults and establishment Shinto in historical context.

Hebert, Jean, *Shinto: At the Fountain-head of Japan*, New York: Stein and Day, 1967. A classic survey of the intricacies of Shinto practice.

Hori, Ichiro, *Folk Religion in Japan*, Chicago and London: University of Chicago Press, 1968. A lively study of Japanese folk traditions, such as shamanism and mountain worship, which contributed to Shinto.

Kitagawa, Joseph M., *On Understanding Japanese Religion*, Princeton, New Jersey and Guildford, Surrey: Princeton University Press, 1987. A scholarly history including Shinto and "new religions," making distinctions between shrine Shinto, folk Shinto, and sect Shinto.

Moore, Charles A., ed., *The Japanese Mind: Essentials of Japanese Philosophy and Culture*, Honolulu: University of Hawaii Press, 1967, 1971. A valuable collection of essays covering Shinto and Buddhism as well as secular aspects of Japanese lifeways.

Nelson, John K., *A Year in the Life of a Shinto Shrine*, University of Washington Press, 1995. Both an in-depth description of the ritual cycle at a major Shinto shrine and an accessible introduction to Shinto.

Picken, Stuart D. B., *Essentials of Shinto: An Analytical Guide to Principal Teachings*. Westport, Connecticut and London: Greenwood Press, 1994. A clear introduction by a minister of the Church of Scotland who is also a *misogi* practitioner.

Smith, Robert J., *Ancestor Worship in Contemporary Japan*, Stanford, California: Stanford University Press, 1974. A sociological study of the continuing tradition of venerating family ancestors in contemporary Japan, including historical chapters that are of help in understanding the roots of State Shinto.

Yamamoto, Yukitaka, *Way of the Kami*, Stockton, California: Tsubaki American Publications, 1987. A highly accessible introduction to Shinto, seen as a universal natural way.

CHAPTER 8
RELIGION IN THE TWENTY-FIRST CENTURY

As the twenty-first century begins, the global landscape is a patchwork of faiths. Religious expressions are heading in various directions at the same time. Yet as we conclude this survey of Eastern-founded religions as living, changing movements, an overview of religion is necessary to gain a sense of how religion is affecting human life now and what impact it may have in the future.

Religious pluralism

A major feature of religious geography is that no single religion dominates the world. Although authorities from many faiths have historically asserted that theirs is the best and only way, in actuality new religions and new versions of older religions continue to spring up and then divide, subdivide, and provoke reform movements.

With migration, missionary activities, and refugee movements, religions have shifted from their country of origin. It is no longer so easy to show a world map in which each country is assigned to a particular religion. In Russia there are not only Russian Orthodox Christians but also Muslims, Catholics, Protestants, Jews, Buddhists, Hindus, shamanists, and members of new religions. Buddhism arose in India but now is most pervasive in East Asia and popular in France, England, and the United States. Hindu temples are being built around the world.

Professor Diana Eck, Chairman of the Pluralism Project at Harvard University, describes what she terms the new "geo-religious reality":

> *Our religious traditions are not boxes of goods passed intact from generation to generation, but rather rivers of faith—alive, dynamic, ever-changing, diverging, converging, drying up here, and watering new lands there.*
>
> *We are all neighbors somewhere, minorities somewhere, majorities somewhere. This is our new geo-religious reality. There are mosques in the Bible Belt in Houston, just as there are Christian churches in Muslim Pakistan. There are Cambodian Buddhists in Boston, Hindus in Moscow, Sikhs in London.*[1]

New Religious Movements

The history of religions is one of continual change. Each religion changes over time, new religions appear, and some older traditions disappear. Times of rapid social change are particularly likely to spawn new religious movements, for people seek the security of the spiritual amidst worldly chaos. In the period since World War II, thousands of new religious groups have sprung up around the world. In Japan, an estimated thirty percent of the population belongs to one of hundreds of new religious movements.

Imported versions of Eastern traditions, such as Hinduism and Buddhism, have made many new converts in Western areas such as North America, Europe, and Russia, where they are seen as "new religions." They have been spread partly by the missionary activities of gurus and teachers, and partly by independent organizations such as the Theosophical Society. It was founded by Madame Helena Blavatsky (1831–1891), psychic daughter of a noble Russian family. She traveled around the globe studying with masters of esoteric schools and said she had undergone initiations with Tibetan masters and unseen Ascended Masters. She founded the Theosophical Society as an attempt, she said, "To reconcile all religions, sects and nations under a common system of ethics, based on eternal verities."[2] The Theosophical Society introduced ancient Eastern ideas to Western seekers, especially Hindu beliefs such as *karma*, reincarnation, and subtle energies. The Theosophical Society now has members in seventy countries. Madame Blavatsky insisted that "Theosophy is not *a* Religion. It is Religion itself."[3]

Other new religions are outgrowths of an older religion. Radhasoami, for example, is an outgrowth of Sikhism. While orthodox Sikhs believe in a succession of masters that stopped with the Tenth Guru and was transferred to the holy scripture, Radhasoamis believe in a continuing succession of living masters. The first of the Radhasoami gurus was Shiv Dayal Singh. In 1861, he offered to serve as a spiritual saviour. After his death, the movement eventually split into what are now over thirty branches, each with its own living master. Initiates are taught a secret yoga practice of concentrating on the third eye with attention to the inner sound and inner light, in order to commune with the all-pervading power of God, or Nam. The Radhasoami movement now claims an estimated 1.7 million initiates in many countries. They gather in *satsangs*, or spiritual congregations, to support each other on the spiritual path.

Yet other new religious movements arise from what are thought to be genuine new spiritual revelations. Many founders of these new religions are women with shamanistic gifts. Miki Nakayama, founder of the Tenrikyo movement in 1838, was acting as a trance medium for the healing of her son when she was reportedly possessed by ten *kami* (spirits worshipped in Shinto tradition), including God the Parent. They proclaimed through her, "Miki's mind and body will be accepted by us as a divine shrine, and we desire to save this three-thousand-world through this divine body."[4] It is said that she later spontaneously composed 1711 poems under divine inspiration, and that these became the sacred scriptures of a new religion. One of these begins with this revelation:

> *Looking all over the world and through all ages, I find no one who has understood My heart. No wonder that you know nothing, for so far I have taught nothing to you. This time I, God, revealing Myself to the fore, teach you all the truth in detail.*[5]

Tenrikyo has continued to be popular since Miki's death, and she is revered as the still-living representative of the divine will.

Another example of a spiritual movement arising from new revelations is the Mahakiri movement, founded in Japan in 1959 by Sukui Nushi Sama, who believes he is the successor to the Buddha and Christ as God's representative on earth. The path he taught has become popular in the Caribbean. It does not claim to be a religion in itself, but rather to bring all religions together. It involves certain distinctive practices centering on spiritual light. Mahikarians are taught to heal by radiating light out of their hands, to send light to disturbed ancestral spirits to help them find peace, and to spread the divine civilization through the world by transmitting light. Practitioners are taught that this spiritual realm is the only reality; science and medicine are considered ignorant superstitions.

Founders of new religious movements are often convinced that they have been directed to save the world, whether others believe them or not. Such is the case with Sun Myung Moon of North Korea. He has proclaimed himself and his second wife, Hak Ja Han, to be collectively the Messiah. He says that in 1935, while he was praying in the mountains, Jesus appeared to him in a vision. Jesus reportedly told him that his mission on earth was left unfinished and asked Rev. Moon to complete the task of establishing God's kingdom on earth. In the 1970s, Rev. Moon and his followers, the Unification Church, staged well-publicized rallies in the United States and saw a rapid growth in membership. Middle-class youths put aside their careers, gave up their worldly possessions and relationships, and devoted themselves to the religious path. They saw their sacrificial and ascetic way of life as a rejection of the materialistic and hedonistic American lifestyle. In time, many were matched by Rev. Moon with other followers, often from different cultures, and married in mass wedding ceremonies. Unificationists view these mass weddings as a movement to create one human family, with couples of all races and nationalities being "engrafted" onto "God's lineage of true love." In the movement's South Korean headquarters, spirits of two deceased family members are said to be assisting Unificationists from the spirit world with the aid of a medium. People cite miraculous physical healings and visions of bad spirits leaving their bodies. There are also liberation ceremonies for ancestors and even historical "infamous personages," such as Hitler, Lenin, and Stalin. A Unification spokesman reports, "The same personages were blessed as the representatives of all wicked people, thereby opening the gate for the 'liberation of Hell.'"[6]

Apocalyptic movements predicting major world changes were particularly common in the years leading up to 2000, the beginning of the third millennium according to the Christian calendar. The expectation of dramatic world changes is imbedded in many older religions—including Hinduism, Judaism, Christianity, Islam, and some indigenous religions. Hindus anticipate that Kali Yuga, the worst of times, will be followed by the return of Sat Yuga, when *dharma* will again prevail over evil. Mahayana Buddhists await the Buddha of the next eon, the Maitreya, the Buddha of Love.

In contrast to these positive expectations, some religions anticipate doomsday—a disastrous end to the present world. In this belief, some new religious groups have undertaken mass suicide in the belief that they will thus transcend the disaster and enter a heavenly existence; some have turned to violence. A notorious example is the Aum Shinrikyo movement, which killed twelve people and injured thousands by releasing sarin gas in the Tokyo subway system in 1995.

The movement had begun with secret meditation training more or less based on Buddhism, but with long night rituals that reportedly include drinking pots of sea water and then vomiting, for purification. Perhaps due to declining membership and attacks in the media, the founder, Shoko Asahara, began propagating apocalyptic teachings that justified murder as beneficial to the *karma* of the victims.

Sociologists are now attempting to determine in advance which new religious movements might become dangerous, either for their members or for others. Robert Jay Lifton proposes that "world-destroying" cults such as Aum Shinnrikyo have these characteristics: (1) "totalized guruism," to the extent that both guru and disciples lose the ability to distinguish between reality and metaphors, (2) "a vision of an apocalyptic event or series of events that would destroy the world in the service of renewal," (3) an "ideology of killing to heal, of altruistic murder and altruistic world destruction," (4) "the relentless impulse toward world-rejecting purification," (5) "the lure of ultimate weapons," (6) "a shared state of aggressiveness," with no scruples against illegal actions, and (7) "a claim to absolute scientific truth," such as Aum Shinrikyo's use of hallucinogens to transform their disciples by "extreme technocratic manipulation."[7]

New religious movements always run into opposition from established religions or governments, whether they are seen as threats to the establishment's power or as threats to their own members and society at large. At the turn of the third millennium, China has taken strong measures to stamp out Falun Gong, one of many movements based on traditional Taoist Ch'i-kung energy practices. Falun Gong has a living charismatic teacher, Li Hongzhi, who now lives in exile in New York City, from whence he has spread Falun Gong to thirty countries. He claims that the energy practices are worthless and perhaps even destructive unless they are practiced in combination with the Buddhist and Confucian virtues of truthfulness, benevolence, and forbearance. In 1999, the Chinese government declared Falun Gong an "evil cult" that has cheated and brainwashed its followers, causing 1,500 deaths by suicide or failure to seek medical care. Not agreeing with this assessment, 10,000 Falun Gong followers staged a silent protest in Tiananmen Square in Beijing. Protestors were jailed and beaten, followed by wave upon wave of peaceful protests by daring members who met the same fate. Some are said to have died from torture while in police custody. Nevertheless, members refuse to give up their new religion. Practitioners claim that Falun Gong has brought them physical healing, inner peace, and answers to the central questions of life.

Hardening of religious boundaries

The increase in new religious movements has contributed to tensions between people of different faiths. As religions proliferate and interpenetrate geographically, one common response has been the attempt to deny the validity of other religions. In many countries there is tension between the religion that has been most closely linked with national history and identity and other religions that are practiced or have been introduced into the country. People from the more established religions seek to find a balance between freedom of religion for all and the threat they perceive to their traditional values, customs, and sense of national identity.

The twentieth-century rush for materialism and secular values also fanned an increase in "fundamentalism." Reactionaries do not want their values and life patterns to be despoiled by contemporary secular culture, which they see as crude and sacrilegious. They may try to withdraw socially from the secular culture even while surrounded by it. Or they may actively try to change the culture, using political power to shape social laws or lobbying for banning of textbooks that they feel do not include their religious point of view. As described by the Project on Religion and Human Rights,

> *Fundamentalists' basic goal is to fight back—culturally, ideologically, and socially—against the assumptions and patterns of life that are taken for granted in contemporary secular society and culture, refusing to celebrate them or to embrace them fully. They keep their distance and refuse to endorse the legitimacy of any culture that opposes what they perceive as fundamental truths. Secular culture, in their eyes, is base, barbarous, crude, and essentially profane. It produces a society that respects no sacred order and ignores the possibility of redemption.*[8]

Although fundamentalism may be based on religious motives, it has often been politicized and turned to violent means. Political leaders have found the religious loyalty and absolutism of some fundamentalists an expedient way to mobilize political loyalties, and fundamentalists have themselves attempted to control the political arena in order to bring the social changes they prefer. Thus, Hindu extremists in India have been encouraged to demolish Muslim mosques built on the foundation of older Hindu temples and to rebuild Hindu temples in their place. The United States, which had prided itself on being a "melting pot" for all cultures, with full freedom of religion and no right of government to promote any specific religion, has witnessed attempts by Christian fundamentalists to control education and politics, and a simultaneous rise in violence against ethnic and religious minorities. Buddhism, long associated with nonviolence, became involved in the violent suppression of the Hindu minority in Sri Lanka.

Interfaith movement

At the same time that boundaries between religions are hardening in many areas, there has been a rapid acceleration of **interfaith dialogue**—the willingness of people of all religions to meet, explore their differences, and appreciate and find enrichment in each other's ways to the divine. This approach has been historically difficult, for many religions have made exclusive claims to being the best or only way. Professor Ewert Cousins, editor of an extensive series of books on the spiritual aspects of major religions, comments: "I think all the religions are overwhelmed by the particular revelation they have been given and are thus blinded to other traditions' riches."[9]

Religions are quite different in their external practices and culturally-influenced behaviors. There are doctrinal differences on basic issues, such as the cause of and remedy for evil and suffering in the world, or the question of whether the divine is singular, plural, or nontheistic. And some religions make apparent claims to superiority which are difficult to reconcile with other religions' claims.

Many people of broad vision have noted that many of the same principles reappear in all traditions. Every religion teaches the importance of setting one's own selfish interests aside, loving others, harkening to the divine, and exercising control over the mind. What is called the "Golden Rule," expressed by Confucius as "Do not do unto others what you do not want others to do unto you," and by the Prophet Muhammad as "None of you truly have faith if you do not desire for your brother that which you desire for yourself," is found in every religion.

Diana Eck, Professor of Comparative Religion and Indian Studies of Harvard Divinity School and Chair of the World Council of Churches committee on interfaith dialogue, observes that there are three responses to contact between religions. One is **exclusivism**: "Ours is the only true way." Eck and others have noted that such a point of view has some value, for deep personal commitment to one's faith is a foundation of religious life and also the first essential step in interfaith dialogue.

Eck sees the second response to interfaith contact as **inclusivism**. This may take the form of trying to create a single world religion. Or it may appear as the belief that our religion is spacious enough to encompass all the others, that it supersedes all previous religions, as Islam said it was the culmination of all monotheistic traditions. In this approach, the inclusivists do not see other ways as a threat. They feel that all diversity is included in a single world view—their own.

The third way Eck discerns is **pluralism**: to hold one's own faith and at the same time ask people of other faiths about their path, about how they want to be understood. As Eck sees it, this is the only point from which true dialogue can take place. And it is a place from which true cooperation, true relationship can happen. Uniformity and agreement are not the goals—the goal is to collaborate, to combine our differing strengths for the common good. For effective pluralistic dialogue, people must have an openness to the possibility of discovering sacred truth in other religions. This is the premise on which this book has been written.

Raimundo Panikkar, a Catholic-Hindu-Buddhist doctor of science, philosophy, and theology, has written extensively on this subject. He speaks of "concordant discord":

> *We realize that, by my pushing in one direction and your pushing in the opposite, world order is maintained and given the impulse of its proper dynamism. . . . One animus does not mean one single theory, one single opinion, but one aspiration (in the literal sense of one breath) and one inspiration (as one spirit). Consensus ultimately means to walk in the same direction, not to have just one rational view. . . . To reach agreement suggests to be agreeable, to be pleasant, to find pleasure in being together. Concord is to put our hearts together.*[10]

Now a large number of interfaith organizations and interfaith meetings draw people from all religions in a spirit of mutual appreciation, for the sake of world harmony.

The landmark global interfaith event was held in 1893 in Chicago: The Parliament of the World's Religions. The figure who most captured world attention was Swami Vivekananda (1863–1902), a learned disciple of Sri Ramakrishna. He brought appreciation of Eastern religions to the West, and made these concluding remarks:

If the Parliament of Religions has shown anything to the world it is this: It has proved to the world that holiness, purity, and charity are not the exclusive possessions of any church in the world, and that every system has produced men and women of the most exalted character. In the face of this evidence, if anybody dreams of the exclusive survival of his own religion and the destruction of others, I pity him from the bottom of my heart.[11]

The largest 1993 centenary celebration of the Parliament of the World's Religions was again held in Chicago. It gathered hundreds of well-known teachers from all faiths and thousands of participants to consider the critical issues facing humanity. It included an attempt to define and then use as a global standard for behavior the central ethical principles common to all religions. The provisional conference document signed by many of the leaders, "The Declaration Toward a Global Ethic", included agreement on what has been called the Golden Rule:

There is a principle which is found and has persisted in many religious and ethical traditions of humankind for thousands of years: What you do not wish done to yourself, do not do to others. Or in positive terms: What you wish done to yourself, do to others! This should be the irrevocable, unconditional norm for all areas of life, for families and communities, for races, nations, and religions.[12]

In such interfaith gatherings, many organizational questions arise. Which religions should be represented? As we have seen, most major religions have many offshoots and branches that do not fully recognize each other's authority. And which, if any, of the myriad new religious movements should be included? Should indigenous religions be included? If so, could one representative speak for all the varied traditions? Would such an organization reflect the bureaucratical patriarchal structures of existing religions, or would it include women, the poor, and enlightened people rather than managers? If the members of the body were not elected by their respective organizations, but were rather simply interested individuals, what authority would they have?

> *"Spirituality is not merely tolerance. . . . It is the absolute recognition of the other's faith in God as one's own."*
>
> *Sri Chinmoy*

Transcending such bureaucratic stumbling blocks to high-level interfaith discussions, at a few places around the globe there are practical efforts to unite ordinary people of different religions. In India, where communal violence between people of varying religions is daily news, the Sikh-based interfaith work of Gobind Sadan is bringing together volunteers of all religions in practical farm work on behalf of the poor, and in celebrations of the holy days of all religions. Baba Virsa Singh, the spiritual inspiration of Gobind Sadan, continually quotes from the words of all the prophets and says:

All the Prophets have come from the same Light; they all give the same basic messages. None have come to change the older revealed scriptures; they have come

*to remind people of the earlier Prophets' messages which the people have forgotten.
We have made separate religions as walled forts, each claiming one of the Prophets
as its own. But the Light of God cannot be confined within any manmade
structures. It radiates throughout all of Creation. How can we possess it?*[13]

Suggested reading

Barney, Gerald O. and others, *Threshold 2000: Critical Issues and Spiritual Values for a Global Age*, Ada, Michigan: CoNexus Press, 2000. Projections of environmental and social crises in the twenty-first century, with multi-faith spiritual perspectives that may offer solutions.

Beversluis, Joel V., ed., *A Sourcebook for Earth's Community of Religions*, second edition, Grand Rapids, Michigan: 1995. Essays on contemporary issues, reflections on how religious people might come together in harmony, and resources guides for religious education, first prepared for the 1993 Chicago Parliament of the World's Religions.

Braybrooke, Marcus, *Faith and Interfaith in a Global Age*, Grand Rapids, Michigan: CoNexus Press and Oxford: Braybrooke Press, 1998. One of the world's central interfaith coordinators surveys the interfaith movement at the turn of the century.

Forward, Martin, *Ultimate Visions: Reflections on the Religions we Choose*, Oxford: Oneworld Publications, 1995. Interesting personal essays by scholars and leaders of many religions, reflecting upon why they like their religion and how it can contribute to a future of harmony among all religions.

Hall, John R. Sylvaine Trinh, Phillip Schuyler, eds., *Apocalypse Observed: Religious Movements, Social Order and Violence in North America, Europe, and Japan*, Routledge, 2000. Articles analyzing situations within which violent new religious movements have developed.

Kelsay, John and Sumner, B. Twiss, eds., *Religion and Human Rights*, New York: The Project on Religion and Human Rights, 1994. A sensitive introduction to conflicts caused by religious "fundamentalism," with positive suggestions as to the potential of religions for insuring human rights.

Khan, Hazrat Inayat, *The Unity of Religious Ideals*, New Lebanon, New York: Sufi Order Publications, 1927, 1979. A master of Sufi mysticism explores the underlying themes in the religious quest that are common to all religions.

Swidler, Leonard, ed., *Toward a Universal Theology of Religion*, Maryknoll, New York: Orbis Books, 1988. Leaders in the evolving interfaith dialogue grapple with the issues of transcending differences.

Tobias, Michael, Morrison, Jane, and Gray, Bettina, eds., *A Parliament of Souls: In Search of Global Spirituality*, Ada, Michigan: CoNexus Press, 1994. Interviews with twenty-eight spiritual leaders from the 1993 Parliament of the World's Religions, plus supplementary material.

Wessinger, Catherine, *How the Millennium Comes Violently: From Jonestown to Heaven's Gate*, Seven Bridges Press, 2000. Develops the theory that violence is catalyzed by certain types of interactions.

World Scripture: A Comparative Anthology of Sacred Texts, New York: Paragon House/International Religious Foundation, 1991. A thematic compendium of appealing excerpts from the scriptures and oral traditions of many religions, in excellent translations selected by major scholars.

NOTES

CHAPTER ONE
THE RELIGIOUS RESPONSE

1   Karl Marx, from "Contribution to the Critique of Hegel's Philosophy of Right," 1884, *Karl Marx, Early Writings*, translated and edited by T. B. Bottomore, London: C. A. Watts and Co., 1963, pp. 43–44; Capital, vol. 1, 1867, translated by Samuel Moore and Edward Aveling, F. Engels, ed., London: Lawrence & Wishart, 1961, p. 79; "The Communism of the Paper 'Rheinischer Beobachter'," *On Religion*, London: Lawrence & Wishart, undated, pp. 83–84.

2   Karl Marx, "Religion as the Opium of the People," in Karl Marx and Friedrich Engels, *On Religions*, Moscow: Foreign Language Publishing House, 1955, p. 42.

3   Emile Durkheim, *The Elementary Forms of Religious Life*, New York: Free Press, 1915, p. 62.

4   Mata Amritanandamayi, *Awaken Children!* vol. IV, Amritapuri, Kerala, India: Mata Amritanandamayi Mission Trust, 1992, pp. 103–104.

5   Jiddu Krishnamurti, *The Awakening of Intelligence*, New York: Harper & Row, 1973, p. 90.

6   Buddha, *The Dhammapada*, translated by P. Lal, 162/92 Lake Gardens, Calcutta, 700045 India. (Originally published by Farrar, Straus & Giroux, 1967, p. 97.) Reprinted by permission of P. Lal.

7   Mahatma Gandhi, quoted in Eknath Easwaran, *Gandhi the Man*, Petaluma, California: Nilgiri Press, 1978, p. 121.

8   *The Bhagavad-Gita*, portions of Chapter 2, translated by Eknath Easwaran, quoted in Easwaran, op. cit., pp. 121–122.

9   Excerpted from Agnes Collard, in "The Face of God," *Life*, December 1990, p. 49.

10 Philippians 4:7, *The Holy Bible*, King James Version.

11 *Brihadaranyaka Upanishad*, Fourth Adhyaya, Fourth Brahmana, 20, 13, translated by F. Max Müller, *Sacred Books of the East*, vol. 15, Oxford: Oxford University Press, 1884, pp. 178–179.

12 William James, *The Varieties of Religious Experience*, New York: New American Library, 1958, p. 49.

13 From *The Kabir Book* by Robert Bly, copyright 1971, 1977 by Robert Bly, copyright 1977 by Seventies Press. Reprinted by permission of Beacon Press.

14 William Wordsworth, "Ode on Intimations of Immortality from Recollections of Early Childhood."

15 Pierre Teilhard de Chardin, *The Heart of Matter*, translated by Rene Hague, New York and London: Harcourt Brace Jovanovich, 1978, pp. 66–67.

16 AE (George William Russell), *The Candle of Vision*, Wheaton, Illinois: The Theosophical Publishing House, 1974, pp. 8–9.

17 Rudolf Otto, *The Idea of the Holy*, translated by John W. Harvey, New York: Oxford University Press, 1958, p. 1.

18 Wilfred Cantwell Smith, *The Meaning and End of Religion*, London: SPCK, 1978, pp. 128, 130.

19 John White, "An Interview with Nona Coxhead: The Science of Mysticism—Transcendental Bliss in Everyday Life," *Science of Mind*, September 1986, pp. 14, 70.

20 Martin Luther, as quoted in Gordon Rupp, "Luther and the Reformation," in Joel Hurstfield, ed., *The Reformation Crisis*, New York: Harper & Row, 1966, p. 23.

21 William James, op. cit., p. 298.

22 Abu Yazid, as quoted in R. C. Zaehner, *Hindu and Muslim Mysticism*, London: University of London, The Athalone Press, 1960, p. 105.

23 Sallie McFague, *Models of God: Theology for an Ecological, Nuclear Age*, Philadelphia: Fortress Press, 1987, p. 133.

24 *Marx and Engels on Religion*, Introduction by Reinhold Niebuhr, New York: Schocken Books, 1964, pp. viii–ix.

25 As quoted by Huston Smith, "The Future of God in Human Experience," *Dialogue and Alliance*, vol. 5, no. 2, Summer 1991, p. 11.

26 Maimonides, "Guide for the Perplexed," 1, 59, as quoted in Louis Jacobs, *Jewish Ethics, Philosophy, and Mysticism*, New York: Behrman House, 1969, p. 80.

27 Guru Gobind Singh, *Jaap Sahib*, English translation by Surendra Nath, New Delhi: Gobind Sadan, 1992, verses 7, 29–31.

28 Bede Griffiths, *Return to the Center*, Springfield, Illinois: Templegate, 1977, p. 71.

29 Pir Vilayat Inayat Khan, "The Significance of Religion to Human Issues in the Light of the Universal Norms of Mystical Experience," *The World Religions Speak on the Relevance of Religion in the Modern World*, Finley P. Ounne, Jr., ed., The Hague: Junk, 1970, p. 145.

30 Antony Fernando, "Outlining the Characteristics of the Ideal Individual," paper for the Inter-Religious Federation for World Peace conference, Seoul, Korea, August 20–27, 1995, p. 9.

31 Joseph Campbell, *The Hero with a Thousand Faces*; second edition, Princeton, New Jersey: Princeton University Press, 1972, p. 29.

32 Rev. Valson Thampu, "Religious Fundamentalisms in India Today," *Indian Currents*, November 2, 1995, p. 3.

33 Quoted in John Gliedman,"Mind and Matter," *Science Digest*, March 1983, p. 72.

34 Ilya Prigogine, abstract for "The Quest for Certainty," Conference on a New Space for Culture and Society, New Ideas in Science and Art, November 19–23, 1996.

35 Murray Gell-Mann, in Kitty Ferguson, *Stephen Hawking: Quest for a Theory of Everything*, London: Bantam Press, 1992, p. 30.

36 Albert Einstein, *The World As I See It*, New York: Wisdom Library, 1979; *Ideas and Opinions*, translated by Sonja Bargmann, New York: Crown Publishers, 1954.

37 Kenneth R. Miller, "Finding Darwin's God: The New Battle over Evolution," Keynote Address at Science Teaching and the Search for Origins, April 14–15, 2000, The University of Kansas, p. 10 on www.aaas.org/spp/dser/evolution/science/kennethmiller.

38 Francis Collins, in "Science and God: A Warming Trend?" *Science*, vol. 277, August 15, 1997, p. 892.

39 Fred Hoyle, quoted in Patrick Glynn, *God, the Evidence*, Rocklin, California: Prima Publishing, 1997.

40 Stephen Hawking, *A Brief History of Time: From the Big Bang to Black Holes*, London: Bantam Press, 1988.

41 Quoted in Merlin Stone, *When God was a Woman*, San Diego, California: Harcourt Brace Jovanovich, 1976, p. x.

42 Rosemary Radford Ruether, *Woman-Church: Theology and Practice of Feminist Liturgical Communities*, San Francisco: Harper & Row, 1985, p. 3.

43 Jonathan Edwards, sermon in Enfield, Connecticut, July 8, 1741. Reproduced in Charles Hurd, *A Treasury of Great American Speeches*, New York: Hawthorn Books, 1959, pp. 19–20.

44 John Welwood, "Principles of Inner Work: Psychological and Spiritual," *The Journal of Transpersonal Psychology*, 1984, vol. 16, no. 1, pp. 64–65.

45 Declaration of The World Conference of Religions on Religious and Human Solidarity, Kochi, Kerala, India, October 1–6, 1991.

46 Dr. Syed Z. Abedin, "Let There be Light," *Saudi Gazette*, Jeddah, June 1992, reprinted in Council for a Parliament of the World's Religions Newsletter, vol. 4, no. 2, August 1992, p. 2.

CHAPTER TWO
HINDUISM

1 English transliteration of the Sanskrit s as "s" or "sh" varies widely and is by no means consistent. In accordance with the inconsistencies long found, this chapter follows existing usage and does not try to standardize it, to conform with popular though inconsistent English usage.

2 Sukta-yajur-veda XXVI, 3, as explained by Sai Baba in *Vision of the Divine* by Eruch B. Fanibunda, Bombay: E. B. Fanibunda, 1976.

3 Sri Aurobindo, *The Immortal Fire*, Auroville, India: Auropublications, 1974, pp. 3–4.

4 *The Upanishads*, translated by Swami Prabhavananda and Frederick Manchester, The Vedanta Society of Southern California, New York: Mentor Books, 1957.

5 Chandogya Upanishad, ibid., p. 46.

6 Brihadaranyaka Upanishad, ibid.

7 The Code of Man, IV.43, as quoted in Roderick Hindery, *Comparative Ethics in Hindu and Buddhist Traditions*, second edition, Delhi: Motilal Banarsidass Publishers, 1996, p. 85.

8 T. M. P. Mahadevan, *Outlines of Hinduism*, second edition, Bombay: Chetana Ltd., 1960, p. 24.

9 A condensation by Heinrich Zimmer of the Vishnu Purana, Book IV, Chapter 24, translated by H. H. Wilson, London, 1840, in Zimmer's *Myths and Symbols in Indian Art and Civilization*, New York: Pantheon Books, 1946, p. 15.

10 Uttara Kandam, Ramayana, third edition, as told by Swami Chidbhavananda, Tiriuuparaitturai, India: Tapovanam Printing School, 1978, pp. 198–199.

11 Chapter III:30, p. 57. All quotes from the Bhagavad-Gita are from *Bhagavad-Gita as It Is*, translated by A. C. Bhaktivedanta Swami Prabhupada, New York: Copyright 1972, The Bhaktivedanta Book Trust. Reproduced with permission of The Bhaktivedanta Book Trust International.

12 Ibid., III:30, p. 57.

13 Ibid., IV:3, p. 64.

14 Ibid., IV:7–8, pp. 68–69.

15 Ibid., VII:7–8, 12, pp. 126, 128.

16 Ibid., IX:26, p. 157.

17 *Srimad-Bhagavatam*, second canto, "The Cosmic Manifestation," part one, chapter 6:3 and 1:39, translated by A. C. Bhaktivedanta Swami Prabhupada, New York: Bhaktivedanta Book Trust, 1972, pp. 59 and 275–276.

18 *Thus Spake Sri Ramakrishna*, fifth edition, Madras: Sri Ramakrishna Math, 1980, p. 54.

19 Swami Prajnananda, introduction to *Light on the Path*, Swami Muktananda, South Fallsburg, New York: SYDA Foundation, 1981, p. x.

20 *The Patanjala Yogasutra with Vyasa Commentary*, translated from Sanskrit into English by Bengali Baba, second edition, Poona, India: N. R. Bargawa, 1949, pp. 96–97.

21 Swami Sivananda, *Dhyana Yoga*, fourth edition, Shivanandanagar, India: The Divine Life Society, 1981, p. 67.

22 Ramana Maharshi, *The Spiritual Teaching of Ramana Maharshi*, Boston: Shambhala, 1972, pp. 4, 6.

23 Swami Vivekananda, *Karma-Yoga and Bhakti-Yoga*, New York: Ramakrishna-Vivekananda Center, 1982, p. 32.

24 *Bhagavad-Gita as It Is*, op. cit., Chapter 2:49 (p. 36), Chapter 5:8, p. 12.

25 Bhakta Nam Dev, as included in Sri Guru Granth Sahib, p. 693, adapted from the translation by Manmohan Singh, Amritsar, India: Shiromani Gurdwara Parbandhak Committee, 1989.

26 Bhakta Ravi Das, as included in Sri Guru Granth Sahib, p. 694, op. cit.

27 Mirabai, *Mira Bai and Her Padas*, English translation by Krishna P. Bahadur, Delhi: Munshiram Manoharlal Publishers Pvt. Ltd., 1998, no. 46, pp. 76–77.

28 Ramakrishna, quoted in Carl Jung's introduction to *The Spiritual Teaching of Ramana Maharshi*, op. cit., p. viii.

29 Leela Arjunwadkar, "Ecological Awareness in Indian Tradition (Specially as Reflected in Sanskrit Literature)," paper presented at Assembly of the World's Religions, Seoul, Korea, August 24–31, 1992, p. 4.

30 *The Thousand Names of the Divine Mother: Sri Lalita Sahasranama*, with commentary by T. V. Narayana Menon, English translation by Dr. M. N. Namboodiri, Amritapuri, Kerala, India: Mata Amritanandamayi Math, 1996, verses 1–2, 8, 158–161, 220–224, pp. 5–6, 11, 82–3, 106–107.

31 Swami Sivasiva Palani, personal communication, October 26, 1989.

32 Appar, as quoted in R. de Smet and J. Neuner, eds., *Religious Hinduism*, fourth edition, Bangalore, India: St. Paul's Society, 1996, p. 321.

33 Swami Palani, op. cit.

34 William F. Fisher, "Sacred Rivers, Sacred Dams: Competing Visions of Social Justice and Sustainable Development along the Narmada," in Christopher Key Chapple, and Mary Evelyn Tucker, eds., *Hinduism and Ecology*, Boston: Harvard University Press, 2000, p. 413.

35 Ibid., p. 410.

36 Aditi Sengupta De, "The 'holy' mess," c/o editor@ip.eth.net, July 31, 2000.

37 "Kumbha Mela," *Hinduism Today*, September 1998, p. 32.

38 Robert N. Minor, "Sarvepalli Radhakrishnan and 'Hinduism': Defined and Defended," in Robert D. Baird, ed., *Religion in Modern India*, New Delhi: Manohar Publications, 1981, p. 306.

39 *Condensed Gospel of Sri Ramakrishna*, Mylapore, Madras: Sri Ramakrishna Math, 1911, p. 252.

40 Ramakrishna, as quoted in Swami Vivekananda, *Ramakrishna and His Message*, Howra, India: Swami Abhayananda, Sri Ramakrishna Math, 1971, p. 25.

41 Lectures delivered by Shastriji Pandurang Vaijnath Athavale at the Second World Religious Congress held at Shimizu City, Japan in October 1954.

42 Shri Pandurang Vaijnath Athavale Shastri, Nivedanam, third edition, Bombay, 1973, p. 6.

43 Shri Pandurang Shastri Athavale, discourse on January 10, 1988, Bombay, on the occasion of Diamond Jubilee Celebration of Shrimad Bhagvad Geeta Pathshala by Sagar-Putras of the Fishing Community, p. 5.

44 Paraphrased from brochure from Vedanta Centre, Ananda Ashram, Cohasset, Massachusetts.

45 Romila Thapar, "Syndicated Hinduism," in Gunther-Deitz Sontheimer and Hermann Kulke, *Hinduism Reconsidered*, New Delhi: Manohar Publishers, 1997, p. 79.

49 All quotations are from an interview with Dr. Karan Singh, November 17, 1998.

46 Shahid Faridi, "RSS is teaching distorted history in its schools," *Asian Age*, August 28, 2000, p. 3.

47 "VHP tells all missionaries to leave India immediately," *Asian Age*, November 12, 1999, p. 2.

48 Aziz Haniffa, "Southern Baptists apologise for anti-Hindu book," *Asian Age*, November 5, 1999, p. 3.

50 Abbreviation of Indian Supreme Court definition of Hinduism, as itemized in "The DNA of Dharma," *Hinduism Today*, December 1996, p. 33.

51 Karan Singh, *Essays on Hinduism*, second edition, New Delhi: Ratna Sagar, 1990, p. 43.

CHAPTER THREE
JAINISM

1 Akaranga Sutra, translated by Padmanabh S. Jaini in *The Jaina Path of Purification*, Berkeley: University of California Press, 1979, p. 26.

2 Akaranga Sutra, Fourth Lecture, First Lesson, in *Sacred Books of the East*, F. Max Müller, ed., vol. XXII, Jaina Sutras part 1, Oxford: Clarendon Press, 1884, p. 36.

3 Acharya Tulsi, as quoted in *Anuvibha Reporter*, vol. 3, no. 1, October–December 1997, p. 54.

4 R. P. Jain, personal communication.

5 Acharya Mahapragya, inaugural speech, Fourth International Conference on Peace and Nonviolent Action, New Delhi, 1999.

6 Samani Sanmati Pragya, interviewed December 11, 1993, Rishikesh, India.

7 Address to the North American Assisi Interfaith Meeting in Wichita, Kansas, October 31, 1988.

8 Avasyaka Sutra, as quoted in Padmanabh S. Jaini, *Collected Papers on Jaina Studies*, Delhi: Motilal Banarsidass Publishers, 2000, p. 223.

9 Amitagati's Dvatrimsika, 1, as quoted in Padmanabh S. Jaini, ibid., p. 224.

10 Gurudev Shree Chitrabhanu, *Twelve Facets of Reality: The Jain Path to Freedom*, New York: Dodd Mead and Company, 1980, p. 93.

11 Lala Sulekh Chand, in "A Rare Renunciation," *The Hindustan Times*, New Delhi, February 17, 1992, p. 5.

12 Muni Amit Sagar, in "A Rare Renunciation," ibid.

13 Padma Agrawal, "Jainism: Mahavira as Man-God," *Dialogue and Alliance*, p. 13.

14 Acharya Kund Kund, *Barasa Anuvekkha* (Twelve Contemplations), M. K. Dhara Raja, ed., New Delhi: Kund Kund Bharati, 1990, p. 32.

15 Ibid., p. 11.

16 Acharya Tulsi, in S. L. Ghandi, "Acharya Tulsi's Legacy," *Anuvibha Reporter*, vol. 3, no. 1, October–December 1997, p. 2.

17 Acharya Shri Sushil Kumar, personal communication, October 30, 1989.

18 Acharya Mahapragya, as quoted in Prof. R. P. Bhatnagar, "Acharya Mahapragya: A Living Legend," in *Anuvibha Reporter*, January–March 1995, p. 8.

CHAPTER FOUR
BUDDHISM

1 *Majjhima-Nikaya* I.80.

2 Muhaparinibbana Sutta, Digha Nikaya, 2.99f, 155–156, quoted in *Sources of Indian Tradition*, William Theodore de Bary, ed., New York: Columbia University Press, 1958, pp. 110–111.

3 "A message from Buddhists to the Parliament of the World's Religions," Chicago, September 1993, as quoted in *World Faiths Encounter* no. 7, February 1994, p. 53.

4 Majjhima-Nikaya, "The Lesser Matunkyaputta Sermon," Sutta 63, translated by P. Lal in the introduction to *The Dhammapada*, op. cit., p. 19.

5 Walpola Sri Rahula, *What the Buddha Taught*, revised edition, New York: Grove Press, 1974, p. 17.

6 Ajahn Sumedho, "Now is the Knowing," undated booklet, pp. 21–22.

7 Ajahn Sumedho, cited in Satnacitto Bhikku, ed., *Buddha-nature*, World Wide Fund for Nature, London, 1989.

8 Sigalovada Sutta, Dighanikaya III, pp. 180–193, quoted in H. Saddhatissa, *The Buddha's Way*, New York: George Braziller, 1971, p. 101.

9 *The Dhammapada*, translated by P. Lal, op. cit., p. 152.

10 Ibid., p. 49.

11 Achaan Chah in *A Still Forest Pool*, Jack Kornfield and Paul Breiter, eds., Wheaton, Illinois: Theosophical Publishing House, 1985.

12 *The Mahavagga* 1.

13 *Suttanipatta* 1093–4.

14 *Majjhima-Nikaya* 1:161–4.

15 *The Dhammapada*, translated by P. Lal, op. cit., pp. 71–72.

16 Samyutta Nikaya, quoted in the introduction to *The Dhammapada*, translated by P. Lal, op. cit., p. 17.

17 Chatsumarn Kabilsingh, *Thai Women in Buddhism*, Berkeley, California: Parallax Press, 1991, p. 25.

18 Joko Beck, as quoted in Lenore Friedman, *Meetings with Remarkable Women*, Boston: Shambhala, 1987, p. 119.

19 "Khandhaparitta, The Group Protection," from Pali *Chanting with Translations*, Bangkok, Thailand: Mahamakut Rajavidyalaya Press, pp. 18–19.

20 His Holiness the Fourteenth Dalai Lama, speaking on February 15, 1992, in New Delhi, India, Ninth Dharma Celebration of Tushita Meditation Centre.

21 As quoted in Lenore Friedman, *Meetings with Remarkable Women*, op. cit., p. 75.

22   Roshi Jiyu Kennett, as quoted in Lenore Friedman, *Meetings with Remarkable Women*, op. cit., p. 168.

23   David W. Chappell, personal communication, July 26, 1995.

24   Tarthang Tulku, *Openness Mind*, Berkeley, California: Dharma Publishing, 1978, pp. 52–53.

25   Lama Drom Tonpa, as quoted in "Gems of Wisdom from the Seventh Dalai Lama," *Snow Lion Newsletter*, vol. 14, no. 4, Fall 1999, p. 14.

26   "Gems of Wisdom from the Seventh Dalai Lama," op. cit., p. 14.

27   *Stories and Songs from the Oral Tradition of Jetsun Milarepa*, translated by Lama Kunga Rimpoche and Brian Cutillo in *Drinking the Mountain Stream*, New York: Lotsawa, 1978, pp. 56–57.

28   His Holiness the fourteenth Dalai Lama, *My Land and my People*, New York: McGraw-Hill, 1962; Indian edition, New Delhi: Srishti Publishers, 1997, p. 50.

29   His Holiness the fourteenth Dalai Lama, evening address after receiving the Nobel Peace Prize, 1989, in Sidney Piburn, ed., *The Dalai Lama: A Policy of Kindness*, second edition, Ithaca, New York: Snow Lion Publications, 1993, p. 114.

30   Platform Scripture of the Sixth Patriarch, Hui-neng, quoted in *World of the Buddha*, Lucien Stryk, ed., New York: Doubleday Anchor Books, 1969, p. 340.

31   From "Hsin hsin ming" by Sengtsan, third Zen patriarch, translated by Richard B. Clarke.

32   Poems by Chinese Zen master Kuon, translated into English by Urs. App, 1996, www.iijnet.or.jp

33   Roshi Philip Kapleau, *The Three Pillars of Zen*, New York: Anchor Books, 1980, p. 70.

34   Bunan, quoted in *World of the Buddha*, Stryk, op. cit., p. 343.

35   Genshin, *The Essentials of Salvation*, quoted in William de Bary, ed., *The Buddhist Tradition in India, China, and Japan*, New York: Modern Library, 1969, p. 326.

36   The Most Venerable Nichidatsu Fujii, quoted in a booklet commemorating the dedication for the Peace Pagoda in Leverett, Massachusetts, October 5, 1985.

37   The Most Venerable Nichidatsu Fujii, ibid.

38   "Rissho Kosei-kai, Practical Buddhism and Interreligious Cooperation," brochure from Rissho Kosei-kai, Tokyo.

39   Thich Nhat Hanh, *Being Peace*, Indian edition, Delhi: Full Circle, 1997, pp. 53–54.

40   Richard B. Clarke, personal communication, October 2, 1981.

41   Alan Wallace in Brian Hodel, "Tibetan Buddhism in the West: Is it working? An interview with Alan Wallace," *Snow Lion*, vol. 15, no. 4, Fall 2000, p. 17.

42   Walpola Rahula, "The Social Teachings of the Buddha," in *The Path of Compassion*, Fred Eppsteiner, ed., Berkeley, California: Parallax Press, 1988, pp. 103–104.

43   *Metta Sutta*, as translated by Maha Ghosananda, in "Invocation: A Cambodian Prayer," *The Path of Compassion*, op. cit., p. xix.

44   Ajahn Pongsak, in Kerry Brown, "In the water there were fish and the fields were full of rice: Reawakening the lost harmony of Thailand," Martine Batchelor and Kerry Brown, eds., *Buddhism and Ecology*, World Wide Fund for Nature, 1992, pp. 94, 90, 98.

45   Maha Ghosananda, *Step by Step*, quoted in "Letter from Cambodia," Coalition for Peace and Reconciliation, January 2001.

46   Sulak Sivaraksa, "Buddhism in a World of Change," in *The Path of Compassion*, op. cit., p. 16.

CHAPTER FIVE
SIKHISM

1   *Songs of Kabir*, translated by Rabindranath Tagore, New York: Samuel Weiser, 1977, p. 45.

2   Puratan, quoted in Khushwant Singh, *Hymns of Guru Nanak*, New Delhi: Orient Longmans Ltd., 1969, p. 10.

3   Guru Nanak, Guru Granth Sahib, p. 150 (as translated by Dr. Gopal Singh, New Delhi: World Book Centre, 1997).

4   Guru Nanak, as quoted in W. Owen Cole and Piara Singh Sambhi, *The Sikhs: Their Religious Beliefs and Practices*, London: Routledge & Kegan Paul, 1978, p. 39.

5   Sri Rag, p. 59, quoted in Trilochan Singh, Jodh Singh, Kapur Singh, Bawa Harkishen Singh, and Kushwant Singh, trans., *The Sacred Writings of the Sikhs*, reproduced by kind permission of Unwin Hyman Ltd., 1973, p. 72.

6   Bhakta Ravi Das, Rag Sorath, Guru Granth Sahib, p. 657.

7   Guru Granth Sahib, p. 724.

8   Guru Har Rai, as quoted in Dr. Gopal Singh, *A History of the Sikh People*, New Delhi: World Sikh University Press, 1979, p. 257.

9   Guru Gobind Singh, *Bachittar Natak*, autobiography.

10   From Dr. S. Radhakrishnan, letter in the Baisakhi edition of "The Spokesman," 1956, reprinted as introduction to Giani Ishar Singh Nara, *Safarnama and Zafarnama*, New Delhi: Nara Publications, 1985, pp. iv–v.

11   Mul Mantra, quoted in Hymns of Guru Nanak, op. cit., p. 25.

12   *Jaap Sahib*, verses 84, 159, English translation by Harjett Singh Gill, New Delhi: Gobind Sadan Institute for Advanced Studies in Comparative Religion.

13   Adi Granth 684, quoted in Cole and Sambhi, op. cit., p. 74.

14   Guru Nanak, Guru Granth Sahib, p. 141.

15   Ibid.

16   Ibid., p. 473.

17   Guru Arjun, Rag Majh, p. 102, quoted in Singh et al., *Sacred Writings of the Sikhs*, op. cit., p. 180.

18   *Anand Sahib*, verse 14.

19   Excerpt from Guru Gobind Singh, *Rahitnamas*, as translated by Gurden Singh.

20   Excerpted from *Rahitnamas*, op. cit.

21   Baba Virsa Singh, quoted by Juliet Hollister in *News from Gobind Sadan*, August 1997, p. 1.

22   Baba Virsa Singh, in *News from Gobind Sadan*, April 1997, p. 3.

23   Op. cit., p. 1.

24   Jap Ji verses 9–10.

25   Baba Virsa Singh, in *News from Gobind Sadan*, May 1994, p. 4.

26   Guru Gobind Singh, *Dasam Granth*.

CHAPTER SIX
TAOISM AND CONFUCIANISM

1   *The I Ching*, translated by Richard Wilhelm (German)/Cary F. Baynes (English), Princeton, New Jersey: Princeton University Press, 1967, pp. 620–621.

2   Excerpt from verse 1 in *Tao-te Ching*, translated by Stephen Mitchell. Translation copyright 1988 by Stephen Mitchell. Reprinted by permission of Harper & Row, Publishers, Inc.

3   *Tao-te Ching*, translated by Lin Yutang, New York: Modern Library, 1948, verse 1, p. 41.

4   Lao-tzu, *Tao-te Ching*, translated by D. C. Lau, London: Penguin Books, 1963, verse 25, p. 82.

5   Lao-tzu, op. cit., p. 82.

6   Chuang-tzu, *Basic Writings*, translated by Burton Watson, New York: Columbia University Press, 1964, p. 36.

7   Chang Chung-yuan, *Creativity and Taoism*, New York: Harper Colophon, 1963, p. 5.

8   Chuang-tzu, *Basic Writings*, translated by Burton Watson, op. cit., p. 40.

9   *The Way to Life: At the Heart of the Tao-te Ching*, non-literal translation by Benjamin Hoff, New York/Tokyo: Weatherhill, 1981, p. 52, chapter 78.

10 *The Way to Life*, translated by Benjamin Hoff, op. cit., p. 33, chapter 35.

11 *Guanzi*, "Inward Training," as quoted in Harold D. Roth, "The Inner Cultivation Tradition of Early Daoism," in Donald S. Lopez, Jr., ed., *Religions of China in Practice*, Princeton, New Jersey: Princeton University Press, 1996, pp. 133–134.

12 *Tao-te Ching*, translated by Stephen Mitchell, op. cit., Chapter 15.

13 *The Secret of the Golden Flower*, translated by Richard Wilhelm/Cary Baynes, New York: Harcourt Brace Jovanovich, 1962, p. 21.

14 Chuang-tzu, op. cit., p. 59.

15 Excerpted from Huai-Chin Han, translated by Wen Kuan Chu, *Tao and Longevity: Mind–Body Transformation*, York Beach, Maine: Samuel Weiser, 1984, pp. 4–5.

16 Sun Bu-er, in *Immortal Sisters: Secrets of Taoist Women*, translated by Thomas Cleary, Boston: Shambhala Publications, 1989, p. 50.

17 Quoted in *T'ai-chi*, Cheng Man-ch'ing and Robert W. Smith, Rutland, Vermont: Charles E. Tuttle, 1967, p. 106.

18 Ibid., p. 109.

19 Excerpted from Al Chung-liang Huang, *Embrace Tiger, Return to Mountain*, Moab, Utah: Real People Press, 1973, pp. 12, 185.

20 Quoted by Da Liu, *The Tao and Chinese Culture*, London: Routledge & Kegan Paul, 1981, p. 161.

21 "Brooms, Gourds, and the Old Ways, An Interview with Daoist Master An," *Heaven Earth: The Chinese Art of Living*, vol. 1, no. 1, May 1991, p. 2.

22 Yu Yingshi, "A Difference in Starting Points," *Heaven Earth*, ibid., p. 1.

23 *The Analects*, VII: 1, in *Sources of Chinese Tradition*, vol. 1, William Theodore de Bary, Wing-tsit Chan, and Burton Watson, eds. , New York: Columbia University Press, 2000, p. 23.

24 Ibid. XIII: 6, p. 32, and Analects II: 1, as translated by Ch'u Chai and Winberg Chai in *Confucianism*, Woodbury, New York: Barron's Educational Series, 1973, p. 52.

25 Confucius, *The Analects*, translated by D. C. Lau, London: Penguin Books, 1979, VIII:19, p. 94.

26 *The Texts of Confucianism, Sacred Books of the East*, Max Müller, ed., Oxford: Oxford University Press, 1891, vol. 27, pp. 450–451.

27 *The Analects*, XI:11, in Ch'u Chai and Winberg Chai, *The Sacred Books of Confucius and Other Confucian Classics*, New Hyde Park, New York: University Books, 1965, p. 46.

28 Ibid., X:25.

29 Ibid., X:103.

30 Mencius, in De Bary, op. cit., p. 91.

31 Ibid., p. 89.

32 From the Hsun Tzu, Chapter 17, in de Bary, op. cit., p. 101.

33 Chang Tsai's *Western Inscription*, in William Theodore de Bary et al., *Sources of Chinese Tradition*, op. cit.

34 A prayer offered by the Ming dynasty emperor in 1538, in James Legge, *The Religions of China*, London, 1880, pp. 43–44.

35 Mao Zedong, "Overthrowing the Clan Authority of the Ancestral Temples and Clan Elders, the Religious Authority of Town and Village Gods, and the Masculine Authority of Husbands," 1927, as quoted in Deborah Sommer, ed., *Chinese Religion: An Anthology of Sources*, New York and Oxford: Oxford University Press, 1995, p. 305.

36 *Quotations from Chairman Mao tse-Tung*, second edition, Peking: Foreign Language Press, 1967, pp. 172–173.

37 *China Daily*, January 30, 1989, p. 1.

38 Xinzhong Yao, "Confucianism and the Twenty-first Century: Confucian Moral, Educational and Spiritual Heritages Revisited," First International Conference on Traditional Culture and Moral Education, Beijing, August 1998, p. 4.

39 Tu Wei-ming, "Confucianism," in Arvind Sharma, ed., *Our Religions*, New York: HarperCollins Publishers, 1993, pp. 221–222.

40 Korean Overseas Information Service, *Religions in Korea*, Seoul, 1986, pp. 55–57.

CHAPTER SEVEN
SHINTO

1   Yukitaka Yamamoto, *Way of the Kami*, Stockton, California: Tsubaki America Publications, 1987, p. 75.

2   Adapted from the *Nihon Shoki* (Chronicles of Japan), I:3, in Stuart D. B. Picken, *Shinto: Japan's Spiritual Roots*, Tokyo: Kodansha International, 1980, p. 10.

3   Sakamiki Shunzo, "Shinto: Japanese Ethnocentrism," in Charles A. Moore, ed., *The Japanese Mind*, Hawaii: University of Hawaii Press, p. 25.

4   Kishimoto Hideo, "Some Japanese Cultural Traits and Religions," in Charles A. Moore, ed., *The Japanese Mind*, op. cit., pp. 113–114.

5   Ise-Teijo, *Gunshin-Mondo, Onchisosho*, vol. x., quoted in Genchi Kato, p. 185.

6   Yamamoto, op. cit., pp. 73–75.

7   Yamamoto, op. cit., p. 97.

8   Unidentified quotation, Stuart D. B. Picken, ed., *A Handbook of Shinto*, Stockton, California: The Tsubaki Grand Shrine of America, 1987, p. 14.

9   Ibid.

10 Hitoshi Iwasaki, "Wisdom from the night sky," Tsubaki Newsletter, June 1, 1988, p. 2.

11 Motoori Norinaga (1730–1801), *Naobi no Mitma*, quoted in Tsubaki Newsletter, November 1, 1988, p. 3.

12 Tensho Kotaijingu oracle, English translation by Norman Havens based on Japanese translation by Kamata Jun'ichi, as reproduced in Brian Bocking, "Changing images of Shinto: Sanja takusen or the three oracles," in John Breen and Mark Teeuwen, eds., *Shinto in History: Ways of the Kami*, Honolulu: University of Hawaii Press, 2000, p. 169.

13 In W. G. Aston, *Nihongi*, Rutland, Vermont and Tokyo: Tuttle, 1972, p. 77.

14 *Ofudesaki*, as quoted in *Aizen Newsletter of the Universal Love and Brotherhood Association*, no. 17, September–October 1997, p. 2.

15 Jinja-Honcho (The Association of Shinto Shrines), "The Shinto View of Nature and a Proposal Regarding Environmental Problems," Tokyo, 1997.

CHAPTER EIGHT
RELIGION IN THE TWENTY-FIRST CENTURY

1 Diana Eck, "A New Geo-Religious Reality," paper presented at the World Conference on Religion and Peace Sixth World Assembly, Riva del Garda, Italy, November 1994, p. 1.

2 H. P. Blavatsky, *The Key to Theosophy*, Los Angeles: The United Lodge of Theosophists, 1920, p. 3.

3 H. P. Blavatsky, "Is Theosophy a Religion," *Lucifer*, November 1888.

4 *Tenri kyoso den* ("Life of the Founder of the Tenri-kyo Sect") compiled by the Tenri-kyo doshi-kai, Tenri, 1913, quoted in Ichiro Hori, *Folk Religion in Japan*, Chicago: University of Chicago Press, 1968, p. 237.

5 Miki Nakayama, *Ofudesaki: The Tip of the Divine Writing Brush*, Tenri City, Japan: The Headquarters of the Tenrikyo Church, 1971, verses 1–3.

6 Andrew Wilson, "Visions of the Spirit World: Sang Hun Lee's 'Life in the Spirit World and on Earth' Compared with Other Spiritualist Accounts," *Journal of Unification Studies 2*, 1998, p. 123.

7 Robert Jay Lifton, *Destroying the World to Save It: Aum Shinrikyo, Apocalyptic Violence and the New Global Terrorism*, New York: Metropolitan Books/Henry Holt and Company, 1999, pp. 202–213.

8 Charles Strozier et al., "Religious Militancy or 'Fundamentalism,'" *Religion and Human Rights*, New York: The Project on Religion and Human Rights, 1994, p. 19.

9 Ewert Cousins, Speech at North American Interfaith Conference, Buffalo, New York, May 1991.

10 Raimundo Panikkar, "The Invisible Harmony: A Universal Theory of Religion or a Cosmic Confidence in Reality?", *Toward a Universal Theology of Religion*, Leonard Swidler, ed., Maryknoll, New York: Orbis Books, 1987, p. 147.

11 Swami Vivekananda, speech for the Parliament of the World's Religions, Chicago, 1893.

12 "Towards a Global Ethic," Assembly of Religious and Spiritual Leaders, at the Parliament of World Religions, Chicago, 1993.

13 Baba Virsa Singh, in Mary Pat Fisher, ed., *Loving God: The Practical Teachings of Baba Virsa Singh*, New Delhi: Gobind Sadan Institute for Advanced Studies in Comparative Religion, pp. 7–8.

GLOSSARY

In the glossary, most words are accompanied by a guide to pronunciation. This guide gives an accepted pronunciation as simply as possible. Syllables are separated by a space and those that are stressed are underlined. Letters are pronounced in the usual manner for English unless they are clarified in the following list.

a *as in*	flat		ow	now
aa	father		u	but
aw	saw		ă, ĕ, ŏ, ŭ,	about (unaccented vowels represented by "ə"
ay	pay			in some phonetic alphabets)
ai	there		er, ur, ir	fern, fur, fir
ee	see			
e	let		ch	church
i	pity		j	jet
ī	high		ng	sing
o	not		sh	shine
ŏŏ	book		wh	where
oo	food		y	yes
oy	boy		kh	guttural aspiration (ch in Welsh and German)
ō	no			

absolutist Someone who holds rigid, literal, exclusive belief in the doctrines of their religion.

Advaita Vedanta (ad vī <u>ee</u> ta ve <u>dan</u> ta) Non-dualistic Hindu philosophy, in which the goal is the realization that the self is Brahman.

Agni (<u>aag</u> nee) The god of fire in Hinduism.

agnosticism (ag <u>nos</u> ti siz ĕm) The belief that if there is anything beyond this life, it is impossible for humans to know it.

ahimsa (ă <u>him</u> să) Non-violence, a central Jain principle.

Amida (ă <u>mee</u> dă) (Sanskrit: Amitabha) The Buddha of infinite light, the personification of compassion whom the Pure Land Buddhists revere as the intermediary between humanity and Supreme Reality; esoterically, the Higher Self.

amrit (<u>am</u> ret) The water, sweetened with sugar, used in Sikh baptismal ceremonies.

anatta (ă <u>nat</u> ă) In Buddhism, the doctrine that nothing in this transient existence has a permanent self.

anekantwad (ă nay <u>kant</u> wăd) The Jain principle of relativity or open-mindedness.

anicca (ă <u>ni</u> chă) In Buddhism, the impermanence of all existence.

aparigraha (ă <u>paa</u> ree gră hă) The Jain principle of non-acquisitiveness.

arhant (<u>aar</u> hănt) (Pali: *arhat* or *arahat*) A "Worthy One" who has followed the Buddha's Eightfold Path to liberation, broken the fetters that bind us to the suffering of the Wheel of Birth and Death, and arrived at nirvana; the Theravadan ideal.

Aryan Invasion Theory Speculation originally advanced by Western scholars that the Vedas were written by people invading India rather than by people already there.

Aryans (<u>ayr</u> ee ăns) The Indo-European pastoral invaders of many European and Middle Eastern agricultural cultures during the second millennium BCE.

asana (<u>aa</u> să nă) A yogic posture.

ashram (<u>ash</u> ram) In Indian tradition, a usually ascetic spiritual community of those who have gathered around a guru.

atheism (<u>ay</u> thee is em) Belief that there is no deity.

atman (<u>aat</u> man) In Hinduism, the soul.

avatar In Hinduism, the earthly incarnation of a deity.

Bhagavad-Gita (ba gă văd <u>gee</u> tă) A portion of the Hindu epic *Mahabharata* in which Lord Krishna specifies ways of spiritual progress.

bhakta (<u>bak</u> taa) Devotee of a deity, in Hinduism.

bhakti (<u>bak</u> tee) In Hinduism, intense devotion to a personal aspect of the deity.

bhakti yoga In Hinduism, the path of devotion.

bhikshu (bi kshoo) (Pali: *bhikkhu*; feminine: *bhikshuni* or *bhikkhuni*). A Buddhist monk or nun who renounces worldliness for the sake of following the path of liberation and whose simple physical needs are met by lay supporters.

Bodhisattva (bŏo dee sat vă) In Mahayana Buddhism, one who has attained enlightenment but renounces nirvana for the sake of helping all sentient beings in their journey to liberation from suffering.

Brahman (braa măn) The impersonal Ultimate Principle in Hinduism.

Brahmanas (braa mă năs) The portion of the Hindu Vedas concerning rituals.

brahmin (braa min) (brahman) A priest or member of the priestly caste in Hinduism.

Buddha-nature A fully awakened consciousness.

canon Authoritative collection of writings, works, etc., applying to a particular religion or author.

caste (kast) Social class distinction on the basis of heredity or occupation.

chakra (chuk ră) An energy center in the subtle body, recognized in *kundalini yoga*.

charisma (kă riz mă) A rare personal magnetism, often ascribed to a founder of a religion.

ch'i (chee) (also *ki*) The vital energy in the universe and in our bodies, according to Far Eastern esoteric traditions.

ch'i-kung (chee kung) A Taoist system of harnessing inner energies for spiritual realization.

cosmogony (kos mog ŏn ee) A model of the evolution of the universe.

darsan (daar shan) Visual contact with the divine through encounters with Hindu images or gurus.

deity yoga (dee i tee yō gă) In Tibetan Buddhism, the practice of meditative concentration on a specific deity.

deva (day vă) In Hinduism, a deity.

Dhammapada (dam ă pă dă) A collection of short sayings attributed to Buddha.

dharma (daar mă) (Pali: *dhamma*) In Hinduism, moral order, righteousness, religion. In Buddhism, the doctrine or law, as revealed by the Buddha; also the correct conduct for each person according to his or her level of awareness.

diaspora (dī ass po ra) Collectively, the practitioners of a faith living beyond their traditional homeland. When spelled with a capital "D", the dispersal of the Jews after the Babylonian exile.

Digambara (di gŭm bă ră) A highly ascetic order of Jain monks who wear no clothes.

dogma (dog mă) A system of beliefs declared to be true by a religion.

dualistic Believing in the separation of reality into two categories, particularly the concept that spirit and matter are in separate realms.

dukkha (dŏo kă) According to the Buddha, a central fact of human life, variously translated as discomfort, suffering, frustration, or lack of harmony with the environment.

Durga (dŏor ga) The Great Goddess as destroyer of evil, and sometimes as *sakti* of Siva.

epic A long historic narrative.

eschatology (es kă tol ŏ ji) Beliefs about the end of the world and of humanity.

exclusivism The idea that one's own religion is the only valid way.

feng-shui (fĕng shwee) The Taoist practice of determining the most harmonious position for a building according to the natural flows of energy.

fundamentalism (fun dă men tăl iz ĕm) Insistence on what people perceive as the historical form of their religion, in contrast to more contemporary influences. This ideal sometimes takes extreme, rigidly exclusive, or violent forms.

Gayatrimantra (gī a tree man tră) The daily Vedic prayer of upper-caste Hindus.

gnosis (nō sis) Intuitive knowledge of spiritual realities.

gurdwara (gŏor dwa ră) A Sikh temple.

guru (gŏo roo) In Hinduism, an enlightened spiritual teacher.

Guru Granth Sahib (goo roo granth sa heeb) The sacred scripture compiled by the Sikh Gurus.

hatha yoga (ha thă yo gă) Body postures, diet, and breathing exercises to help build a suitable physical vehicle for spiritual development.

heretic (hair i tik) A member of an established religion whose views are unacceptable to the orthodoxy.

Hinayana (hee nă ya nă) In Mahayana Buddhist terminology, the label "lesser vehicle," given to the orthodox southern tradition now represented by Theravada; in Tibetan terminology, one of the three vehicles for salvation taught by the Buddha.

immanent Present in Creation.

incarnation Physical embodiment of the divine.

inclusivism The idea that all religions can be accommodated within one religion.

Indra (in dră) The old Vedic thunder god in the Hindu tradition.

interfaith dialogue Appreciative communication between people of different religions.

Jap Ji (jap jee) The first morning prayer of Sikhs, written by Guru Nanak.

jen (yen) Humanity, benevolence—the central Confucian virtue.

Jina (jī nă) In Jainism, one who has realized the highest, omniscient aspect of his or her being and is therefore perfect.

jiva (jee vă) The soul in Jainism.

jnana yoga (ya na yō gă) The use of intellectual effort as a yogic technique.

Juchiao (jee tzŭ yow) The Chinese term for the teachings based on Confucius.

Kali (kaa lee) Destroying and transforming Mother of the World, in Hinduism.

Kali Yuga (kaa lee yoo gă) In Hindu world cycles, an age of chaos and selfishness, including the one in which we are now living.

kami (kaa mee) The Shinto word for that invisible sacred quality that evokes wonder and awe in us, and also for the invisible spirits throughout nature that are born of this essence.

kannagara (kă nă gă ră) Harmony with the way of the *kami* in Shinto.

karma (kaar mă) (Pali: *kamma*) In Hinduism and Buddhism, our actions and their effects on this life and lives to come. In Jainism, subtle particles that accumulate on the soul as a result of one's thoughts and actions.

karma yoga (kaar mă yō gă) The path of unselfish service in Hinduism.

kensho (ken shō) Sudden enlightenment, in Zen Buddhism.

kevala (kay vă lă) The supremely perfected state in Jainism.

Khalsa (kalsă) The body of the pure, as inspired by the Sikh Guru Gobind Singh.

kirtan (keer tan) Devotional singing of hymns from the Guru Granth Sahib in Sikhism.

koan (kō aan) In Zen Buddhism, a paradoxical puzzle to be solved without ordinary thinking.

kshatriya (ksha tree ă) A member of the warrior or ruling caste in traditional Hinduism, Jainism, and Buddhism.

kundalini (koon dă lee nee) In Hindu yogic thought, the life-force that can be awakened from the base of the spine and raised to illuminate the spiritual center at the top of the head.

Lakshmi In Hinduism, the consort of Vishnu.

lama (laa mă) A Tibetan Buddhist monk, particularly one of the highest in the hierarchy.

langar (lan găr) In Sikh tradition, a free communal meal without caste distinctions

li (lee) Ceremonies, rituals, and rules of proper conduct, in the Confucian tradition.

liberal Flexible in approach to religious tradition; inclined to see tradition as metaphorical rather than literal truth.

lingam (ling ăm) A cylindrical stone or other similarly shaped natural or sculpted form, representing for Saivite Hindus the unmanifest aspect of Siva.

Mahabharata (mă haa baa ră tă) A long Hindu epic that includes the *Bhagavad-Gita*.

Mahayana (maa hă ya nă) The "greater vehicle" in Buddhism, the more liberal and mystical Northern School, which stressed the virtue of altruistic compassion rather than intellectual efforts at individual salvation.

mandala (man daa lă) A symmetrical image, with shapes emerging from a center, used as a meditational focus.

mantra (man tră) A sound or phrase chanted to evoke the sound vibration of one aspect of creation or to praise a deity.

materialism The tendency to consider material possessions and comforts more important than spiritual matters, or the philosophical position that nothing exists except matter and that there are no supernatural dimensions to life.

maya (mī yă) In Indian thought, the attractive but illusory physical world.

metta (met ă) In Buddhist terminology, loving-kindness.

misogi (mee sō gee) The Shinto waterfall purification ritual.

moksha (mōk shă) In Hinduism, liberation of the soul from illusion and suffering.

monistic (mon iz tik) Believing in the concept of life as a unified whole, without a separate "spiritual" realm.

monotheistic (mon ō thee iz tik) Believing in a single God.

muni (moo nee) A Jain monk.

mystic One who values inner spiritual experience in preference to external authorities and scriptures.

mysticism The intuitive perception of spiritual truths beyond the limits of reason.

myth A symbolic story expressing ideas about reality or spiritual history.

naga (naa gă) A snake, worshipped in Hinduism.

Nam (naam) The Holy Name of God reverberating throughout all of Creation, as repeated by Sikhs.

nirvana (ner <u>va</u> na) (Pali: *nibbana*) In Buddhism, the ultimate egoless state of bliss.

nontheistic Perceiving spiritual reality without a personal deity or deities.

oharai Shinto purification ceremony.

OM (ōm) In Hinduism, the primordial sound.

orthodox Adhering to the established tradition of a religion.

Pali (<u>paa</u> lee) The Indian dialect first used for writing down the teachings of the Buddha, which were initially held in memory, and still used today in the Pali Canon of scriptures recognized by the Theravadins.

Panth In Sikhism, the religious community.

Parvati (<u>paar</u> vă tee) Siva's spouse, sweet daughter of the Himalayas.

phenomenology An approach to the study of religions that involves appreciative investigation of religious phenomena to comprehend their meaning for their practitioners.

pluralism An appreciation of the diversity of religions.

polytheistic (<u>pol</u> ĕ thee iz ĕm) Believing in many deities.

Prakriti (<u>praak</u> ri tee) In Samkhya Hindu philosophy, the cosmic substance.

prana (<u>praa</u> nă) In Indian thought, the invisible life-force.

pranayama (<u>praa</u> nă ya mă) Yogic breathing exercises.

prasad (pră <u>saad</u>) In Indian traditions, blessed food.

profane Worldly, secular, as opposed to sacred.

puja (<u>poo</u> jă) Hindu ritual worship.

Puranas (pŏŏ <u>raa</u> năs) Hindu scriptures written to popularize the abstract truths of the Vedas through stories about historical and legendary figures.

Pure Land A Buddhist sect in China and Japan that centers on faith in Amida Buddha, who promised to welcome believers to the paradise of the Pure Land, a metaphor for enlightenment.

Purusha (poo <u>roo</u> shă) The Cosmic Spirit, soul of the universe in Hinduism; in Samkhya philosophy, the eternal Self.

Ramayana (raa <u>maa</u> yă nă) The Hindu epic about Prince Rama, defender of good.

reincarnation The transmigration of the soul into a new body after death of the old body.

Rig Veda (rig <u>vay</u> dă) Possibly the world's oldest scripture, the foundation of Hinduism.

rishi (<u>rish</u> ee) A Hindu sage.

ritual A repeated, patterned religious act.

sacred The realm of the extraordinary, beyond everyday perceptions, the supernatural, holy.

sacred thread In Hinduism, a cord worn over one shoulder by men who have been initiated into adult upper-caste society.

sadhana (<u>saad</u> hă nă) In Hinduism, especially yoga, a spiritual practice.

sadhu (<u>sad</u> oo) An ascetic holy man, in Hinduism.

Saivite (<u>sīv</u> īt) A Hindu worshipper of the divine as Siva.

Sakta (<u>sak</u> ta) A Hindu worshipper of the female aspect of deity.

sakti (<u>sak</u> tee) The creative, active female aspect of Deity in Hinduism.

samadhi (sa <u>maa</u> dee) In yogic practice, the blissful state of superconscious union with the Absolute.

Samkhya (<u>saam</u> khyă) One of the major Hindu philosophical systems, in which human suffering is characterized as stemming from the confusion of Prakriti with Purusha.

samsara (săm <u>saa</u> ră) The continual round of birth, death, and rebirth in Hinduism, Jainism, and Buddhism.

Sanatana Dharma (să <u>na</u> tă nă <u>daar</u> mă) The "eternal religion" of Hinduism.

sangat A Sikh congregation, in which all are ideally considered equal.

sangha (<u>sung</u> ă) In Theravada Buddhism, the monastic community; in Mahayana, the spiritual community of followers of the *dharma*.

sannyasin (sun <u>yaa</u> sin) In Hinduism and Buddhism, a renunciate spiritual seeker.

Sanskrit (<u>san</u> skrit) The literary language of classic Hindu scriptures.

sant A Sikh holy person.

satori (să <u>taw</u> ree) Enlightenment, realization of ultimate truth, in Zen Buddhism.

shabd (shaabd) The Sikh term for a Name of God that is recited or a hymn from the Guru Granth Sahib, considered the Word of God.

shaktipat (<u>shaak</u> tă păt) In the Siddha tradition of Hinduism, the powerful, elevating glance or touch of the guru.

Shang Ti In ancient China, a deity (or perhaps deities) with overarching powers.

shudra (<u>shoo</u> dră) A member of the manual laborer caste in traditional Hinduism.

Sikh (seek) "Student," especially one who practices the teachings of the ten Sikh Gurus.

Siva (<u>shee</u> vă) In Hinduism, the Supreme as lord of yogis, absolute consciousness, creator, preserver, and destroyer of the world; or the destroying aspect of the Supreme.

soma (sō ma) An intoxicating drink used by early Hindu worshippers.

stupa (stoo pă) A rounded monument containing Buddhist relics or commemorative materials.

sunyata (soon yă tă) Voidness, the transcendental ultimate reality in Buddhism.

sutra (soō tră) (Pali: *suta*) Literally, a thread on which are strung jewels—the discourses of the teacher; in yoga, *sutras* are terse sayings.

Svetambara (swe taam bă ră) Jain order of monks who are less ascetic than the Digambara.

symbol Visible representation of an invisible reality or concept.

T'ai-chi chu'an (tī chee hwaan) An ancient Chinese system of physical exercises, which uses slow movements to help one become part of the universal flow of energy.

Tantras (tan trăs) The ancient Indian texts based on esoteric worship of the divine as feminine.

Tantrayana (tăn tră ya nă) *see* Vajrayana.

Tao (dow) (also Dao) The way or path, in Far Eastern traditions. The term is also used as a name for the Nameless.

thang-ka (tang ka) In Tibetan Buddhism, an elaborate image of a spiritual figure used as a focus for meditation.

theistic (thee is tik) Believing in a God or gods.

Theravada (ter ă vă dă) The remaining orthodox school of Buddhism, which adheres closely to the earliest scriptures and emphasizes individual efforts to liberate the mind from suffering.

Tipitaka (ti pi ta ka) (Sanskrit: *Tripitaka*) the foundational "Three Baskets" of Buddha's teachings.

Tirthankaras (tir tăn kăr ăs) The great enlightened teachers in Jainism, of whom Mahavira was the last in the present cosmic cycle.

transcendent Existing outside the material universe.

transpersonal Referring to an eternal, infinite reality, in contrast to the finite material world.

Triple Gem ("Three Refuges") The three jewels of Buddhism: Buddha, *dharma*, *sangha*.

tsumi (tzoo mee) Impurity or misfortune, a quality that Shinto purification practices are designed to remove.

Udasi (oo daa see) An ascetic Sikh order.

untouchable The lowest caste in Brahmanic Hindu society.

Upanishads (oo pan i shăds) The philosophical part of the Vedas in Hinduism, intended only for serious seekers.

Vaishnavite (vīsh nă vīt) (or Vaishnava) A Hindu devotee of Vishnu, particularly in his incarnation as Krishna.

vaishya (vīsh yă) A member of the merchant and farmer caste in traditional Hinduism.

Vajrayana (văj ră yaa nă) (or Tantrayana) The ultimate vehicle used in Mahayana, mainly Tibetan, Buddhism, consisting of esoteric tantric practices and concentration on deities.

Vedas Ancient scriptures revered by Hindus.

vipassana (vi pas ă nă) In Buddhism, meditation based on watching one's own thoughts, emotions, and actions.

Vishnu (vish noo) In Hinduism, the preserving aspect of the Supreme or the Supreme Itself, incarnating again and again to save the world.

wu-wei (woo way) In Taoism, "not doing," in the sense of taking no action contrary to the natural flow.

yang In Chinese philosophy, the bright, assertive, "male" energy in the universe.

yantra (yan tră) In Hinduism, a linear cosmic symbol used as an aid to spiritual concentration.

yi (yee) Righteous conduct (as opposed to conduct motivated by desire for personal profit), a Confucian virtue stressed by Mencius.

yin (yin) In Chinese philosophy, the dark, receptive, "female" energy in the universe.

Yoga (yō gă) A systematic approach to spiritual realization, one of the major Hindu philosophical systems.

yoga (yō gă) Ancient techniques for spiritual realization, found in several Eastern religions.

yoni (yō nee) Abstract Hindu representation of the female vulva, cosmic matrix of life.

yuga (yoo gă) One of four recurring world cycles in Hinduism.

zazen (zaa zen) Zen Buddhist sitting meditation.

Zen (zen) (Chinese: Ch'an) A Chinese and Japanese Buddhist school emphasizing that all things have Buddha-nature, which can only be grasped when one escapes from the intellectual mind.

zendo (zen dō) A Zen meditation hall.

CREDITS

The author and publishers wish to acknowledge, with thanks, the following photographic sources.

Half-title: Robert Harding Library/ James Strachan
Title: Robert Harding Library/ Gavin Hellier.

Chapter 1
13 Alexandra Engel; 14 Idemetsu Museum of Fine Arts, Tokyo; 16 Alexandra Engel; 19 Hirschhorn Museum and Sculpture Garden, Smithsonian Institution (Gift of Joseph H. Hirschhorn); 20 Tate Gallery/ Photo: John Webb; 22 Magnum Photos Ltd./Ian Berry; 25 JCK Archives; 27 Iranian, Hanging for prayer niche. Mihrab design with Tree of Life, 19th century. Wool embroidered in silk. 75 ? 50 ins. The Metropolitan Museum of Art, Rogers Fund, 1910. (10.33.1). Photograph © 1975 The Metropolitan Museum of Art; 30 Space Telescope Science Institute/Corbis; 34 Werner Forman Archive; 35 V&A Picture Library.

Chapter 2
44 The Mansell Collection; 46 Mary Pat Fisher; 49 Alexandra Engel; 51 Hutchison Library; 53 V&A Picture Library; 54 Mary Pat Fisher; 55 Ann/Bury Peerless; 58 Photo of Paramhansa Yogananda, copyright © 1953 renewed 1981 Self-Realisation Fellowship, copyright © 1984 Self-Realisation Fellowship. All rights reserved. Reprinted with permission; 59 (top) Ann and Bury Peerless; 59 (bottom) Mary Pat Fisher; 60 Circa Photo Library/Bipin J. Mistry; 62 Mary Pat Fisher; 63 V&A Picture Library; 66 Mary Pat Fisher; 68 (top) Metropolitan Museum of Art, New York, Harry Brisbane Dick Fund, 1964 (64.251). 68 (bottom) JCK Archives; 69 (left) Rex Features; 69 (right) Mary Pat Fisher; 70 Hutchison Picture Library/Christine Pemberton; 74 Hutchison Picture Library/Dave Brinicombe; 75 Hutchison Picture Library/ Nancy Durrell McKenna; 76 Gurmeet Thukral; 77 Panos Pictures/Paul Smith; 78 (top) Peter Peterson; 78 (bottom) Gurmeet Thukral; 79 Mary Pat Fisher; 80 Gurmeet Thukral; 81 Panos Pictures/D. White; 85 Sandhya S., Kannada Matruvani, Mata Amritanandamayi Mutt; 87 Mary Pat Fisher.

Chapter 3
90 Mary Pat Fisher; 91 Musée Guimet, Paris/Werner Forman Archive; 92 Ann and Bury Peerless; 97 V&A Picture Library; 101 Mary Pat Fisher.

Chapter 4
104 (top) Sarnath Museum; 104 (bottom) Hutchison Picture Library/Ivan Strasbourg; 108 Circa Photo Library/William Holtby; 109 Hutchison Picture Library/R. Constable; 111 Alexandra Engel; 115 V&A Picture Library; 116 Alexandra Engel; 119 Nevada Weir/Corbis; 120 Alexandra Engel; 124 Hutchison Picture Library/Juliet Highet; 125 (left) Alexandra Engel; 125 (right) Hutchison Picture Library/R. Ian Lloyd; 126 (top) Patrick Field, Eye Ubiquitous/Corbis; 126 (bottom) Chinese, Northern Wei Dynasty, Maitreya Altarpiece, dated 524 AD, gilt bronze, H.76.9 cm). The Metropolitan Museum of Art, Rogers Fund, 1938. (38.158. 1a-n). Photograph by Lynton Gardiner. Photograph © The Metropolitan Museum of Art; 128 V&A Museum; 129 Alexandra Engel; 132 (left) Panos Pictures/Alain le Garsmeur; 132 (right) V&A Picture Library; 133 Rex Features; 136 Hutchison Picture Library/Bernard Regent; 137 Christie's Images/Corbis; 141 Tim Page/Corbis; 142, 143 Zen Mountain Monastery, Mount Trumper; 145 Panos Pictures/Paul Quayle.

Chapter 5:
152 Picture reproduced from the book entitled *Biography of Guru Nanak* by Kartar Singh and published by Hemkunt Press, New Delhi 110028; 156 Painting by Mehar Singh, courtesy of Gobind Sadan, New Delhi; 158 Mary Pat Fisher; 160 Alexandra Engel; 161 Alexandra Engel; 164 Mehar Singh/Gobind Sadan; 165 Ann and Bury Peerless; 169 Sondeep Shankar.

Chapter 6
176 The Mansell Collection; 178 JCK Archives; 181 Nelson Atkins Museum of Fine Arts, Kansas City (Nelson Fund); 183 Photo Si Chi Ko, courtesy of C. Al Huang, Celestial Arts Publications, Berkeley, California; 185 Barnaby's Picture Library; 188 Archiv für Kunst und Geschichte; 192 Panos Pictures/Jon Spaull; 194 Hutchison Picture Library/ Felix Greene; 195 Topham Picturepoint.

Chapter 7
201 Popperfoto; 202 Hutchison Picture Library/Jon Burbank; 204 Barnaby's Picture Library; 206 Ernest Haas/Hulton Archive; 208 © Tsubaki America; 210 Hutchison Picture Library/ Jon Burbank.

INDEX